Test Flying in Lanc

from Samlesbury and Warton A

Military Aviation at the Leading Edge

"They will rise on wings like eagles..."

Volume 1: WW1 to the 1960s

JAMES H. LONGWORTH

BAE SYSTEMS

CONTENTS

Foreword 4

Introduction 6

1917-1926 – Early Days, from 7
Tramcars to Flying Boats

People, Aircraft, Places

- Messrs Dick, Kerr & Co Ltd, 7
  Strand Road, Preston
- Felixstowe F.3/5 Flying Boats 7
- English Electric Co Ltd 8
- Capt Thomas Newton 9
- Lytham Works 9
- English Electric Wren, 12
  Ayr and Kingston
- Sqn/Ldr Maurice Wright 12
- Marcus Manton 13
- Maj H. G. Brackley 14

1926-1939 – Decline and Resurgence 21

- Handley Page Ltd, Hampden 21
  and Halifax
- Samlesbury Aerodrome 23

English Electric – a new force in 24
British Military Aviation

Aircrew and Events of the 1940s/'50s

People, Aircraft, Places

- Arthur Sheffield 24
- J. D. Rose 24
- J. Easdown 24
- 'Doug' Potter 24
- De Havilland Vampire 24
- Geoffrey de Havilland Jnr 28
- R. L. C. Blyth 29
- Sir George Nelson 30
- W. E. W. 'Teddy' Petter 31
- H. G. Nelson 32
- English Electric A1/Canberra 33
  'TC' Corporation Street, Preston
- F. W. 'Freddie' Page 33

- B. O. Heath 34
- Ray Creasey 34
- 'Dai' Ellis 34
- Frank E. Roe 35
- Ivan R. Yates 38
- J. W. C. 'Johnny' Squier 38
- Wg/Cdr R. P. Beamont 42
- English Electric P.1/Lightning 48
- Warton Aerodrome 50
- Peter D. Hillwood 58

Strategic Imperatives – Altitude, 73
Speed, Range

Aircrew and Events of the 1950s/'60s

People, Aircraft, Places

- Sqn/Ldr Dennis Watson 99
- T. B. O. Evans 103
- Pete Lawrence 105
- Jock Still 122
- Don Knight 122
- Wally Gibb 124
- Mike Randrup 125
- Walter Shirley 125
- Sqn/Ldr 'Dick' Whittington 130
- Tim Ferguson 132
- John Hall 133
- Desmond 'Dizzy' de Villiers 134
- English Electric P.1/Lightning 140
- John Walter 'Johnny' Hackett 185
- Peter Moneypenny 185
- Keith Isherwood 198
- Fred Ritchie 212
- Wg/Cdr Jimmy Dell 214
- Len Houston 222
- John Nicholls 222

Acknowledgements 226

Warton's Heritage Department 229

FOREWORD

Such is the long and distinguished record of test flying associated with BAE Systems' plants at Samlesbury and Warton near Preston in Lancashire that an account of its development requires little by way of justification.

However, during the preparation of my previous book *Triplane to Typhoon*, published in 2005 by Lancashire County Developments Ltd on behalf of Lancashire County Council, with the support of BAE Systems, it was evident that by concentrating primarily on the aircraft themselves, limitations of space inevitably left much of the human story of test flying, both experimental and production, prior to release and entry into service of the aircraft, largely unrecorded. *Test Flying in Lancashire* now seeks to fill that gap. Today, test flying in Lancashire, enacted most dramatically by daily sorties of the Eurofighter Typhoon from BAE Systems' Warton Aerodrome, is the highly visible manifestation of a large, long-established world-class advanced technology industry with proven capability in design, manufacture and assembly of the most advanced aircraft in the world. The aerospace industry in Lancashire and the North West now supports, directly and indirectly, some 60,000 jobs and has a turnover of £7 billion, making up over a third of UK aerospace production. As well as BAE Systems it includes other 'primes' such as Rolls-Royce and Airbus, with a supply chain of hundreds of small and medium-sized enterprises across the region and beyond.

Moreover, an account of test flying in the area has been motivated, at least in part, by the 65th Anniversary of the start of experimental test flying at the former English Electric Company's site at Warton Aerodrome. That most significant event took place on 28 August 1947 with the first flight by the company's then newly-appointed first Chief Experimental Test Pilot, Wg/Cdr Roland Prosper Beamont, of an eleven-month research programme conducted at Warton using a borrowed Gloster Meteor fighter as an experimental trials aircraft. Ever since then, in fact from around 1940, there has been unbroken continuity of aircraft manufacturing, final assembly and test flying in Lancashire, involving such aeronautical icons as the Hampden, Halifax, Vampire, Canberra, P.1/Lightning, TSR2, Jet Provost/Strikemaster, Jaguar, Tornado, EAP, Hawk, Harrier, Nimrod MRA4 and Typhoon.

In compiling the story of test flying in Lancashire, it has not been my intention to repeat in detail all the material contained in previously published aviation titles, particularly the many books written by Wg/Cdr Beamont himself, or indeed others dealing with the life and times of key figures notably Wg/Cdr James 'Jimmy' Dell. These and other related books will be listed in a bibliography in due course. Rather, my intention has been to produce a comprehensive framework of the main events, detailed where appropriate with previously unpublished information, an objective that has been aided by access to many, though not all, of the flight logs of the key persons involved. The considerable amount of information that has come to light has proved too much for a single volume. This therefore, the first of a series, starts by briefly outlining events from the earliest days of aircraft production by Messrs Dick, Kerr & Co and the English Electric Aircraft Department at Preston and Lytham during WW1 and in the 1920s, before looking in more detail at Samlesbury and Warton from WW2 up to the 1960s. Accounts of later decades will in due course bring the story up to date. It is the intention later to compile a detailed index.

Inevitably, the volume of text devoted to particular people varies according to the amount of information that has come to light. What follows therefore is not necessarily a measure of the full worth or contribution made by specific individuals. In that respect it does not represent a value judgement either by myself or BAE Systems. Indeed I hope that its circulation among a wide readership will itself 'tease out' further information and memories suitable for publication in the future. I would be most grateful to have any such material sent to me at the BAE Systems Heritage Department, Warton, the full address of which is on the back cover of this publication.

Together with a few innocuous but hopefully moderately amusing anecdotes, I have restricted content to those factual events that I have been able to draw from the archives or that have been presented to me. As with most professions, test flying anecdotes are legion and any that have strayed towards the nocuous or controversial – doubtless all apocryphal anyway! – have nevertheless been left out of the narrative, albeit with some regret.

What follows is my own perspective on the history of test flying at Samlesbury and Warton, taking into account all the assistance, information and material I have received. Any content that might be construed as comment or opinion, unless specifically attributed, should therefore be considered mine, not necessarily reflecting any official policy or view held by BAE Systems plc.

James H. Longworth
BAE Systems Heritage Department
Warton
Lancashire
June 2012

INTRODUCTION

For seven decades, from the dawn of the jet age to the present day, test flying at the former English Electric Company's Samlesbury and Warton Aerodromes, near Preston in Lancashire [from 1960 the British Aircraft Corporation (BAC), 1977 British Aerospace (BAe) and, since 2000, BAE Systems] has been at the centre of the development of the UK military aircraft industry.

Today, test flying in Lancashire continues at the leading edge of an industry that attracts more superlatives than most other forms of man's economic activity, notably in terms of the scale, output and value, technology and skills, and the sheer spectacle of its products, underpinning the area's manufacturing economy and making Lancashire one of the world's great centres of aerospace. Its story has been compiled from information held in the BAE Systems Heritage Department archive at Warton, notably from house journals, press releases and aircrew *curricula vitae*, together with flight logs and other material made available by many of the personnel referred to, and from a wide range of other sources, the totality of which is either already within the public domain or otherwise compliant with regulations restricting the publication of sensitive or classified information.

The narrative is one of men and machines entering unexplored realms of speed and altitude, encountering issues of compressibility, critical Mach number, 'shock stall' and the 'dreaded sound barrier' sensationalised so direfully by the Press and Cinema in an era well before that of sophisticated predictive computer simulation. Inspired, intuitive, yet often unproven advances in aircraft design, supported by formative developments in aerodynamic and structural testing, materials technology and manufacturing were coupled with the most demanding and courageous experimental test flying. With Lancashire at its centre, the story also extends far beyond the North West of England, encompassing long-range intercontinental record-breaking flights, world altitude and speed records, delivery of aircraft to markets worldwide in support of UK exports, and not least the securing of the country's air defences.

The very origins of test flying by English Electric and its successors in Lancashire can however be traced back even before the Second World War, before the development of Samlesbury and Warton Aerodromes, to the period of the previous great conflict of 1914-18. Briefly, for completeness and context, those early beginnings are as follows:

1917-1926 – EARLY DAYS, FROM TRAMCARS TO FLYING BOATS

As the land forces and ordnance of the First World War combatant powers remained dug-in on the Western Front, amid scenes of the most appalling human attrition, the war at sea and in the air was fast-moving. At sea, British warships and mechantmen were vulnerable to the blockading tactics of German *Unterseebooten* or U-boats, evidenced by the losses of 1915. After a brief interlude, in 1916 the German Naval Command resumed unrestricted submarine warfare on a 'sink on sight' basis, aimed at strangling Britain's supply lines and forcing her out of the war within months. Among a number of countermeasures adopted by the Lloyd George government, in 1917 the electrical engineers Messrs Dick, Kerr & Co Ltd of Preston and the Phoenix Dynamo Manufacturing Co Ltd of Bradford, both already heavily engaged on munitions work, particularly ordnance, were instructed by the Admiralty to co-operate on the design and production of coastal patrol anti-submarine flying boats to supplement production elsewhere in the country. Dick, Kerr had considerable experience fabricating large wooden structures for electric tramcars while Phoenix were already producing Short Type 184 Dover seaplanes and Maurice Farman S.7 Longhorns for the Royal Naval Air Service (RNAS). As a result, between the years 1917 and 1926, the aircraft department of Dick, Kerr & Co (from 1918 the English Electric Co Ltd) built 63 Felixstowe F.3/F.5s (to the designs of Squadron Commander John Porte of the RNAS, based on those of Glenn H. Curtiss in America), one Fairey N.4 *Atalanta*, one Ayr M.3 and seven Kingston P.5 naval patrol and reconnaissance flying boats, together with four Wren S.1 light trainer aircraft, at the company's works at Strand Road (then known as West Strand Road), Preston, and in hangars at Lytham. In 1917 the aircraft department, occupying newly constructed premises in the form of two 400ft-long bays totalling 48,000 sq ft off Marsh Lane in Preston, was a relatively small part of an extensive older industrial complex manufacturing tramcar carriages, electric traction equipment and a wide range of wartime munitions, the whole bisected into an 'East' and 'West' Works by the busy thoroughfare of Strand Road.

For some years the complex had comprised several enterprises which, though corporately independent, were synergetically linked in the supply of electric tramway equipment to markets worldwide. Registered as the North of England Railway Carriage & Iron Co Ltd in 1863, liquidated in 1878, the disused and derelict 'East Works' or 'Wagon Works' was acquired in 1897 by the then Kilmarnock engineers W. B. Dick and John Kerr for renovation, management and occupation the following year by the Electric Railway and Tramway Carriage Works Ltd. As a result of several mergers, from 1905 this became the United Electric Car Co Ltd. To the west of Strand Road, on land reclaimed following the diversion in 1892 of the River

Ribble to create Preston's Albert Edward Dock, a large new factory was built in 1900 by the Equipment Syndicate Ltd of Manchester, to be occupied for production of electric traction equipment by the English Electric Manufacturing Co Ltd, a company absorbed by Dick, Kerr & Co in 1903. When Dick, Kerr also gained overall control of the 'Carriage Works' by share acquisition in 1917, they had complete charge of all manufacturing operations on both sides of Strand Road. That was the position until the end of 1918 when Dick, Kerr themselves merged with a number of other companies across the North of England and the Midlands – Phoenix Dynamo, the Coventry Ordnance Works Ltd and steam engineers Willans & Robinson Ltd of Rugby – to form the English Electric Co Ltd, from 1919 with head offices at Queen's House, Kingsway, London. In 1920 these initial mergers and acquisitions were completed by English Electric's purchase, from the British Government's compulsorily acquired stock, of the Siemens Bros' Dynamo Works at Stafford.

The Electric Railway and Tramway Carriage Works Ltd (the old Preston Wagon Works), looking east from reclaimed land on West Strand Road, Preston, 1899

West Strand Road, Preston in the early 1900s, after construction of the English Electric Manufacturing Co factory (left) in 1900. On the right is the Carriage Works, from 1905 the United Electric Car Co Ltd

In 1917 Dick, Kerr's new aircraft department was located to the rear of other premises fronting the east side of Strand Road belonging to their neighbours, H. Viney & Co Ltd, haulage contractors of Preston, Liverpool and Manchester. Adjoining both, commanding the junction of Strand Road and Marsh Lane, was the Neptune Hotel. With no local flying facilities, Preston-built Felixstowe flying boats were initially transported on a three-day journey across the Pennines by a fleet of Viney's steam lorries for final assembly at the Royal Naval Air Station at South Shields on Tyneside, from where they were given their first test flights by RNAS pilots. The first of some 35 F.3 aircraft so delivered, *N4230*, flown by **Capt Thomas Henry Newton** at South Shields on 20 February 1918 and subsequently named *Pauline* after his wife, was wrecked at its mooring in the harbour during a storm six days later. Road haulage to South Shields ceased following the Government's requisition, towards the end of the war, of land fronting the Ribble estuary at Lytham for the construction of two hangars totalling 150,000 sq ft, with a slipway, an altogether simpler means of final assembly, flight test and delivery of the remaining F.3/F.5 flying boats to be built by Dick, Kerr. The completed aircraft were collected from Lytham by RNAS pilots for production flight test and delivery to South Shields.

The new factory (centre) occupied by Dick, Kerr's aircraft department, Strand Road, Preston in 1917, the birthplace of aircraft manufacturing in Central Lancashire. [NB: In Manchester, A.V. Roe & Co began series production of aircraft in 1910]

Felixstowe F.3 flying boat N4259 *nearing completion in Dick, Kerr's aircraft department, Strand Road, c. July 1918*

Lytham flying boat assembly sheds, looking east along Warton Street with Lytham Hospital on the left, c. 1918

After the Armistice, Felixstowe production drifted on at a reduced rate into 1919. Thereafter, the single Fairey N.4 *Atalanta* remained in assembly at Lytham until 1921 when declining work dictated the closure of the aircraft department at Strand Road and the Lytham Works. Both were reinstated in 1923 after English Electric secured contracts for prototypes of the Ayr, Kingston and Wren. All three types were designed at Queen's House, London, by English Electric's Chief Designer, William Oke Manning, formerly of Coventry Ordnance and Phoenix Dynamo, who had also worked on a redesign of the Felixstowe hulls at Preston. On 5 April 1923 the prototype Wren, *J6973*, technically the first aircraft of English Electric design and therefore the first type to carry the company's name, was taken from the Strand Road Works to Ashton Park, Preston, for its maiden take-off and landing trials. On 8 April it was flown from Lytham Sands for seven minutes by Air Ministry test pilot **Sqn/Ldr Maurice Wright**, assigned by the Ministry to flight-test the Wren and assess its suitability as a training aircraft. Wright was born in 1893 and educated at Marlborough and Caius College, Cambridge. As an air-minded undergraduate, in 1913 he flew a Wright (Orville and Wilbur)-type glider at Eastchurch, Isle of Sheppey, where he met Richard (later Sir Richard) Fairey, beginning a friendship that was to last over 40 years. In 1914 Wright volunteered for the RNAS and, as a Flight Sub-Lieutenant, flew on operations over the North Sea, the Dardanelles, Bulgaria, Syria, Aden and Egypt. His duties included flying long observation missions in Short 184 seaplanes operating from HMS *Roberts* and HMS *Ben-my-Chree*. Fitted with primitive radios with a reach of 20 miles and having to contend with the excessively turbulent air over the Dardanelles, they spotted for the Royal Navy's guns which were shelling over a range of 15 miles. [*Ben-my-Chree*, the third vessel of that name operated by the Isle of Man Steam Packet Co, built by Vickers at Barrow in 1908, was converted into a seaplane carrier by Cammell Laird in 1915, following requisition by the Admiralty. In 1917, under bombardment from Turkish positions near the Greek island of Kastellorizo, she sank in shallow water in the Mediterranean. Raised in 1920, she was scrapped at Venice in 1923. The Steam Packet Co replaced her with *Ben-my-Chree (4)*, built by Cammell Laird in 1927, herself to serve as the headquarters ship for the 512th Assault Flotilla at Omaha Beach on D-Day, 6 June 1944.] Invalided home, Maurice Wright was later appointed test pilot for seaplanes, flew Felixstowe F.2A flying boats from the Isle of Grain and in 1916 flew Fairey's first aircraft, the Campania seaplane, from Grain to Scapa Flow. He became Chief Test Pilot at the Admiralty and transferred to the RAF in 1918, later joining the Air Ministry.

Wright maintained his gliding and light aircraft interests after the war and taking off in the Wren from Lytham Sands into a strong wind on 8 April 1923, in the course of a seven-minute flight found that the aircraft handled very well, attaining 300ft at a little over 40mph. On 11 May he addressed the Institution of Aeronautical Engineers on the subject of 'Flying with Low-Power'. On 14 June he was airborne for over an hour, climbing to 2,350ft at up to 52mph. The following day, flying for 68 minutes at up to 300ft, the Wren consumed seven-eighths of a gallon of petrol.

Prototype English Electric S.1 Wren J6973, sitting outside the aircraft department at Strand Road, adjacent to Viney's, 1923

In October, two Wrens, piloted by Sqn/Ldr Wright and Flt/Lt Longton, were entered in the 1923 Light Aeroplane competition held at Lympne, the prize for lowest fuel consumption being shared between Longton and A. H. James who was flying an ANEC monoplane. With long experience of seaplanes and flying boats, in 1924 Wright became Chief Technical Officer at the Marine Aircraft Experimental Establishment (MAEE) at Felixstowe. In 1925 he was invited by Richard Fairey to join the Fairey Aviation Company, established in 1915, as a Director. For the next 23 years Wright experienced many different Fairey aircraft, bringing his total of types flown to 170. Maurice Wright died in post in 1957, still a Director of Fairey, Chairman of Avions Fairey and a member of the Council of the Society of British Aircraft Constructors (SBAC).

At the beginning of 1924, **Marcus Dyce Manton**, onetime 'famous boy aviator', who had learned to fly in a 1910 Howard Wright biplane at the Grahame-White Flying School at Hendon in 1912, gaining Aviator's Certificate No. 231, was appointed Superintendent of the English Electric aircraft department. 10 years earlier, in 1914, Manton, together with Bentfield Charles 'B. C.' 'Benny' Hucks, the latter born in 1884 at Bentfield Green, Stansted, Essex, famed as the inventor of the 'Hucks Starter' auxiliary motor and the first British airman to 'loop the loop', had gained notoriety for their pre-war combined spiral 'S-loop' displays. Such 'aerial acrobatics' involved diving their aircraft clean past the vertical until inverted – the so-called 'outside loop' or 'bunt' – together with extended inverted flights, manoeuvres that astonishingly failed to collapse their Bleriot 'parasol' monoplanes. Ironically, when Hucks *did* meet his demise later in 1914, it was the result of his having succumbed to the 'Spanish 'flu'. Manton reputedly prepared for inverted flight by lashing himself into a chair, the whole ensemble then being suspended upside down from a strong beam at his home.

Early in 1924, **Maj Herbert George Brackley**, Air Superintendent of Imperial Airways, was retained to flight-test the prototype English Electric Kingston, *N168*, together with some of the later production series. Born in 1894 and educated at Sevenoaks School, in the First World War Brackley served with the RNAS and RAF and was awarded the DSO and DSC. In 1919, he and his Handley Page V/1500 were potential candidates to make the first transatlantic air crossing but were pre-empted by Alcock and Brown in their Vickers Vimy. Instead, Brackley flew the V/1500 from Newfoundland to New York. The following year, in a Handley Page 0/400, he attempted a flight from London to Cape Town but engine trouble caused him to crash near Khartoum. He then joined Handley Page Transport as Chief Pilot and was a member of the British aviation mission in Japan where he survived the Great Kanto Earthquake of 1923. Returning to the UK just as a number of companies were being amalgamated into Imperial Airways, he was appointed Air Superintendent of the new airline.

Maj H.G.Brackley, engaged to test fly the prototype, second and third P.5 Kingston Mk 1 flying boats, 1924

On 22 May 1924, prototype Kingston *N168* was launched down the slipway at the Lytham flight sheds for taxying trials and its maiden flight from the Ribble estuary. With everything apparently in order, Maj Brackley, assisted by observer **C. J. Blackburn** and engineer **W. A. Bannister**, pointed the aircraft seawards and opened up its two Napier Lions to their raucous maximum. Picking up speed into a stiff north-westerly breeze, moving well over the slightly choppy waters, fully committed and just about to leave the surface, *N168* came to a sudden halt in a cloud of spray. The aircraft remained afloat but with its nose underwater and tailplane vertical. Having been thrown into the water, the crew was rescued by the company launch and, although reportedly arguing vociferously as they came ashore, they and the Kingston, which was later recovered, were found blameless in the incident. The official inquiry concluded that the accident was caused by the aircraft hitting flotsam, not, as suggested by onlookers, the north training wall of the navigable channel of the Ribble, built of stone and submerged at high tide but with its western extremity marked by a beacon. Both Brackley and Manton also tested later Kingstons. Brackley subsequently returned to Imperial Airways, renewing his association with the North West in 1928 when he inaugurated an Imperial Airways service between Liverpool and Belfast using a Short Calcutta flying boat. During the Second World War he was appointed Deputy Air Officer (Admin) and Senior Air Staff Officer (SASO) of No.19 Group, Coastal Command, under Air Chief Marshal Sir Frederick Bowhill, with whom he also later served as SASO in Transport Command. He was appointed CBE in 1941 and in 1947 organised the evacuation by BOAC of some 42,000 people during the partition of India and Pakistan. Brackley became assistant to the Chairman of BOAC and then succeeded Air Vice-Marshal Donald Bennett as Chief Executive of British South American Airways (BSAA). He was a lifelong advocate of flying boats. 'Brackles' to his friends, though not very well-known to the general public, was an influential force in military and civil aviation. Tragically, in 1948, during a tour of BSAA routes and stations in South America, Air Commodore H. G. Brackley, CBE, DSO, DSC, FRGS, AFRAeS, drowned while swimming off Copacabana Beach, near Rio de Janeiro.

Towards the end of 1924 Marcus Manton became English Electric's Chief Test Pilot and Inspector, responsible, together with colleagues **Alan Calder** and **C. J. Blackburn**, for testing the company's Kingston flying boats. Calder is believed to have also served with the Fairey Aviation Co. Manton also tested the unsuccessful prototype English Electric Ayr *N148*, whose reluctance to 'unstick' from the waters of the Ribble estuary proved insuperable. It is not known for certain whether Service test pilots had any greater success with the Ayr in trials elsewhere. During the Second World War, Manton held the post of Service Liaison Officer with Armstrong Whitworth Aircraft, after when he was employed by Hawker Siddeley until his retirement in 1946.

Maj Brackley taxies prototype Kingston N168 off Lytham, 22 May 1924…

…and begins the take-off run…

...before ending up vertical in the estuary after striking an underwater obstruction.
An inauspicious start for the Kingston

After recovery, back in the Lytham sheds the damage sustained by the hull of N168 is evident

Exhaust rises from the gas starter engine priming the Napier Lion engines of third Kingston, N9710, prior to its first flight by Maj Brackley, Lytham, 13 November 1924

Marcus Manton (centre), Alan Calder (left) and C. J. Blackburn at Lytham Works, 1924/25

Kingston and Ayr flying boats at the Lytham Works, standing at the slipway to the Ribble, February 1925

English Electric M.3 Ayr N148, *happy enough on its beaching trolley on the apron at Lytham…*

…less so under power on the water

1926-1939 – DECLINE AND RESURGENCE

Precipitated by the total collapse of Air Ministry contracts for the Kingston, in April 1926 the English Electric aircraft department at Strand Road closed for the second time and the company finally abandoned its Lytham Works which became a film studio and in 1930 a bakery. English Electric remained outside the aircraft industry for the next twelve years, its former aircraft department being converted to assemble railway locomotives. By 1936 the Preston factory was turning out not only diesel locomotives but also domestic electrical appliances. Then, in 1938, the rapidly deteriorating political situation in Europe led to the decision by the English Electric Board of Directors at Stafford, where the company had acquired the Siemens Bros' Dynamo Works in 1920, to put its experience and capacity at the disposal of the Government in expediting the defence programme. The company's offer was conveyed by its Chairman and Managing Director, Mr George Nelson, at a meeting with the Air Minister, Sir Kingsley Wood. In the summer of 1938, having concluded that large companies in the electrical and motor industries offered the greatest potential for expanding aircraft production, the Air Ministry directed that English Electric should, as subcontractors, build Handley Page's Hampden twin-engined medium bomber, hitherto built at Radlett, Hertfordshire, under the 'shadow factory' scheme. Planning started right away for the resumption of aircraft manufacturing at Strand Road, Preston.

H.Viney & Co Ltd, hauliers, Strand Road, Preston, 1939

Plans were drawn up in 1940 by the Preston architect George (later Sir George) Grenfell Baines for the redevelopment of Viney's for aircraft production by English Electric

Becoming an integral part of English Electric's Strand Road Works, it would continue to be referred to as 'Vineys' for years to come

Immediate high-level contacts were instigated between the two companies, followed by transfer of a small number of key personnel from Handley Page to English Electric. The first priority was to expand the Strand Road 'East Works' production facilities, which included the original aircraft department. Among a number of developments, Viney's haulage premises were requisitioned in 1939 and demolished, their site built over and incorporated within the greatly expanded English Electric factory as assembly and final erection shops. That part of the Works would continue to be referred to as 'Vineys' for years to come. Soon after, in anticipation of contracts also to build the larger four-engined Handley Page Halifax heavy bomber at Strand Road, it was decided to bring the 'West Works' into aircraft production.

Faced then with an urgent need for an extensive final assembly facility with adjacent flying ground for production test and delivery despatch of land-based aircraft, there was renewed inerest on the part of the authorities in a site extending over some 350 acres at Samlesbury for development as an aircraft works and aerodrome. Situated some 20 miles from the Lancashire coast, between the towns of Preston and Blackburn, on a low plateau 250ft above sea level overlooking the meandering River Ribble and its scenic rural valley, from as early as 1922 land at Manor Farm, adjoining the historic Samlesbury Hall, seat of the Southworths since the 14th Century, had been the subject of various abortive inter-war proposals for a shared municipal aerodrome. As the international situation in Europe soured, in 1938 the site was pressed into service for construction of an aircraft assembly works and aerodrome for English Electric. A mile or so to the east, rising ground peaked at the 730ft summit of Mellor Moor, a hilltop which would merit respect and a wary eye on the part of future generations of pilots 'in the circuit', particularly under East Lancashire weather conditions. Samlesbury Aerodrome was laid out with three runways, the main one 1,300 yards in length, considered suitable in due course for the installation of radio landing aids, the others each of 1,000 yards. When the aerodrome became operational in 1940, tarmacadam runways having been completed in January, wrapped within strict wartime security the busy air traffic in the Samlesbury 'circuit' afforded some interesting sights for travellers and residents along the Whalley/Myerscough Smithy Road (later the Whalley Bypass A59) and Preston New Road (A677), which bounded the aerodrome to the north and south respectively. Aircraft movements at Samlesbury, inevitably dominated by production and delivery flying of Hampden and Halifax bombers, were supplemented between 1941 and 1944 by those of Spitfires, Hurricanes, Masters, Defiants, Oxfords, Ansons, Hornet Moths and Tiger Moths attached to the Communications Squadron of No.9 Group, RAF Fighter Command, headquartered at Barton Hall just to the north of Preston. The main runway was concreted by May 1943, reflecting the growth in volume and weight of traffic. Additionally, repaired and refurbished Bristol Beaufighters, reassembled by Burnley Aircraft Products, a small aero-engineering company located on Preston New Road next to Samlesbury Hall, were flown from the aerodrome on flight test and delivery.

ENGLISH ELECTRIC – A NEW FORCE IN BRITISH MILITARY AVIATION

AIRCREW and EVENTS of the 1940s /'50s

New-build Aircraft Programmes Current:
Handley Page Hampden, Handley Page Halifax, de Havilland Vampire, English Electric B3/45 B5/47 A1 Canberra, English Electric F23/49 P.1

During the Second World War, at Preston and Samlesbury, English Electric licence-built 770 Handley Page Hampden and 2,145 Halifax bombers, together with six de Havilland Vampire fighter jets. Larger-scale production of the Vampire followed in the early post-war years, a total of 1,369 of the jets having been completed by English Electric – more than by de Havilland themselves – when production ceased in 1952.

Manufactured in sub-assemblies at Strand Road and in component form in a number of satellite factories in the area, wartime Hampden and Halifax bombers were fully assembled at the company's new airfield at Samlesbury. It is reputed that late in 1939, with the first Hampden due to be nearing completion early the following year, the Chief Inspector at Strand Road approached the Works Manager, the redoubtable Arthur Sheffield, known throughout the works as 'Sheff', pointing out that the contract required the aircraft to be test flown by the company prior to delivery. What were to be the arrangements? Sheffield, a production man *par excellence*, but no aviator, is believed to have suggested that the Chief send a pair of his inspectors on a pilots' course! Fortunately, more realistic counsels prevailed and several experienced Ministry of Aircraft Production (MAP) and RAF test pilots were brought in, including **J. D. Rose, J. Easdown** and **'Doug' Potter**. It was they who would bear the brunt of the production-testing of all English Electric output from Samlesbury Aerodrome during the war, with some assistance from other RAF personnel and men and women civilian pilots of the Air Transport Auxiliary (ATA), one of whom was Jim Mollison, husband of the legendary Amy Johnson. At first, flying aids at Samlesbury were primitive and flying was permitted only if the Chief Test

J. D. Rose and Halifax at Samlesbury

Pilot could see Mellor Mill chimney. With no lighting or ground-to-air R/T, Hampden and early Halifax pilots reported faults by flying low over the aerodrome and dropping written messages contained in small white bags weighted with lead shot.

Chief Test Pilot **John Dumella 'Mella' Rose**, MBE, was at Samlesbury from late 1939 until 30 September 1946, flying frequently with **George Gilbraith** as test observer/flight engineer. It was not unknown for Rose to take the occasional staff member as a passenger on a test flight. Rose had learned to fly in an Avro 504N 'Lynx' at No.1 FTS Netheravon in 1929 and, from 1935 to 1939, as a Flying Officer in the RAF Reserve, had also been a test pilot with the Blackburn Aircraft Co. During his time at Samlesbury he presided over an exemplary flight safety record, although on one occasion a Halifax he was testing blew a tyre on touchdown, swinging off the runway and colliding with a cement mixer. Rose was unhurt and the aircraft, though badly damaged, was repairable. After the war he joined the Ministry of Aviation Air Accidents Investigation Branch, based in Shell Mex House in the Strand, London. In 1964 he revisited Samlesbury and, both there and at Warton, met many former associates. In 1940 **J. Easdown** joined the Samlesbury pilots, living nearby at Nab's Head and serving throughout the war until 1945. Wartime production test pilot and local man **'Doug' Potter** remained with the company after the war, engaged on sales particularly in South American markets, subsequently establishing and running the Spares Department. Flight test engineers and observers **Len Dean** and

Rose and Gilbraith at Samlesbury

Rose, relaxing between production flights at Samlesbury

Arthur Talbot were also members of the wartime production test team who stayed on with English Electric after the war.

The first 'English Electric' Hampden, *P2062*, flew on 22 February 1940 and the first Halifax, *V9976*, on 15 August 1941. Initially the Hampdens were flown to No.37 Maintenance Unit (MU) at RAF Burtonwood to be fitted with heating systems, armour plate and guns. The first four aircraft arrived there from Samlesbury on 26 May 1940. During the war years, the production test flying team lived virtually 'on-site' at Samlesbury Hall Cottage, formerly two smaller properties that once housed gardeners employed at the nearby Samlesbury Hall. From there the pilots were on immediate call in order to deal with routine production and delivery flying of works output that peaked at 80 Halifaxes during the month of February 1944, together with any backlog of aircraft that might accumulate due to adverse East Lancashire weather conditions, a constraint that from time to time would continue to affect post-war flying at Samlesbury. Delivery ferries were often flown single-handed to one of a number of RAF MUs including West Freugh and Castle Kennedy in Dumfries and Galloway, Troon and Prestwick in Ayrshire, for final fitting out. Sometimes, if the aircraft performed satisfactorily during the first half-hour of a morning test flight from Samlesbury, the flight would continue as a delivery ferry up to one of the MUs. The pilots returned by train to Preston to be met by car at the station and driven back to Samlesbury in order to fly another machine north of the

Early Handley Page-built Hampden L4135, flown by the company's Chief Test Pilot, Maj James Cordes, airborne from Radlett, April 1939. Northbound on the London - St Albans line is LMS Beyer Garrett 2-6-0 + 0-6-2 engine 7982, hauling coal wagons

Border in the afternoon, then back again on the train late afternoon or early evening. Altogether a punishing schedule, but the company's flight-test record remained unimpaired for the whole of the war: not one of over 2,900 aircraft to emerge from the Samlesbury assembly lines was lost or written off before delivery to the RAF. Every hundredth aircraft also had to be flown to Handley Page's aerodrome at Radlett so that HP test pilots could carry out quality control checks, a somewhat pointless exercise given the superior quality of the English Electric-built aircraft. Flight Engineer Len Dean flew on about 1,000 test flights and Arthur Talbot was present on another 100 tests and deliveries. After such intense activity, as the war ended there were mixed emotions among the workforce when some of the final Halifaxes were towed away to the far side of the airfield to be cut up for scrap.

Although not an English Electric test pilot, Leonard Pomeroy was reputedly responsible for test flying Beaufighters reassembled by Burnley Aircraft Products at Samlesbury, establishing a reputation for flying the formidable twin-engined heavy strike fighter down to 30ft along the runway. Armed with two cannon and six machine guns, it was named 'The Whispering Death' by the Japanese, due to its relatively quiet approach but shatteringly noisy departure. Sub-assemblies rebuilt by the firm at its Gannow, Burnley factory, were brought to Samlesbury by road on 'Queen Mary' transporters for final assembly and fitting with new Hercules engines, hydraulics and electrics. Highly classified – indeed one of the war's best-kept

Hampden 1 AE394 *(foreground) and Halifax 11* V9978 *nearing completion at Samlesbury, September 1941*

Halifax 11s undergoing final pre-delivery checks, Samlesbury. JB928 (foreground), delivered to No.78 Sqn in April 1943, failed to return from a raid on the Ruhr in June

secrets – was the fitting out of some of the Beaufighters at Samlesbury with airborne radar. At the time it suited the British authorities to attribute RAF night-fighter successes by pilots such as John 'Cats Eyes' Cunningham to enhanced night vision resulting from a substantial dietary intake of carrots, a myth perpetuated to the present day. Post-war, Burnley Aircraft Products became the Lancashire Aircraft Corporation, building the Lancashire Prospector agricultural utility and crop-sprayer aircraft. Later, as Samlesbury Engineering, they diversified into truck and bus components. In 1954 they were noted particularly for their sheet metal work and assembly of Donald Campbell's *Bluebird* turbojet hydroplane, which was also fitted with its Metropolitan-Vickers Beryl power plant at the Samlesbury works.

The maiden flight of the first English Electric-produced Vampire F.1, *TG274*, was made at Samlesbury on 20 April 1945 by **Geoffrey de Havilland Jnr**, the designers' Chief Test Pilot, who held that post from 1937 to 1946. John Rose, having been totally absorbed in production-testing multi-engined medium and heavy bombers throughout the war, was reputedly unimpressed by the diminutive single-engined jet. Perhaps the official code-name of *Spider Crab* for the curious little aeroplane did not help. Three days later, *TG274* was flown to the de Havilland Co at Hatfield for trials by its designers and, a month later, to the Aircraft and Armament Experimental Establishment (A&AEE) at Boscombe Down for engine and handling assessment. On 3 December, in the hands of Polish test pilot **Sqn/Ldr Janusz (Jan) Zurakowski**, who had flown Spitfires with the RAF in the Battle of Britain, during a demonstration of its low speed handling before a delegation of Soviets at Boscombe, *TG274* stalled over their heads, bellying into the ground in a cloud of dust and debris with the Russians scattering in all directions. It was written off. Zurakowski survived and became a noted aerobatic pilot, famed for the 'Zurabatic Cartwheel', a manoeuvre he is believed to have perfected while production-testing the twin-engined de Havilland Hornet fighter. He achieved the spectacle at the top of a vertical climb, just before the stall 'chopping' the throttle of one of the two engines, simultaneously opening up the other, spinning the aircraft around its vertical axis, which was parallel to the ground, in vertical descent. On no occasion was it displayed to greater astonishment, even alarm, than at the 1951 Farnborough Air Show when 'Zura' initiated proceedings above cloud, toppling out below cloud base in front of the crowd in ground attack fighter Gloster Meteor *G-7-1*, heavily and improbably laden with rockets and wingtip tanks. He got away with it. Following demobilisation from the RAF, another production test pilot, **Richard L. C. 'Dickie' Blyth**, DSO, DFC, came to Samlesbury late in 1945 to test Vampires but left in March 1947, for the next ten years working for de Havilland as a sales and RAF liaison pilot. He returned briefly to Samlesbury on 24 May 1948 to carry out a ten-minute production test of RAF Vampire FB.5 *VV215*. In 1953, a distinctive figure in his tweed cap, Blyth demonstrated the short take-off, slow and 'fast' handling of the Leonides-powered DH Canada Beaver 2 at the SBAC Farnborough Air Show.

Vampire F.1 final assembly at Samlesbury, October 1945, with the 19th production aircraft TG292 in the foreground

Early in 1944, meeting in the boardroom at Stafford Works, the Directors of the English Electric Co under the Chairman and Managing Director **Sir George Horatio Nelson** (later **Baron Nelson of Stafford**), took the momentous decision to capitalise further on their profitable and greatly expanded production facilities at Preston and Samlesbury by continuing to manufacture aircraft after the war. [Nelson had relocated the headquarters of English Electric from London to the Stafford Works in the 1930s.] Their decision was communicated to the world at a luncheon held twelve months later on 6 April 1945 at Strand Road, Preston, attended by VIPs and members of the press, at which Sir George disclosed the previously classified information that nearly 3,000 bombers had been produced by the Preston Works. In arriving at their decision the Directors were acutely aware that, not being a member of the established 'family' of pre-war aircraft companies such as Avro, Bristol, de Havilland, Gloster, Handley Page, Hawker, Shorts, Vickers or Westland, despite their magnificent wartime production record of Hampdens and Halifaxes and while post-war subcontracts for the Vampire seemed assured (a contract was received in June 1944), English Electric could not take for granted the continuity of such 'grace and favour' work under licence. Even less could they be guaranteed long term survival in a competitive world with reduced military requirements. That could only be achieved by establishing their own design team, capable of conceptualising entirely new aircraft types unique to English Electric, followed by the winning of contracts for production by the company of its own designs.

Strand Road, Preston, 6 April 1945, Sir George Nelson announces English Electric's intention to continue in the aircraft industry after the war

Accordingly, in July 1944, the 35-year-old **William Edward Willoughby 'Teddy' Petter**, BA, FRAeS, from 1936 Technical Director of Westland Aircraft Ltd of Yeovil, Somerset, where he designed the Lysander, Whirlwind and Welkin, was appointed as Chief Engineer of English Electric's Aircraft Division at Preston, with responsibility for generating new designs and a brief to recruit the necessary skills.

Impressed by English Electric's wartime production record, the Ministry of Aircraft Production (MAP) was keen to support the company's continued post-war involvement in the industry and to marry such continuity with Petter's vision of a twin-jet tactical fighter bomber to replace the Mosquito, a concept on which he had been working at Yeovil with the support of the Ministry to its Specification B1/44 of March 1944. However in 1938 Teddy's father, Sir Ernest Petter, against his son's wishes, had sold out the controlling family interest in Westland to the John Brown shipbuilding group who made a number of new appointments to the Board, notably two of their own Directors, the father and son industrialists Sir Holberry Mensforth and Eric (later Sir Eric) Mensforth, the latter as Joint Managing Director. Seemingly it led to various boardroom tensions. [Eric Mensforth established the domestic appliance division of English Electric in 1931, later became production adviser to the MAP and, in the USA in 1946/47, negotiated a licence with Igor Sikorsky for Westland to build helicopters, a decision that would prove to be of fundamental importance to the long-term future of the company.]

By 1944 the Westland Directors were more interested in developing a naval fighter, later to result in the Wyvern, than in Petter's ideas for the jet fighter bomber. On returning from a few weeks away from the company in April/May 1944, reputedly on a trip with his wife to visit her family in Switzerland, although details of their mysterious wartime travel arrangements are unknown, Petter was incandescent to find that during his absence, despite Ministry support for his jet fighter bomber, the Westland Board had secured the Royal Navy's approval to work up designs for the Wyvern. The company lacked the capacity to tackle both projects. When, characteristically as future events would show, Petter walked out, leaving Westlands to get on with the problematical Wyvern, he was allowed to take the design rights for the fighter bomber with him to English Electric. Truly, Yeovil's loss was to become Preston's gain.

It seems likely that senior contacts of Petter's at the Ministry, where his stock was high, notably its Director, Air Marshal Sir Wilfrid Freeman, together with Air Marshal Sir Ralph Sorley, Controller of Research and Development (himself a test pilot and in 1944 just recently the instigator of the Empire Test Pilots School), and Technical Development Director N. E. (Nero) Rowe, put him in touch with Sir George Nelson, paving the way for his appointment to English Electric. Moreover, among the labyrinthine connections between boards of directors of British companies, it was Sir Holberry Mensforth, as Chairman of English Electric from 1930-33, who had appointed George Nelson, who had worked for him at the British Westinghouse Co at Trafford Park, as Managing Director of English Electric. When Mensforth left to join the Board of John Brown in 1933, Nelson succeeded him as Chairman and Managing Director. All the leading protagonists were well known to each other…

Having cast the die so determinedly, Sir George, together with his son **Henry George Nelson** (known with some affection among the workforce as 'Half' Nelson, Superintendent and Deputy Works Manager at Preston during the early war years and a future Chairman and MD of English Electric), together with the Board, would prove unstinting in providing the capital necessary for recruitment and new facilities for R&D, test and design. Sir George was adamant that English Electric should not be dependent on shared national test facilities, for use of which projects had to 'join the queue', so the company invested in its own range of wind tunnels, structural test rigs and early computers such as the English Electric-built Digital Electronic Universal Computing Engine (DEUCE).

Located initially at English Electric's London offices at Queen's House in Kingsway, Petter shared a secretary, Anne Seagrim, with the Cambridge University scientist and novelist C. P. Snow who, as wartime Chief of Scientific Personnel for the Ministry of Labour, was then also personnel adviser to the company. Miss Seagrim was later Private Secretary to the Duke of Windsor and, afterwards, Field Marshal Lord Alexander of Tunis. On arriving in Preston early in 1945, Petter took rooms in the Park Hotel where, in the green surroundings of Miller Park, with sweeping views over the River Ribble and rural Lancashire, he developed on paper many of his early ideas for the new aircraft project. With a private access to the adjacent Preston Station the Park Hotel was convenient for essential business visits to London. Air traffic overhead, in and out of Samlesbury and to and from the USAAF 8th Air Force Base Air Depot No.2 at Warton, some seven miles to the west of Preston, would have been an ever present, though unnecessary, reminder of the reason for his coming to Lancashire. Soon after arriving in Preston he established his design office on the upper floor of the 40,000 sq ft former showroom and garage of Barton Motors in Corporation Street, close to the town centre. In a less than sylvan setting, adjoining the Dock Street Coal Sidings, their cobbled access road, weighbridges and shunting yard, with a monumental mason as another neighbour, the somewhat war-weary but nevertheless striking art deco premises built in the 1930s had been requisitioned around 1940 as a Government Training Centre, familiarly known as 'TC', to equip men and women with engineering skills for the wartime 'shadow' aircraft factories. In the mid-'40s the building and its watch-house stood behind a makeshift fence and a miscellany of emergency water tanks and pipes. As production of the Halifax peaked, during 1944 the requirement for training was scaled back and, in April, to allow work on the bombers to proceed unimpeded at Strand Road, English Electric leased 'TC' as workshop facilities for limited production of airframe structures for the Vampire jet fighter. After the war ended, all Vampire work, post-50th aircraft set, was relocated from 'TC' to take up vacated floorspace back at Strand Road and Samlesbury. Thereafter 'TC' quickly and discreetly assumed its new mantle as the company's design office, a total lack of salubriousness providing more than adequate cover for its new highly classified secret role. On the ground floor were mould loft, mechanical test and weight groups. The upper floor, accessed by an internal staircase and 'up' ramp from the street, was the drawing office containing a sea of around 50 drawing boards (off which the coal dust had to be blown each morning), together with stress, aerodynamics and half glass-partitioned senior staff offices. Supported on pillars, a distinctive semicircular bow-fronted projection of the upper floor, overlooking Corporation Street, is believed to have been the senior staff dining room. To the rear of the building, accessed by a 'down' ramp, was a large lower ground floor, the original garage service workshop, overlooked by the offices, used as the experimental, mock-up and prototype shop. It also contained a small 30 x 30inch wind tunnel purchased from the Weybridge Airscrew Co in 1946.

At a time when other manufacturers such as Avro, Handley Page, Vickers and Shorts began to focus on large four-engined designs, later to evolve as the 'V'-bombers, the field was wide open for English Electric's design team at 'TC' to concentrate fully on developing Petter's proposed experimental twin-jet high altitude, high speed aircraft. It met closely an official Ministry of Supply (MoS) experimental specification of that time for a high altitude light bomber, E3/45 (the fighter element having been dropped), towards which the company received an initial design investigation contract in June 1945. Much of the first technical brochure, submitted to the MoS in the autumn of 1945, was reputedly written by the team in the Victoria and Station Hotel on Fishergate, Preston. That was followed in January 1946 by a contract for detail design and build of four prototypes (to be designated within the company initially as the A1 and later as the English Electric Canberra B.1). In March 1946 it was formalised as bomber specification B3/45 for a twin-jet, high speed, high altitude unarmed light bomber, still seen as a replacement for the Mosquito, incorporating radar navigation and bomb aiming equipment capable of high-altitude delivery of bombs and guided projectiles onto targets out of vision or obscured by cloud. So close to the specification had been Petter's original proposals for a fighter bomber, they were easily modified to meet the official requirement for an unarmed light bomber, requiring few changes other than the abandonment of any ideas for fixed gun armament.

In October 1944, in London and Kingston, more by informal discussion than interview, Petter secured the interest of **Frederick William 'Freddie' Page** in the jet bomber project. Having taken a 'first' in the Mechanical Sciences Tripos at St. Catharine's College, Cambridge, from 1938 Page had worked under Sydney Camm in the design office of the Hawker Aircraft Company as Stress and Project Engineer on aircraft such as the Hurricane, Typhoon and Tempest. Both Teddy Petter and

H. G. Nelson were also Cambridge Mechanical Sciences Tripos graduates. In 1945, Petter recruited Harry Harrison from Westlands as Chief Draughtsman and, in April, Page joined English Electric as Chief Stressman, the third member of Petter's new team, soon to expand rapidly with specialists in structural design and aerodynamics. Alec Atkin, a future aerodynamicist (1950); Project Manager Lightning (1959); Special Director (1964); Divisional Managing Director (1976) and Chairman (1978), started in 1945 as an assistant aerodynamicist with a Diploma in Aeronautics from Hull Technical College, later returning to do a degree course at Hull University. In July 1945, Bernard Oliver Heath, from Nottingham University and Imperial College, London, having been interviewed by C. P. Snow in London, was directed to the company and assigned to Page as stressman, Canberra, later becoming an aerodynamicist on the P.1 (1948); Aerostructures Group Leader (1951); Chief Project Engineer (1957); Assistant Chief Engineer, Canberra and TSR2 (1959); Project Manager TSR2 (1963); Special Director (1965); Leader, Jaguar Technical Team (1965); Project Manager AFVG (1966); Director of Systems Engineering (Warton), Panavia (1969); Project Director for MRCA (1970); Director of Engineering (1974) and Professor of Aeronautical Engineering, Salford University (1983). In October 1945 Glen Hobday, of Westland, joined as a stressman, subsequently attaining senior positions with the company. Don Crowe, from Handley Page, who had acted as Design Liaison Engineer/Technical Representative during English Electric's wartime work on the Hampden and Halifax, returned as Chief Structural Designer. Dai Ellis (mid-1945) and Ray Creasey (mid-1946) came from Barnes Wallis' Vickers team at Weybridge, Ellis as Chief Aerodynamicist, succeeded in that capacity in 1946 by Creasey. Ellis subsequently went on to design and commence building the company's low and high speed wind tunnel facilities at Strand Road, later to be erected at Warton. Creasey became the dominant force in the detail design of English Electric's first two jet aircraft types, the A1/Canberra and P.1/Lightning, going on to make major contributions to TSR2 and Tornado before his untimely death in 1976 when Director of Engineering. Roy Fowler, from the National Physical Laboratory, joined in November 1945 to oversee low-speed and the first transonic wind tunnel developments. Ron Dickson, later Director of Research, came straight from Cambridge University. Bob Hollock was in charge of prototype manufacture, including assembly of the first wing sets at 'TC' and other major assemblies at Strand Road. John King from RAE Farnborough took charge of mechanical and structural test. Ted Loveless, a future Deputy MD of Panavia, worked under Page in the Stress Office. In 1948 A. E. Ellison came from Airspeed as Assistant Chief Designer. Denis B. Smith, a former RAF Wing Commander, came earlier to oversee administrative matters. Air Commodore Strang Graham, wartime MAP overseer at English Electric, was appointed as aviation adviser to Sir George Nelson and to liaise with the Ministry and RAF. Some of the early key appointees literally were 'directed' by the Government to take up work with English Electric, while for others special dispensation had to be obtained from the strictures of the Control of Employment Act, which made wartime mobility of labour subject to compliance with national strategic industrial policies.

In September 1946, having served for a short period at Boscombe Down, **Frank E. Roe**, from Bishop Auckland, County Durham, holder of a postgraduate Diploma in Aeronautics from Imperial College, University of London, where he was interviewed by Freddie Page, was one of the first three to be engaged as graduate apprentices in aircraft engineering at English Electric's 'TC' premises. To gain practical experience, rather than going straight into the technical offices, they opted for an apprenticeship, working for a year with skilled fitters on the shop floor before moving round the technical departments. After working on tooling for the Vampire and jigs for the prototype Canberra at 'TC', followed by a spell on Vampire final assembly at Samlesbury and in mechanical test back at 'TC', in 1948 Frank Roe became an aerodynamicist working on the wind tunnel at Warton where in 1949 he was put in charge of the construction of the first high speed tunnel, powered by a Rolls-Royce Nene jet engine. He became Head of the Wind Tunnel Department at Warton in 1950, succeeding Roy Fowler who left for the RAE. Roe was later appointed Chief Development Engineer; a Special Director (1964), Director of Resources (1968), becoming Deputy Managing Director (1978) and Managing Director of the Military Aircraft Division (1981). He joined the Boards of the British Aerospace Aircraft Group and Panavia GmbH and was appointed CBE (1985) and a Deputy Lieutenant of Lancashire, retiring in 1987.

These personnel were the nucleus of a group that by mid-1947 numbered around 100, located in the overcrowded conditions and highly charged atmosphere of 'TC', with responsibility for developing Petter's original concept from his time at Westland into a viable design for production by English Electric. Today, Frank Roe remembers vividly the team spirit in the new design organisation, its strong leadership and bright young graduates unfettered by tradition or practice, with everything to play for at the dawn of the jet age. Having been warned by his Professor that to go to Preston might be something of a gamble – the new English Electric Aircraft Division could just as easily fall flat on its face as succeed – Frank nevertheless took a calculated risk and joined a team where opportunities would be seized, problems solved and things made to happen.

Petter and Page were gaining confidence all the time, particularly after positive discussions in 1945 with Stanley Hooker and Adrian Lombard at Rolls-Royce Barnoldswick, and A. A. Griffiths at R-R Derby, concerning the adoption of twin axial-flow R-R AJ65 (Axial Jet 6,500 lb thrust) turbojets, later to be named Avons, as specified subsequently by B3/45. As the team became established, from 1946 Petter, Page and Creasey began to firm up the detail design for the new aircraft to meet the Ministry's requirement for an unarmed high speed, high altitude bomber

Teddy Petter at 'TC', Corporation Street, Preston in 1947. Visible are a Lysander photograph and desk models of the A1 (Canberra) and (left) English Electric's submission for a five-crew, six-engine, high-wing 'T'-tail aircraft to meet Spec. B35/46 for a medium/long range bomber which later resulted in the 'V'-bombers. The submission was rejected because the company's capacity was decreed to be fully taken up by the A1

Freddie Page in the spartan accommodation at 'TC' in 1947

to specification B3/45. However, following problems of bulk, weight and development delays arising with the radar (which was later installed in the larger 'V'-bombers), in 1947 the B3/45 'blind' bomber metamorphosed into the B5/47 tactical bomber, later to appear as the Canberra B.2, with conventional visual bombsight in a glazed nose and provision for an additional crew member. In March 1948, apart from the first four B.1 prototypes being produced to B3/45, that specification was cancelled and superseded by B5/47.

Further indication of progress was the establishment in August 1947 of the Preston Branch of the Royal Aeronautical Society with a membership of 60, represented by a committee of eight including Teddy Petter and Freddie Page. Many of the new staff would stay long-term to make vital contributions to successive programmes extending from Canberra to Lightning, TSR2, Strikemaster, Jaguar, Tornado and others which remain ongoing to the present day. In 1950, **Ivan R.Yates**, born in Suffolk and educated in Surrey, at the Collegiate School, Liverpool and Liverpool University, began as a B.Eng graduate apprentice at Preston. From working on the Canberra and P.1, in 1957 he became responsible for aerodynamic work on what was to become TSR2, for which he was later appointed Chief Project Engineer. He became Jaguar Project Manager (1966); a Special Director of BAC Preston Division (1970); a Director of SEPECAT SA (1976); a Director of Panavia (1977); Managing Director of British Aerospace Warton (1978) and Director of Engineering and Project Assessment, Aircraft Group (1981). Appointed CBE in 1982, he succeeded (the then) Sir Frederick Page as Chief Executive of the British Aerospace PLC Aircraft Group (1982), was a Director of Eurofighter GmbH (1986) and later Deputy Chief Executive of British Aerospace and Visiting Professor in Design, Cambridge University.

As post-war large-scale licensed production of the Vampire gathered pace, with effect from 1 September 1946 **John William Copous 'Johnny' Squier** was appointed Production Test Pilot, responsible for pre-delivery flight clearance of the jet fighter at Samlesbury. Born in 1920 at Bulphan, near Brentwood in Essex, Squier had been considered a delicate child by his parents who retained a private tutor for his education. Reputedly keen to prove them wrong, as a boy he drove a farm tractor and worked in a local garage. Educated at Southminster Grammar School, from December 1936 he served an apprenticeship in the motor trade at Chelmsford. During the evenings he studied at the Mid-Essex Technical College and obtained the City and Guilds Automobile Repair Certificate. Squier joined the RAFVR in April 1939, commencing elementary flying training with a 30-minute flight in a Tiger Moth on 21 May, followed by his first solo on 27 July, all completed during weekends and evenings before the outbreak of war. Called to full-time service on 1 September, he flew in a Harvard for the first time at No.10 FTS, Ternhill, on 13 December, soloing on type four days later. He was awarded his flying badge or 'wings' on 25 April 1940. Further training included cross-country flying during which on 17 May he made the first of what would be a number of forced landings in his career. Posted to No.5 OTU at Aston Down, Gloucester, he first flew a Spitfire Mk.1 on 13 July and made his first contact with the enemy when he engaged a Ju 88 only twelve days later. With just over two weeks' experience on the Spitfire and 19 hours' flying time on type, on 29 July he was posted as a Sergeant Pilot to No.64 Sqn at Kenley, Surrey, to be projected into the Battle of Britain at its most intense. On 5 August he tangled with a group of Me109s and, on 8 August, in Spitfire Mk.1 *SH-E*, flying out of Kenley, he crash landed in a field on the coast while attempting an emergency recovery to Hawkinge due to engine failure sustained over the Channel. Suffering severe face and arm injuries, he was taken to Canterbury Hospital and became one of the early 'Guinea Pig Club' patients of plastic surgery pioneer Archie (later Sir Archibald) McIndoe at the Queen Victoria Hospital, East Grinstead. Little more than three months later, after making a full recovery, on 26 November Squier returned to flying, then with No.72 Sqn. After several dog-fights, on Christmas Day 1940, flying Spitfire Mk.II *P7597* with No.603 Sqn, he engaged with the enemy again, this time over the North Sea some 15 miles east of St. Abb's Head, as a result of which he was credited and subsequently confirmed as having destroying a Ju 88.

After a few weeks instructing on Magisters with No.141 Sqn, from March 1941 Squier served as a wartime production test pilot with RAF Maintenance Command at RAF units around the country, flying almost every conceivable type of aircraft. Based at No.33 MU Lyneham, No.5 MU Kemble and No.48 MU Hawarden, and with No.4 FPP Ferry Pool, he flew Spitfire, Hurricane, Defiant, Battle, Blenheim, Anson, Lysander, Rapide and Proctor. He flew a Wellington for the first time on 20 June, an aircraft which, together with the Hurricane, would occupy most of his time for the next two or three years. Among others were Master, Oxford, Botha, Airacobra, Beaufighter, Liberator, Halifax and Lancaster. Commissioned from Warrant to Pilot Officer in June 1942, he flew his first Halifax on 13 August, was certified as First Pilot on type on 14 September and from 7-8 December visited Samlesbury to collect and deliver three of the type, two to Leeming and one to Hawarden. In February 1943 he was one of a four-man team from Hawarden who flew 17 Halifaxes from Samlesbury to Woburn Abbey for temporary storage. In May, by then a Flying Officer, Squier was accredited as 'above the average' as a test pilot. During this period he alighted at many other airfields and landing grounds in the North West including Knowsley, Tatton, Ringway, Woodford, Sealand, Silloth, Squires Gate, Barton and Speke.

In late March/early April 1944 he was attached to Messrs A. V. Roe at Woodford, production-testing Lancasters as second pilot to the Chief Test Pilot, the legendary Capt Harry Albert 'Sam' Brown, and other pilots including Bill Thorn, Syd Gleave and Reg Knight. Returning again to Woodford during September/October, by then a Flight Lieutenant, Squier first-flighted and re-tested yet more Lancasters. In January/February 1945 he was attached to the Avro factory at Yeadon, flying

Lancasters and Ansons. As the war drew to its close, for the remainder of his RAF service up to 1946, Squier served with Nos.5, 39 and 51 MUs, the latter at Lichfield, and in late 1945 and early 1946 with No.3 Ferry Pool. On 29 January 1946 he flew Lincoln *RF474* from Lichfield to Samlesbury for an electronics upgrade. Between October 1945 and December 1948 Samlesbury traffic included some 200 Avro Lincoln heavy bombers, English Electric having secured contracts to modify or fit a number of electronic systems including Loran, Rebecca and Gee radio navigation and H2S ground mapping radar. Many of these aircraft were reputedly flown by a Flt/Lt Sheerboom, a name that itself perhaps heralded the approach of the supersonic era. Also on 29 January 1946 Squier flew Vampire F.1 *TG302* out from Samlesbury to No.29 MU, High Ercall, at Wellington near Shrewsbury, his first flight on type and first experience of a jet aircraft. No two-seater conversions in those days! He left the RAF at the end of August 1946, immediately joining English Electric.

On arrival at Preston in September, Squier and his wife bought a cottage on the fringe of Samlesbury Aerodrome. His first flight, an 'experience' sortie in Vampire F.1 *VF302*, took place on 17 September. Six days later, in Swedish F.1 *28009*, an early machine of a batch of 70 built for export to that country under a subcontract received from de Havilland early in 1946, he started a series of production test flights that would continue until the final discharge in 1952 of all English Electric contracts to build the Vampire. Inevitably there were a number of highlights in the programme. On 10 April 1947 he tested the first English Electric-produced Vampire F.3, *VF315*. In September 1947 he production-tested 34 Vampires in no less than 88 sorties, followed by another 33 aircraft in 84 sorties in October. On 3 November 1947, seconds after lifting off from the 1,200-yard Runway 26 on the second flight of Vampire F.3 *17043*, one of a batch of 85 ordered by the Royal Canadian Air Force, Squier was faced with a major emergency. A fuel pump drive had sheared on take-off, causing instant engine flame-out only 20ft above the runway, leaving him with no alternative but to make a forced landing. Barely clearing the Samlesbury Aerodrome fence, he steered the aircraft through a 30-yard gap between a tree and a farmhouse before it thumped into a shallow dried-up pond, forcing the pilot through the bottom of his seat and shattering the canopy. Airborne briefly once more and with more trees approaching, acutely aware that his wooden cockpit shell had three quarters of a ton of very hot metal in the form of a Goblin engine in close pursuit, Squier decided to bring matters to a conclusion by digging in a wing, applying full aileron to starboard. This had the desired effect as the aircraft spun round, sliding backwards to come to a halt with its tailplane six inches from a tree. He and the aircraft had come to rest not far from his own back garden. Luckily he suffered only minor injuries and a slight back strain, but the Vampire, having absorbed some very heavy ground-handling, was written off and replaced at the end of the batch by *17086*. On 14 November, in F.3 *VT812*, the elevator jammed as a

Aftermath of Johnny Squier's rural excursion in Vampire F.3 17043, its Goblin engine clearly open for inspection, Samlesbury, 3 Nov 1947

Investigation and retrieval of the wreckage

result of a loose screw finding its way into the pulley assembly and on the 25th, in two unusual but identical incidents on the same day, the canopies of consecutive Canadian F.3s *17050* and *17051* both cracked in flight during the climb at 31,000ft and 28,000ft respectively. On re-test the following day, *17051*'s fuel pump drive also sheared, fortunately on its ground run after landing. Squier dealt with all these emergencies with characteristic stoicism.

Into 1948, on 12 February Squier flew an 'experience on type' sortie in Meteor F.4 *EE545*, an aircraft English Electric at Warton had borrowed from Glosters to carry out a programme of high altitude trials for the Ministry of Supply. Squier flew the aircraft on two further sorties on 14 May. Acting on the instructions of Petter and accompanied by Walker and Dean, from 26-30 April, Squier employed his extensive wartime experience on the Halifax by conducting trials with English Electric-built Halifax *ST808* fitted with a Servodyne powered elevator, to assess its potential for future use on the forthcoming English Electric jet bomber, the A1, then in build to Ministry Specification B3/45. Further trials were carried out during October/ November, but in the outcome the Servodyne was considered unsuitable for the A1 which, at least until later developments came along, would continue to rely on pilot muscle-power for control.

Meanwhile, in further building his team, in 1946 Petter had shortlisted two possible candidates for the post of Chief Experimental Test Pilot. They were **Wg/Cdr Roland Beamont** and **Sqn/Ldr A. F. (Tony) Martindale**. Beamont had a long and distinguished war record as a fighter pilot and wartime test pilot for Hawkers. Martindale, a highly experienced engineer and test pilot, O/C of the Aero Flight at RAE Farnborough, had gained notoriety flying a Spitfire at 606mph in a 45-degree dive while investigating compressibility and had been awarded the AFC. Both were equally impressive, but on the basis that English Electric had access to plenty of engineering expertise already, Beamont got the job.

Wg/Cdr Roland Prosper 'Bee' Beamont – correctly referred to as 'Bee', 'RPB' or sometimes just 'B', but not 'Bea', and never under any circumstances as 'Roly' or '*Beau*mont'! – joined English Electric on 1 May 1947. Born at Enfield in North London on 10 August 1920, he was brought up in Summersdale, near Chichester and between 1934 and 1938 educated at Eastbourne College. He had been determined to join the RAF ever since, as a child, he had received a wave from the pilot of a passing silver-painted Hawker Fury. He was granted a short-service General Duties Commission in the RAF in 1938, commencing flying training the following year with No.13 FTS at White Waltham and Drem, flying Tiger Moths and Hawker Harts during which he was graded 'exceptional'. He converted to Hawker Hurricanes with No.11 Group, St. Athan. Thereafter, his distinguished war record with Fighter Command included flying Hurricanes with No.87 Sqn of the Advanced Air Striking Force (the Air Component of the British Expeditionary Force) at Lille

Seclin in France, including a stationing at Le Touquet, seeing action in the Battle of France and in Belgium. Like many others, he managed to escape France by the skin of his teeth during evacuation on 23 May 1940, a necessarily hurried event when personal effects including his first flying log book were lost. He served with No.87 Sqn at Exeter in the Battle of Britain during which he was credited with shooting down five aircraft and mentioned in despatches. From spring 1941, based at RAF Warmwell, he took part in the first offensive sweeps over occupied Europe. He became a Flight Commander with No.79 Sqn, flying Hurricanes from Fairford Common before being posted to the newly-formed No.56 (Typhoon) Sqn at Snailwell. On 1 July 1942 he went to No.609 (West Riding) Sqn as Flight Commander on ground attack Typhoon fighter-bombers, commanding the squadron from 17 October. It was with No.609 that he became highly proficient at locomotive-busting by day and night, destroying 25 trains over a three-month period. His active service was interspersed with wartime test flying of Hurricanes, Typhoons and Tempests as a production and experimental test pilot for Hawker Aircraft Ltd at Langley, Buckinghamshire, during two 'rest periods' from December to June 1941/42 and May to February 1943/44. The latter posting required his relinquishing command of No.609. On 14 March 1942, in a single day he production-tested eleven Hurricanes to their maximum straight, level and diving speeds, trim, stall and engine performance limits. In *UK Flight Testing Accidents 1940-71* (Air-Britain, 2002) it is recorded that on 24 December 1942, in a production test of Hurricane Mk.IIA *Z5075* by Sqn Ldr R. P. Beamont, DFC (MAP Approved Test Pilot), Hawker, Langley, having completed the dive test at 400mph the starboard undercarriage leg extended inadvertently, causing a violent yaw. With no hydraulics and the u/c leg showing a red, the aircraft was landed back at Langley but weather-cocked towards the flight line and collided with another new Hurricane, sustaining Category 3 damage but without casualties.

Among Beamont's duties was the investigation of 23 instances of catastrophic failures during the early development stages of the Typhoon, when aircraft lost their tails in high speed dives. It involved diving the aircraft, fitted with strain-gauges, as fast as possible in 45-degree descents from 30,000ft, reaching Mach 0.74 and approaching compressibility. Luckily for Beamont, his 'low-hours' test aircraft remained intact, the problem later revealing itself to be fatigue fracturing of the elevator mass-balance brackets with onset of serious elevator flutter leading to detachment of the tail. Beamont later became Project Pilot for development of the Tempest.

Promoted to Squadron Leader at the age of 22 and Wing Commander at 23, from February 1944 his further active service on Typhoons and Tempests included flying with 85 Group and 25 Wing, commanding the first RAF Wing (No.150, at Newchurch, Kent, comprising Nos.3, 56 and 486 Sqns) to be equipped with the Tempest Mk.V (later No.122 Wing, comprising Nos.3, 56, 486, 86 and 274 Sqns),

Wg/Cdr Roland Prosper Beamont DFC, aged 23, Tempest Wing Leader, 1944

intercepting and shooting down V1 'doodlebug' flying bombs. Two days after D-Day, on 8 June 1944 near Rouen, he shot down an Me109, the first enemy aircraft to fall to the Tempest. One of the first to engage in the practice of 'wing tipping' the V1 to send the missile spinning off its pre-determined track to explode in open countryside or the sea, Beamont, in an action on 17 June 1944, was reputedly an initiator of the technique of sliding the wingtip of the fighter some six inches beneath that of the V1, but without actually making contact, causing boundary layer airflow disturbance sufficient to topple the missile's guidance system. Beamont first flew a Meteor F.1 on 26 August, his first experience of jet propulsion, describing it as having "extremely smooth motors – but a poor fighter". Many ground targets were also attacked. His wartime total of 491 missions ended when, having taken his Wing to Holland in September, based at the Dutch airfield of Volkel, on 12 October 1944 he was shot down over Germany when his radiator was hit by small arms ground fire while strafing a German troop train. After crash-landing his Tempest, stepping out unharmed and activating its incendiary, he was captured when he walked straight into the path of a patrol of Wehrmacht who addressed him with the classic "For you the war is over!" Beamont spent what was left of the war as a PoW at Luckenwalde near Potsdam, to be released after seven months when the camp was overrun by the advancing Russian Army. He was repatriated in a Lancaster bomber on 29 May 1945. Credited with ten enemy aircraft, 32 'doodlebugs', 35 locomotives and many other ground targets destroyed, he was awarded the DSO (1943) and Bar (1944), DFC and Bar (1943) and the DSO (USA) (1946).

During his spells with Hawkers the possibility had been mooted of Beamont being offered a permanent test flying post with the company. Not surprisingly, on returning from his enforced absence he found that the position had of necessity already been filled. Posted immediately to the Central Flying Establishment (CFE) at West Raynham, Beamont was back in the air within days of his return from Germany, flying a variety of aircraft including the Tempest, Meteor, Spitfire, Mustang and even an Me109, Ju88, Fw190 and a Sikorski R4B helicopter. After briefly commanding the Chilbolton Tempest Wing, and flying a Tempest in the 'Battle of Britain' formation over London on 15 September, which he described as "in close gaggle below cloud at 1,800ft – a bit fraught", with effect from 24 October 1945 he was posted to command the Air Fighting Development Squadron (AFDS) at the CFE. Shortly afterwards, Beamont turned down a permanent commission and was released from the Service.

Leaving the RAF on 16 January 1946, four days later he joined the Gloster Aircraft Co as senior experimental project test pilot on Meteor F.3/4 twin-engined jet fighters which he flew from the company's flight test centre at Moreton Valence in Gloucestershire. By then, the Gloster G.41 Meteor, the RAF's first jet-powered aircraft and the only jet aircraft of the Allied Powers to have seen operational service in the Second World War, was in large-scale production. Between March and June he made numerous flights in Meteor F.4 *EE455*, an experimental clipped-wing aircraft in which he attained speeds up to 585mph in level flight. At Moreton Valence on 14/15 May 1946, he made two flights in Meteor F.1 *EE227* powered experimentally by two Rolls-Royce Trent turbine airscrew (turbo-prop) engines but, with less power than the pure-jet version and performance far inferior to propeller-driven piston-engined aircraft such as the Tempest, he felt that it had little to commend it – other than as a test bed for the Trent. Beamont demonstrated Meteor F.4 *EE522* at the Royal Aircraft Establishment (RAE) Display at Farnborough in June. In a series of tests in the Meteor F.4, researching the effects of compressibility at low level and up to 35,000ft, as input to the RAF High Speed Flight's forthcoming attempt to gain the World Air Speed Record, in July he reached speeds (in *EE549*) of up to 608mph IAS. In reality it was believed to be 632mph, higher than the then World Record and higher even than that of 616mph officially established later on 7 September in *EE549* by Gp/Capt E. M. Donaldson. But Beamont was No.2 Experimental Test Pilot at Gloster Aircraft, in a hierarchy under Chief Test Pilot Walter Greenwood and his Deputy, Bill Waterton, that offered little scope for early advancement. Accordingly, in August 1946 he moved to the Sales and Commercial Division of de Havilland Aircraft as the company's No.1 Demonstration Pilot flying the Vampire, the Dove prototype and the first Chipmunk trainer to arrive in the UK from Canada, and also as a test pilot. Having made his first flight on type on 30 April while still at Glosters, he demonstrated Vampire F.1 *TG285* at the SBAC/RAeS display at Radlett on 13/15 September. But a familiar problem soon arose in that he could anticipate no early promotion opportunity to transfer fully from the commercial side to experimental test flying under dH Chief Test Pilot John Cunningham.

When word came that English Electric at Preston, then still regarded by many in the industry as 'those upstarts in the north', were seeking to appoint a new Chief Experimental Test Pilot, Beamont saw it as an opportunity well worth investigating. He came north to Preston by train in October, putting up at the Victoria and Station Hotel on Fishergate. After sleeping only fitfully amidst the night-long racket of the shunting of railway coal wagons, he was interviewed the following day by Teddy Petter, whom he found rather cold and impersonal, at 'TC', the former car showroom and garage a mere 250 yards round the corner in Corporation Street. There, screened off but nevertheless dominating the well-guarded experimental workshops at the rear of the building, Beamont was impressed to be shown the full-scale wooden mock-up of Petter's forthcoming twin-engined jet bomber – the A1 – designed to Ministry Specification B3/45. Work on the mock-up of the front fuselage, including crew positions and accommodation for the radar bombing system scanner in the nose, had started in September 1945 by when, to all intents and purposes, the general configuration had been 'frozen'. In essence, it was

The 'Wooden Bomber' – full scale wood and paper mock-up of the A1 in the workshop at the rear of 'TC', as first shown to RPB by Petter in October 1946

based on an unswept, low aspect broad chord wing, thick enough to accommodate main landing gear, outboard engines – including fatter profile centrifugals as insurance against any delays in development of the preferred slimmer axials – together with 'wet wing' fuel tanks in later versions. The whole was optimised for long range high altitude cruising at high speeds just below the onset of the limiting factors of compressibility and shock wave formation. Beamont's interest was further kindled by Petter's confirmation of the aircraft's low wing-loading and high power-to-weight ratio, a combination promising speed, altitude, good take-off and landing performance at moderate speeds, with a high roll rate, agility and manoeuvrability comparable with a fighter. It was in this part of the premises that the original assembly jigs, tools and components were also being made, together with castings being prepared for machining. During 1948 all these were moved to that part of the Strand Road site formerly occupied by H. Viney & Co, for complete assembly of the actual prototype aircraft there in the Spring of 1949.

The outcome of the interview was at first inconclusive. Initially, Petter was inclined more to Martindale, but deferred to the view of Freddie Page who, by then Assistant Chief Designer, favoured Beamont because of his background in both operational and test flying. Page had also worked with Beamont during the latter's wartime test flying of Typhoons and Tempests at Hawkers and was well aware of Beamont's capabilities. After hearing nothing further for six months, Beamont was summoned north once again by the austere Petter and offered the job – evidently no great urgency was foreseen. After all, the A1 was not yet available for test flying, while Samlesbury Aerodrome, at that time English Electric's only flying ground, despite having served for Hampden, Halifax and Vampire aircraft, was very much a production rather than experimental facility and in any event not considered extensive enough for the future test flying of larger and faster jet aircraft. Beamont took up his appointment as the English Electric Company's first Chief Experimental Test Pilot on 1 May 1947, with an office at 'TC', coming to live, as had Johnny Squier the year before, near Samlesbury Aerodrome. From then on, recognisably clad in white trenchcoat and RAF-style blazer, Beamont spent considerable time inside the Canberra mock-up, developing its cockpit design. [From August 1947 to September 1950, in addition to his duties at English Electric, Beamont was a member of the RAuxAF, firstly with No.609 (West Riding) Sqn at RAF Yeadon and then as O/C, No.611 Sqn at RAF Woodvale.]

Teddy Petter was one of the aircraft industry's great visionaries – a perfectionist who demanded absolute excellence. He recognised the practical potential of the jet turbine right from the start of its development as an aero-engine during the Second World War, promising both speed and range if wed to a suitably aerodynamic airframe. From the beginning of 1946 he had been musing over and sketching ideas about the sort of future fighter aircraft that would be needed to intercept a new generation of bombers with the potential height and speed of the A1. He believed that although aircraft such as the Meteor were adequate interceptors at normal altitudes, they would be useless against intruders of the calibre of the A1. In 1947 he delivered a prescient lecture in Paris on 'Long Range Jet Aircraft', in which he held out the prospect of nowhere in the world being beyond 24 hours' travelling time. Two aircraft of his initial design would become synonymous with the factors of altitude, range and speed that he believed represented the future of aviation: the A1/Canberra high altitude bomber to Specification B3/45 (also considered by English Electric in 1946/7 as the basis for a civil airliner) and the supersonic P.1/ Lightning to Specification ER 103. Between 1951 and 1953, the Canberra would dramatically demonstrate its global reach with a number of world record time-over-distance and altitude flights. From 1954 the P.1/Lightning, though lacking in range, would regularly achieve both supersonic speed – eventually Mach 2 – as well as high altitude performance. In designing them, the English Electric team of Petter, Page, Creasey and their colleagues brought to practical fruition – albeit in two different aircraft types – those very features of altitude, range and speed that two decades later would be combined to spectacular effect by Concorde.

All that was very much in the future. Like the rest of the industry, frustrated by the Government's cancellation in February 1946 of the potentially world-beating Miles M.52, then Britain's sole supersonic aircraft project, and its subsequent decision to terminate further research into supersonic flight supposedly on grounds of cost and the dangers involved for test pilots, Petter immediately sought means of circumventing the edict. Not only did the Minister of Aircraft Production, Sir Stafford Cripps, cancel M.52, he also instructed Miles to hand over their designs to the Bell Aircraft Company of America, for whom Capt Chuck Yeager of the USAF made the world's first supersonic level flight in the Bell X-1 (unsurprisingly a Miles M.52 straight-wing look-alike) in October 1947. Sir Ben Lockspeiser, Director-General of Research at the Ministry of Supply, famously indicated that the Government had not the heart to ask pilots to fly the high-speed models which would instead be radio-controlled, involving no further risks to test pilots and achieving economy in purpose. But if the UK Government was concerned at the risks for pilots in entering the unknown realms of transonic flight, particularly with straight-wing aircraft, the US had no such inhibitions and as a result the UK lost its lead in the race to be the first to achieve supersonic flight. [With military work declining in Britain, George Miles subsequently worked on civil aircraft such as the Messenger, Gemini and the Airspeed Ambassador, and later had an interest in Beagle Aircraft.]

So, early in 1947 Petter took his own proposals for a swept-wing supersonic interceptor to what had then become the Ministry of Supply (MoS). Fully aware of the compressibility trials conducted up to 35,000ft by Beamont at Glosters, Petter felt that for his new design team to make progress similar research was essential at higher altitudes. Ostensibly to extend the envelope previously explored by Glosters, he successfully negotiated a Ministry contract to undertake 30 hours of research into the effects of high Mach numbers on stability at high altitudes. The contract was received in mid-1947 when Beamont, newly arrived in Lancashire, was put on standby to conduct the exercise pending availability of a suitable aircraft. Then, in August 1948, in a complete reversal of its stance two years earlier, the Government also awarded English Electric a further contract to undertake a design study for a transonic research aircraft. Proposals were completed and submitted to the MoS in the form of a brochure towards the end of the year. Preliminary work on this, the company's second major new aircraft project, the experimental P.1 swept-wing interceptor, was therefore in hand nearly a year before even the maiden flight of its first, the A1 bomber.

On arriving at English Electric in May 1947, with the A1 then still a couple of years from completion and Petter's proposals for high speed/high altitude trials still to be resolved, Beamont found that the only flying opportunities lay within Johnny Squier's domain – the production-testing of Vampires which were then starting to come off the Preston and Samlesbury lines in greater numbers. At first the General Manager, Arthur Sheffield, to whom Production Test Pilot Johnny Squier reported direct, did not welcome Beamont, whom he regarded as Petter's experimental pilot, becoming involved on the production side. However, due to the numbers involved and a growing backlog of aircraft to be cleared for delivery, Sheffield had to accept it as inevitable. Moreover, Beamont was highly proficient on the Vampire from his time with de Havillands and had displayed the Vampire F.1 at the 1946 SBAC Show at Radlett. Accordingly, he commenced Vampire production flying on 15 May 1947 with two flights, each of 20 minutes, in F.3 *VF367*. On 22 May he conducted the maiden flight of Vampire *28065*. At Samlesbury, the typical production test routine in the uncongested skies over the North of England in those days, before the advent of controlled airspace and the Amber One airway, involved taking off on a westerly course under full power to 30,000ft over the Irish Sea, with full instrumentation checks including ASI and jet-pipe temperature. After turning onto the reciprocal, further ascent to 40,000ft would be followed by a dive, so far as cloud permitted, to the Mach limit of 0.74, then instrument descent to cloud base with slow-speed handling and stall tests in the Samlesbury area. In the absence of navigation aids – all Samlesbury then had was VHF – everything rested on the pilot, not least the essential need to break out from cloud base well away from the rising ground of the Pennines to the east. On 5 November 1947 Beamont carried out his first flight of the Nene-powered Vampire F.2 *TX807*, a one-off aircraft to be used for development trials by English Electric and subsequently allotted to de Havilland at Hatfield.

As work on the the A1 proceeded apace, interspersed with his routine production test flying of Vampires, from August 1947 Beamont commenced preliminary investigations on the Petter-inspired, by then Government-sponsored, research contract into compressibility and manoeuvrability at altitudes in excess of 40,000ft. For this he used Meteor F.4 *EE545*, allocated to English Electric for the duration of the trials, an aircraft which as well as its usefully high subsonic speed and high altitude capability, although smaller, had the added handling advantage of similarity of configuration to the forthcoming bomber. By this time, English Electric had acquired an additional airfield at Warton, to the west of Preston, and it was there that the trials took place.

Located just over eleven miles to the west of English Electric's Samlesbury Aerodrome, mid-way between Preston and Blackpool, Warton Aerodrome occupied an extensive area of flat land comprising some 700 acres between the village of Warton and the River Ribble about two miles from the point at which its channel discharged into the Ribble estuary. Enjoying uninterrupted approaches to and from the east and west, and crucially with a 6,000ft-long runway potentially ideal for testing the new fast jets, it was an otherwise undistinguished tract of land rising barely 30ft above sea level and the sand and mudflats of the estuary. During the Second World War it had been developed initially as a relief landing ground for the RAF but, from September 1942, had been operated by the USAAF on a vast scale as Base Air Depot (BAD) 2 in conjunction with BAD 1 at Burtonwood, near Warrington, in South Lancashire. After the war, in February 1946 it reverted to RAF use for storage of everyday 'domestic' equipment, operated by Nos.55 & 90 MUs. English Electric started to plan for the use of Warton at the beginning of 1947.

When they took it over a little later in the year, some of its buildings were dilapidated, runway and taxiway surfaces were starting to break up with lots of loose stones around and there were no radio, radar or other navigation or homing devices. Only Samlesbury had VHF. It was against this rather unsatisfactory background that Beamont, having to drive to Warton almost daily, based in Hangar No.25, began the Meteor trials – English Electric's first post-war experimental test flying programme – fortunately with the support of a dedicated ground team comprising a fitter, a rigger and a tractor driver, led by foreman Bill Eaves who had worked on English Electric's wartime aircraft production. Eaves also doubled as Air Traffic Controller at Warton, signalling reds and greens from the airfield on an Aldis lamp that Beamont had 'borrowed' from the RAF. Airfield security consisted of the Works' policeman on a bicycle. Eaves went on to enjoy a long career at Warton, becoming Superintendent of Experimental Aircraft, working on all types up to the Tornado until his retirement in the 1980s.

On 6 August 1947 Beamont personally collected and delivery-flew the Hucclecote-built Derwent V-powered G.41F Meteor F.4 *EE545* from Glosters' flight test centre at Moreton Valence to Warton in a flight lasting 35 minutes. His previous attempt on 25 July had been aborted when bad weather forced a return to Moreton Valence. The Gloster Aircraft serial block prefix EE was entirely coincidental, not relating to English Electric. *EE545* was one of an early production batch of F.4s built in 1946. On Thursday 28 August Beamont took the aircraft up from Warton on the first of a series of 44 experimental test flights which he made from the Lancashire airfield up to July 1948. The flight, again 35 minutes in duration, was the very first experimental test flight from Warton, so 28 August 2012 marks the 65th anniversary of a most significant event in company and British aviation history. The programme that followed involved a series of test flights ranging from brief 15 or 20-minute air tests to sorties of up to 55 minutes during which Beamont attained, for those days, some impressive altitudes of up to 47,200ft. Even by today's standards, quite high operating ceilings could be achieved by some of the early post-war British jet fighters. Meteor F.4s with their original 43-ft wingspans could reach 52,000ft, although later versions, with wings clipped to 37ft 2in to alleviate airframe stress and meet RAF pilots' demands for improved roll-rates, struggled to get to 45,000ft. Moreover the wingspan modification came at the cost of reduced climb rate and higher take-off and landing speeds. Early de Havilland Vampires could also achieve well over 40,000ft and the fifth production 'English Electric' Vampire F.1, *TG278*, built at Samlesbury in 1945 and delivered to de Havilland on 9 August for subsequent use as a trials aircraft, established, albeit in modified form with wider than standard wingspan, a new World Altitude Record of 59,446ft in the hands of de Havilland test pilot John Cunningham on 23 March 1948.

RPB taking off from Warton in Meteor F.4 EE545, 1947/48 (W. Eaves, via BAE Systems)

Meteor EE545 being prepared for another of RPB's test flights from Warton, 1947/48

Beamont's trials series in Meteor *EE545* included many climb tests to altitude, instrument, general handling, stick force per 'g' and other checks. On his 21st flight, one of 30 minutes' duration on 26 November 1947, at 35,000ft he experienced a starboard engine flame-out that proved impossible to relight. In an outcome that tested his already legendary airmanship to the utmost he not only proved his mastery of the single-engined asymmetric handling of a twin-jet under such conditions, an experience that would later be of value to him with the Canberra, but was also able to land the aircraft safely back at Warton in a Fylde Coast winter gale-force crosswind. The event portended the levels of skill Beamont would repeatedly bring to bear during his flight test career at Warton over the next two decades. On his 27th flight, on 3 February 1948 he took the Meteor to 46,700ft. During the trials the Meteor was typically flown at Mach 0.79 at 45,000ft, pulling to the shock-stall at 1.9g at which point it would roll into a steep dive recoverable only after losing 10,000ft and allowing speed to fall again to below Mach 0.79. The trials were carried out at what were then the frontiers of flight, beyond conventional limits of safety, in conditions of extreme cold soak with consequent misting, even icing-up inside the canopy during the descent, all the time requiring continuous attention to dead-reckoning navigation in the certain knowledge of there being a total lack of navigational aids back at Warton. The pilot, battling with a primitive demisting system, then had to hope that he had enough fuel left for a high speed run at relatively low level to generate sufficient 'ram' air temperature in the airframe to disperse condensation to enable him to find the runway. Such was the nature of test flying early jets in the late 1940s! However, among the benefits to come out of the trials was the establishment of known compressibility limits for the Meteor at all altitudes from sea level to its operational ceiling.

In May 1948, part way through the Meteor trials at Warton and in the run-up to the B3/45 A1 test programme, Beamont found time to go on a UK MoS-sponsored, Pentagon-approved visit to the USA to gain experience of the latest American experimental jet bombers and fighters. To gain the necessary flying approvals, in January he first had to undertake a conversion course on a heavy bomber, in the shape of Avro Lincoln *RF503* of No.138 Sqn at RAF Wyton. There, at the end of the month, following general handling, circuits, landings, overshoots and three-engine drills, Sqn/Ldr Baker certified that "… this officer is a competent pilot of Lincoln II aircraft". Beamont set off to the States on 3 May, flying from Heathrow to New York via Shannon and Gander in BOAC Constellation *G-AHEL Bangor*. While in the USA, he experienced flights in the Boeing B-50 Superfortress, Lockheed P-80 Shooting Star *460* (surging its engine and bursting its nose tyre on landing, for which he had to make due apology to Col. Albert 'Al' Boyd, O/C of the Flight Test Center at Wright Patterson Air Force Base), Republic P-84 Thunderjets *514*, *515*, North American B-25 Mitchell *22858* and four-jet bomber XB-45 Tornado *7001*. Through sheer persistence, Beamont also managed to persuade the American authorities to agree to his flying, on 22 May, the second prototype of the North American XP-86 swept-wing interceptor, *PU598*, to be named the F-86 Sabre in March 1949, at the North American Aviation Experimental Flight Test Center, later to become Edwards AFB, located in the vast white salt expanse of Muroc Dry Lake in California's Mohave Desert. The first prototype, *PU597*, had made its maiden flight in the hands of North American Project Pilot Major George Welch, Beamont's host at Muroc, on 1 October the previous year. That first flight had come just two weeks before Capt Charles 'Chuck' Yeager of the USAF had, on 14 October 1947, also at Muroc Lake, become the first person in the world to exceed Mach 1 in level flight by achieving Mach 1.06 in the rocket-powered Bell X-1. Only a month or so before Beamont's visit, on 25 April 1948 George Welch had reputedly exceeded Mach 1 in a shallow dive in *PU597* over the Mohave. It has been suggested that Welch had also exceeded Mach 1 in shallow dives on several occasions before then, possibly even before Yeager did so in level flight, although there is no official evidence and the matter may have been suppressed by the US authorities who at that time were strongly behind the Bell X-1 project. Welch was also noted, as portrayed in the 1970 film *Tora! Tora! Tora!* as the first pilot to have taken off from Oahu, Hawaii, flying a Curtiss P-40B Tomahawk and still wearing his mess uniform, to engage Japanese aircraft during the attack on Pearl Harbor on 7 December 1941. Welch died in the crash of a North American F-100 Super Sabre on 12 October 1954.

Amidst such heady atmosphere at the frontiers of supersonic flight, Beamont more than adequately described the setting at Muroc: "On the morning of May 21 [sic], soon after dawn under a clear sky, with the desert golden under the early sun and the mountains etched clear and blue, seemingly just beyond the immense dry salt-lake airfield but actually 60 miles away, briefing on the XP-86 began at the North American test centre…" For the flight that followed, Beamont's flight log entry states: 'Mach No of Unity reached at 29,000ft … M 0.99-1.0 at 29,000ft.' In his subsequent flight report, Beamont stated that he had initiated a maximum power dive from 36,000ft to 29,000ft, at which the Mach meter showed unity or a little over, yet, despite a slight roll and minor buffeting at the tail, the aircraft appeared to be perfectly comfortable in transonic state. At that point he had certainly achieved the fastest speed of any British pilot.

But had Beamont gone truly supersonic? Had he done so he would have been possibly the third or fourth person in the world, certainly the first Briton, to have broken the 'sound barrier'. Not by nature a reticent person, in the immediate aftermath he curiously made little of his transonic experience at Muroc Lake. Possibly for diplomatic reasons, the authorities on both sides of the Atlantic also remained strangely uncommunicative when questioned on the matter. The sensitivities at the time were revealed by the remark made by 'Chuck' Yeager to Beamont: "You must be the limey pilot they let loose on the '86 before even *I've* had the chance to fly it!"

Some of these issues were explored briefly in *Against the Sun – The story of Wing Commander Roland Beamont DSO, OBE, DFC* by Edward Lanchbery (Cassell, 1955). Stating that Beamont's flight had *not* been accompanied by the tell-tale sonic boom, it concluded: 'Subsequent investigations proved that the pitot head on the P.86 [sic] was situated in a position where it was liable to be affected by shock waves and turbulence in the airflow. With a resultant error of up to…0.04…in the Machmeter reading, this meant that the true speed of dives in the P.86 had been nearer Mach 0.98.'

Other accounts have described Beamont as 'the first Englishman to *reach* the speed of sound'. As Beamont himself put it in one of his eleven published books (*Testing Years*, Ian Allan, 1980): "As no Machmeter/ASI 'jump up' had occurred (or I had not seen it) it was probable that we had not gone fully supersonic, but we had undoubtedly reached transonic speed and with the fuel state reducing fast and much work yet to be done [i.e. on that particular sortie – Author] that had to be enough." Yet in his final book *The Years Flew Past* (Airlife), published just before his death in 2001, in somewhat different terms Beamont stated: "In a fascinating flight I reached more than Mach 1 in a comfortably controlled dive, becoming the fourth pilot to do so (and the first British pilot to reach Mach 1)." Beamont's entry in *Who's Who* described him as '1st British pilot to fly at speed of sound (in USA), May 1948.'

A few months after Beamont's trip to the States, on 6 September 1948 between Farnborough and Windsor, de Havilland test pilot Sqn/Ldr John D. Derry, DFC, dived the tailless DH.108 'Swallow' *VW120* almost vertically from 40,000ft, doubtlessly entering the realms of uncontrollability in the process, before the aircraft levelled out at 20,000ft, attaining Mach 1.1 in conjunction with a sonic bang. As a result, Derry was credited as the first British pilot to fly a British aircraft faster than sound. *VW120* was the last of three DH.108s built by de Havillands at Hatfield with wooden front fuselages 'lifted' from the early post-war Vampire production line at Samlesbury, all three at various times between 1946 and 1950 to be involved in crashes fatal for their pilots G. E. C. 'Jumbo' Genders, AFC, DFM [O/C Aero Flt, RAE Farnborough and a graduate of Empire Test Pilots School (ETPS) No.4 Course at Cranfield in 1946]; G. de Havilland Jnr., OBE and J. S. R. Muller-Rowland, DSO, DFC, [O/C Aero Flt, RAE Farnborough and a graduate of the ETPS No.6 Course at Farnborough in 1947.] Lanchbery stated that in the light of Derry's flight and subsequent experience, Beamont personally grew certain that his own dive in the XP-86 had not been quite supersonic and accepted Derry's achievement. On 6 September 1952, four years later to the day of his having broken the sound barrier, Derry together with flight test observer Anthony Richards and some 30 spectators were killed when the DH.110 prototype *WG236* broke up over the crowd at the Farnborough Air Show. It was a shocking reminder of the dangers inherent in test flying and demonstrating early jets at that time. Ironically, Beamont had been scheduled to fly with Derry in *WG236* a few days earlier, but had been prevented by the weather.

Back in the UK, in July 1948 Beamont's test flying of the Meteor from Warton was combined with his related high altitude trials from Samlesbury, at heights up to 44,000ft, of the English Electric-made Vampire F.3 *VT861* fresh off the Samlesbury production line. He flew 567 Vampire Mks.F.1, 2, 3, FB.5, 9 and F.20 production test and demonstration flights from Samlesbury between November 1947 and December 1951, distinctively signing off many of them with a fast run across the aerodrome followed by a half loop and roll off the top in the course of which lowering the undercarriage. They were not without incident. On 7 June 1948, Vampire F.3 *VV218* ran off the runway sustaining damage when the brakes failed on touchdown. Potentially more serious was an experimental test flight in Vampire FB.5 *VV453* on 30 July 1948 when a crack in the *Perspex* resulted in the cockpit canopy bursting with explosive decompression at 43,000ft, the aircraft entering a steep dive, causing Beamont to briefly lose consciousness. Coming to, he was able to level out at 33,000ft above a continuous cloud sheet. But he was by no means out of danger. Not knowing his precise whereabouts, he had to descend very cautiously through 4,000ft of cloud, for safety steering west towards the sea, rather than east towards high ground. Breaking cloud at 2,000ft over the Wyre estuary, he made a welcome but thoroughly unpleasant, cold and draughty low-level return to Samlesbury. Amazingly, Beamont's eardrums had remained intact, though he suffered severe headaches for days afterwards. On 30 August he made the first delivery of a Vampire FB.5, *VV457*, to the RAF at Hullavington.

On 16 September 1948 Beamont returned the Meteor, which had been loaned to English Electric for the period of the trials, back to Glosters in a 30-minute delivery flight from Warton to RAF Pershore in Worcestershire. From 1944-48 Pershore was the site of No.1 Ferry Unit, responsible for collecting and delivering all types of aircraft. It subsequently became an Advanced Flying School and from 1957-78 was the location of the Royal Radar Establishment Flying Unit (RREFU). *EE545* later went to RNAS Bramcote, near Nuneaton in Warwickshire, a technical training centre for naval airmen and aircraft mechanics. When the Navy took Bramcote over from the RAF in 1946, the Naval Officer Commanding, Capt G. N. Brewer, DSO, informed those assembled: "You have seen the White Ensign hoisted for the first time about as far from the sea as is possible in England. You are serving in the most inland 'stone frigate' in the country!" *EE545* was subsequently used as an instructional airframe before being scrapped in 1955.

Although *EE545* was not built in the North West, it is regrettable that an aircraft of such significance for the test flying of jet aircraft in Lancashire should not have been preserved. However, four aircraft further down the Hucclecote production line, Meteor F.4 *EE549* flown by Gp/Capt E. M. Donaldson of the RAF High Speed Flight, who took the Absolute World Air Speed Record to a shade under 616mph on 7 September 1946, can today be seen preserved at the Tangmere Military Aviation Museum. Another Meteor F.4, *EE531*, the second-oldest intact Meteor still in

'TC' in Corporation Street, Preston, after being vacated by Petter's design team, bound for Warton in 1948

existence, is preserved at the Midland Air Museum, Coventry. The oldest is the first of eight G.41 F.9/40 prototypes, *DG202/G*, at the RAF Museum, Cosford.

'TC' at Preston remained in use by English Electric only until the end of 1948. By then, in a removal that had begun after the Whitsuntide weekend in May, Petter and all his team, numbering around 250, had departed to the far more extensive Warton Aerodrome. The move widened further a void that had already opened up between Chief Engineer and Designer Petter at 'TC' and General Manager Arthur Sheffield, responsible for all production at the Strand Road and Samlesbury works. Petter's objective was to secure his own independent experimental workshop with manufacturing capacity dedicated to the production of prototypes, something that Sheffield fiercely resisted. Fortunately there was sufficient co-operation between the various key members of their respective staffs. That remained the position even after the move to Warton, where Petter's team occupied an office block and 25 Hangar in which the first facility to be erected was the new 9 x 7ft wind tunnel that Ellis had started building at 'Vineys' in Strand Road in 1946, completed in May 1948, together with a large structural test frame. The wind tunnel was put to immediate use in testing the B3/45 A1 design a full twelve months before the prototype's maiden flight. 'TC' reverted to its pre-war use as a car showroom and garage until, much degraded in condition, it was demolished in the 1980s, one of many acts of civic vandalism that have taken out so many architecturally and historically significant buildings from town and city centres in the UK.

Beamont's final Vampire production test was in FB.9 *WG871* on 1 December 1951, some two months before English Electric completed its Vampire contracts in February 1952. In discharging the overall programme for 1,369 macines between 1944 and 1952, the sterling production test flying by English Electric pilots Rose, Squier, Beamont, Hillwood, Evans, Blythe and Randrup (the latter also Chief Test Pilot of Napier Aero Engines, an English Electric associate company) was on occasion supplemented by de Havilland pilots. Geoffrey de Havilland Jnr, John Cunningham and John Derry, together with Messrs Olver, Cartwright, Murray, Martindale, Pike and Wilson, all assisted by relieving production test bottlenecks, at the same time providing checks on quality control. Cunningham flew F.3s *VT795* and *VT797* on 2 September 1947 and *VV200* on 19 April 1948. Derry tested RAF and Canadian F.3s *VT831* and *17066* respectively on 22 January 1948 and later flew four FB.5s: *VV219* from Samlesbury to Hatfield on 18 August 1948, *VV661* on 25 March 1949, *VX970* on 8 July 1949 and *WA204* on 20 September 1950. Understandably, Beamont's contribution to Vampire testing was much reduced after the A1 took to the sky in 1949, although he continued to make occasional Vampire flights thereafter. Similarly Hillwood had less to do with the Vampire after January 1951, the brunt of the remaining production flying then falling on Squier and Evans. Beamont and Squier went on to have long and distinguished careers of production and experimental flight testing and in management, spanning some three decades with English Electric and its successor companies in Lancashire.

Peter D. Hillwood, born in London in 1920, joined English Electric in March 1949 as an experimental test pilot and Assistant Chief Test Pilot to Beamont at Warton Aerodrome. Having gained his initial flying certificate on a DH.60 Gipsy Moth at the Cambridge Aero Club in May 1938, he joined the RAFVR later that year and was posted to RAF Fighter Command where he served as a sergeant-pilot with No.56 Sqn on Hurricanes, seeing service in the Battle of France. In the period leading up to Dunkirk, flying on patrol near Cambrai in Hurricane Mk. 1 *L1899* on 17 May 1940, he received damage from a Do17 of 5/KG76 and an Me109 of 1/JG3, and had to make a forced landing near Vitry. His aircraft caught fire and, like many other fighter pilots in the era before self-sealing fuel tanks, he suffered burns to face and hands. Returning to fight in the Battle of Britain, based at North Weald he was credited with several 'kills' including a Ju 87 and Bf 109 in June and July 1940. On 13 August, flying Hurricane *R4093*, his aircraft was hit during an engagement over the Straits of Dover. He baled out off Sheppey and swam two miles to the shore. Hillwood then served as a flying instructor in Canada under the Empire Air Training Scheme. Commissioned, he returned to Fighter Command in 1943, going on to fly Spitfires with the Second Tactical Air Force, seeing service in France, Belgium and Holland. As a Flight Lieutenant and Flight Commander with No.127 Sqn, he flew aircraft including his personal clipped-wing Spitfire Mk.XVI *SM179 9N-T* 'Lady Jane', and a

Peter Hillwood (left) with RAF fighter pilot colleagues Flt/Lt Edward John 'Jumbo' Gracie DFC and Flt/Sgt Higginson, No 56 Sqn, North Weald, 1940

similar machine *RR257* in which he carried out a dive-bombing attack on railway lines at Arnhem. He was awarded the DFC on 24 November 1944. The citation stated: 'Hillwood has completed very many sorties against the enemy and has led his flight with outstanding skill and courage. He has shown determination in always pressing home his attacks, often at low level, in the face of intense enemy anti-aircraft fire. Flight Lieutenant Hillwood is an excellent flight commander.' He was seconded to the MoS in 1945 as an RAF test pilot, subsequently becoming a test pilot with Supermarine and Cunliffe-Owen Aircraft Ltd at Eastleigh, Hampshire, where Spitfires and Seafires were built and refurbished. *Flight Magazine* commented on the excellent work he undertook with Cunliffe-Owen.

In *UK Flight Testing Accidents 1940-71* (Air-Britain, 2002), it is recorded that on 22 June 1945, piloted by Flt/Lt P. Hillwood, DFC, (Test Pilot) Vickers-Armstrongs, on a production test flight at Hursley Park, Spitfire Mk.XIV *TZ140* sustained Category 4 damage when the pilot forgot to lower the undercarriage when landing. There were no casualties. It would appear that wheels-up landings were not only the province of novice pilots – even those with considerable battle experience and overworked test pilots were not immune. Hillwood, then of Fisher's Pond near Southampton, was released from RAF service in October 1946. On arriving at English Electric in March 1949, while awaiting the forthcoming B3/45 A1 jet bomber, Hillwood was assigned to Squier and Beamont, production testing Vampires at Samlesbury. On 9 March he

A1 prototype VN799 in 25 Hangar, Warton, being prepared for flight in April 1949 following its transfer from Strand Road (Vineys). Evident is the rounded profile of the original fin/rudder

started work with two flights of 58 and 41 minutes in FB.5 VV635. From then he went on to make nearly 900 Vampire flights up to 31 October 1951, when he cleared *WG846* in a 41-minute sortie, some four months before English Electric completed the Vampire contracts for 1,369 machines on 19 February 1952. The account of Hillwood's test flying with English Electric is continued later.

With work on the B3/45 A1 jet bomber progressing quickly and satisfactorily at Preston, on 24 September 1948 **Roland Beamont** flew to the Rolls-Royce airfield at Hucknall in Vampire *VV460*, later that day flying as second pilot to Capt R.T. Shepherd (Chief Test Pilot, Rolls-Royce 1935-1951) on a 45-minute experimental test flight in an Avro Lancastrian which was being used as a flying test bed for the new Avon engines to be used in the A1. On 22 October Beamont and Squier made a further assessment of a Servodyne elevator fitted in a Halifax. In the late spring of 1949, having been completed in 'Vineys' at Strand Road, the A1 airframe was dismantled and transported to No.25 Hangar at Warton for final assembly, engine installation and systems checks. At the beginning of May, Beamont started engine ground runs and taxying tests, from 9-12 May easing it up to 15ft above the 1,900-yard runway in short 500-yard 'straights', to get the feel of the controls. In 1949 it was a rather novel means of progressively familiarising with a new aircraft. In a local hostelry, having observed several days of seemingly unsuccessful attemps to become fully airborne, a pessimistic local resident was overheard saying "Nowt'll come o' that lot, they can't even get it off t'ground after tryin' for a week!"

Another view of VN799 *in 25 Hangar*

VN799 *being prepared on 29 April 1949 for its first engine runs*

VN799's *first engine runs, 2 May 1949*

VN799 *being prepared for final taxying trials and runway 'hops', 12 May 1949, at a Warton that retains its wartime appearance*

At 11.46hrs on Friday 13 May 1949, superstitious connotations of which he dismissed as irrelevant, Beamont, call sign *Tarnish 1*, lifted the prototype A1 *VN799* off the Warton runway for its full maiden flight, with Johnny Squier flying in attendance in Vampire FB.5 *VV696* from Samlesbury. It was possibly the first instance in the history of British test flying of a 'chase' aircraft being used to accompany a first flight. Having left Beamont and the ground crew to get on with their preparations undisturbed on the flight line, the normally undemonstrative Petter, watching discretely in the distance, succumbed to raising his trilby hat in salutation as the A1 became airborne. Apart from some linear control problems the flight proved better than anyone had dared hope. Rudder over-balance was noted by Beamont, the rudder being effective for small applications either side of neutral but not during more generous use. Although perfectly manageable, it would not have offered adequate control in the event of a single engine situation developing, a factor that curtailed the flight. Having conducted various handling tests at up to 245kt and 8,000ft, Beamont landed uneventfully back at Warton after 27 minutes in the air. The rudder issue was quickly dealt with by a redesign to reduce the horn balance area which had intentionally been made of wood for ease of modification, incorporated in time for the second flight on 18 May. During that sortie the aircraft reached 15,000ft, but experienced significant vibration or 'flutter' at speeds in excess of 400kt. The following day, on the third flight, Beamont attained Mach 0.77 at 20,000ft but another problem emerged, that of slight directional oscillation or 'snaking'. Clearly these issues had to be investigated as a matter of urgency and, after further general handling tests, on 30 May the ninth flight was made with fixed camera recording vibrograph sensors fitted around the rear fuselage, these measuring oscillation of eight cycles vertical, with some of 24 cycles, believed to be elevator flutter. To demonstrate the problem, as described in *English Electric Canberra* (Beamont/Reed, Ian Allan 1984), the following day Beamont flew with Chief Aerodynamicist Dai Ellis in the navigator's seat as observer. After having initially induced the symptoms, Beamont suggested repeating the experience, but Ellis, somewhat reluctant, advised that further investigation be made back on the ground.

In another account of early problems of oscillation, the *Aerospace Heritage* magazine (BAe North West Heritage Group, Issue 3, May 1999), described how, in the early stages of working up the prototype, Beamont experienced a pitching oscillation around Mach 0.8, as evidence of the onset of compressibility at a lower speed than had been anticipated. For a first-hand assessment 'Bee' invited aerodynamicist *Ray Creasey* to join him on the next flight. Creasey looked at his colleague Ron Dickson, who had never flown in an aeroplane of any sort before, and said "You too!" It was at a time not long after Geoffrey de Havilland Jnr had been killed at a somewhat similar Mach number after encountering severe oscillation in the DH.108.

VN799 airborne as RPB makes a final short 'hop' on 12 May 1949 before its full maiden flight the following day

VN799 *takes off from Warton on its maiden flight, 13 May 1949*

RPB and VN799 *after early redesign of the rudder horn balance area which resulted in a squared-off, less rounded appearance*

RPB and VN799 over Blackpool, Summer 1949, preparing for their first display at the Farnborough Air Show in September

Ron Dickson, a graduate of Cambridge University with a first class honours degree in mathematics, joined the English Electric Aerodynamics Department from the RAE in June 1946, working with Creasey, Ellis and Atkin. Dickson was also an accomplished musician and church organist. When he retired as Divisional Research Director of the Warton Division of BAe in 1985, after 39 years' service, he described to *Intercom* (December 1985) how, in the summer of 1949, Beamont returned from a flight complaining of vibration with a frequency that he could hear, rather than feel. Dickson recalled:

"The aircraft instrumentation in those days was very simple and we didn't even know the frequency of the oscillation, which would have enabled us to cure the problem. However, Dai Ellis had an inspiration and decided that since Bee could hear the oscillation, he should accompany me to the local church. The idea was that he would recognise the sound again from the notes I was going to play on the organ. I must say I didn't have much faith in the idea, but along we went. I played various low notes at random several times and Bee was consistent in selecting the same one each time. I worked the frequency out and we returned to Warton and did a few flutter calculations to ascertain what part of the airframe might be affected. After a few more calculations we had our answer. So, it can be said that one of the Canberra's incipient flutter problems was cleared with the aid of a church organ!"

By August all such problems had been resolved, at least to an acceptable degree, chiefly by modifications to the elevator horns and mass balances, with the addition of a simple cockpit canopy fairing to control the 'snaking'. On the 11th, within twelve weeks of its first flight, Beamont took *VN799* above 40,000ft for the first time, to 42,000ft; on the 21st for the first time to Mach 0.8; and on the 22nd, following high Mach handling at 40,000ft, on his way back to Warton he carried out its first aerobatics, rolling and looping the aircraft like a fighter. At Warton on the 23rd, Beamont demonstrated the A1's controllability by pulling a 360-degree turn within the aerodrome boundary in a near-vertical bank at 200kt, gaining confidence all the time in the jet bomber's unique fighter-like aerobatic capability. Planning a spectacular inaugural display at the Farnborough Air Show, but anticipating official opprobrium and possible censure if seen to be 'risking' such an important new aircraft, for the next couple of weeks Beamont reverted to sedate flying anywhere public or near Warton. Colleagues, including Petter, suspecting what he was up to elsewhere, remained discreet. On 31 August the aircraft achieved its initial design speed of 470kt IAS at 4,500ft, 20 kt above the proposed initial Service requirement.

As early as 1949, Australia was showing interest in acquiring the A1 to replace the RAAF's force of Lincoln bombers built under licence by the Government Aircraft Factory at Fisherman's Bend, near Melbourne. At home the question had arisen of choosing a name for the A1, having regard to certain conventions whereby bombers were traditionally named after inland cities and naval aircraft after coastal towns. Given that most suitable British cities had already been 'used', it was perhaps no co-incidence that Sir George Nelson, a great supporter of the Commonwealth, suggested 'Canberra' which was emblazoned on its nose for the Farnborough Show. However, it would be 1951 before the name was formally adopted.

After intensive initial test flying, by the time of the 1949 SBAC Show an impressive debut was almost guaranteed. In September, the crowd at Farnborough, expecting to see a fairly sedate 'bomber' display from this 'over-sized' Meteor, which to many disappointingly eschewed the much-vaunted and exciting new swept wings, was astonished. That was in spite of fuel transfer problems causing a very smoky engine flame-out right at the start while still on the tarmac, requiring the flight to be delayed until the end of the show, together with the loss later of a number of ancillary pieces of test instrumentation seen to fall from the bomb bay, the opening of which Beamont demonstrated on the landing approach. Neither matter was as serious as it appeared, the instrumentation in particular merely not having been sufficiently secured to withstand the buffeting. But Beamont, accompanied by Chief Flight Test Engineer Dave Walker, enthralled the crowd with a collation of tight high-g banking dumb-bell turns, high speed runs, vertical climbs into half loops and a 360-degree roll along the flight line, all within the airfield limits, displaying to spectacular effect the speed, rate of climb and manoeuvrability of the world's first jet bomber, its Petter-inspired cerulean blue finish specially polished for the occasion.

Senior staff at Farnborough 1949. L to R: Crowe, Ellis, Harrison, Ellison, Petter, RPB, Smith, Page, Howatt.
'Canberra' has been added to the aircraft's nose

Petter, Sir George and H. G. Nelson, with senior managers and directors of English Electric, Marconi,
Cable & Wireless, Rolls-Royce and EE support staff, Farnborough 1949

VN799 starting its take-off run at Farnborough 1949 – the smoke seemingly issuing from the rear of the Canberra is in fact from the Royal Aircraft Establishment's chimneys in the distance

With the aviation world and spectators beside themselves with excitement, Beamont was later told by the display control committee to "just cool it!" *Flight Magazine* commented that 'Wg/Cdr Beamont's introductory performance in our first jet bomber was historic… a new aircraft has never been more convincingly demonstrated.' In displaying the Canberra in the years that followed, Beamont became an exponent of the even more exciting 'cartwheel', as perfected in Meteor aircraft by the Polish aerobatic pilot Zurakowski, at the top of a steep climb throttling back one engine and simultaneously opening up the other, to drop a wing for a fast return along the runway. Little did the industry know it, but Farnborough 1949 was the start of a process that would generate worldwide recognition and interest in the remarkable Canberra.

Johnny Squier flew the Canberra for the first time in a one-hour 'experience on type' sortie in *VN799* on 7 October 1949, so becoming the second person to fly the type. He made two further flights in it in December. Flown by Beamont, *VN799* attained 45,000ft for the first time on 19 October and 47,500ft on the 21st. Beamont delivered the aircraft to the A&AEE at Boscombe Down on the 28th for a 'Service Preview', there to be appraised by seven RAF test pilots including Wg/Cdr Davies, Sqn/Ldr Saxelby and Flt/Lt Callard in 30 hours of flight testing over an 18-day period. Having provided them with initial conversion training, he left them to their own devices to undertake comparative performance, rate of climb and manoeuvrability tests with a Meteor F.8, which the Canberra outflew on all criteria. Typically in the tests, the Canberra attained 40,000ft under normal climbing power in the time the Meteor took to reach 38,500ft at maximum power. After the first test, the Meteor pilot could not believe it and returned to base to make sure that his aircraft was not suffering from drag induced by an ill-fitting undercarriage door. All doors were found to fit perfectly! Moreover, in trying to out-turn the Canberra at such heights the Meteor invariably stalled out. The RAF was very impressed. Later, well into the 1950s, during annual defence exercises over the North Sea, RAF Canberras had to operate well below their optimum altitudes to allow the RAF fighters of the time a sporting chance of interception.

VN799 as demonstrated for the first time by RPB at Farnborough in 1949. Their highly praised participation presaged more than six decades of dramatic displays by aircraft of English Electric and its successor companies at Farnborough to the present day

Beamont flew the second of the four B.1-standard Canberra prototypes, the Nene-powered *VN813*, the first Canberra to be finished in the RAF black and grey colour scheme, on its maiden flight from Warton on 9 November 1949, noting a degree of dive-brake buffet. The Nene centrifugal-flow power units were an insurance against development delays with the Avon axials, the latter experiencing recurring surge problems right from bench testing in 1947 through into the early 1950s, but the Nenes' greater frontal area and larger nacelles adversely affected aerodynamics and speed. On 22 November he flew the Avon-powered third prototype *VN828* on its 35-minute maiden flight, the first Canberra flight from Samlesbury, from where all subsequent prototype and production Canberras would be first-flighted, landing at Warton. *VN828* was the first Canberra to dispense with the slender dorsal fin of its predecessors, a modification that Beamont assessed together with rudder and flutter performance on its second flight on 1 December. On 28 November Beamont took Peter Hillwood up in *VN799* for a one-hour air experience sortie and on 14 December was continuing to investigate oscillation in *VN799*. Johnny Squier had the honour of being the first pilot, after Beamont, to first-flight a Canberra when he made the maiden flight, airborne for 43 minutes, of the fourth and final B.1-standard prototype *VN850* from Samlesbury to Warton on 20 December, the aircraft curiously still retaining the dorsal fin of the first two prototypes.

Second Canberra prototype VN813, with Nene centrifugal engines inside fatter nacelles, augmented later, as shown in this photograph, by a DH Spectre rocket motor

Third Canberra prototype VN828, *dispensing with the fin fillet*

Fourth Canberra prototype VN850, *retaining the fin fillet*

STRATEGIC IMPERATIVES
– ALTITUDE, SPEED, RANGE

AIRCREW and EVENTS of the 1950s/'60s

New-build Aircraft Programmes Current:
Vampire, Canberra, P.1/Lightning

By 1950 the Canberra seemed assured of success, attracting orders for the RAF on such a scale as to make it evident that the production resources of English Electric alone would not be able to meet the demand. With the onset of the Cold War, the Berlin Airlift and war in Korea, in September arrangements were hurriedly entered into for the company to subcontract the manufacture of 300 aircraft shared equally between the three companies A.V. Roe (Avro), Handley Page and Short Bros & Harland. It was ironic that after English Electric had built Hampdens and Halifaxes on behalf of Handley Page during the war, the venerable firm of Handley Page would now be making Canberras for English Electric! In 1944, little had the English Electric directors realised that their fateful decision to remain in the industry after the war would prove so successful that within six years they themselves would be subcontracting out the first of their post-war designs for large scale production by no less than three of the 'founding family' of British aircraft manufacturers.

Surprisingly, as the Canberra's initial success mounted, in February 1950 Teddy Petter formally tendered his resignation to Sir George Nelson. Having been little seen at Warton since the end of 1949, he left the company immediately. After a period of contemplation, in September 1950 he was appointed Deputy Managing Director (Managing Director designate) at Folland Aircraft at Hamble, where he succeeded H. P. Folland as MD in July the following year. His position as Chief Engineer of the English Electric Aircraft Division, with responsibility for design, was taken by Freddie Page, then aged 32, who from early 1949 had been Assistant Chief Designer (Technical and Projects) and *de facto* deputy to Petter. Ray Creasey became deputy to Page, with A. E. Ellison as Assistant Chief Designer. Fortunately, Page's abilities as a designer, a manager capable of running multiple overlapping programmes and as a politically astute businessman, ensured a smooth transition and successful future. Petter had never been able to accept, as he saw it, the Warton design team being unable to operate fully independently of the deeply entrenched (and highly successful) production facility at the Strand Road Works, Preston, controlled by the General Manager, Arthur Sheffield. Late-stage design changes introduced in 1947/48 for manufacture to the revised Specification B5/47, even though imposed by the Ministry, may also not have helped relationships. It was Sheffield who had been largely responsible for English Electric's magnificent wartime production record, an achievement recognised by his being awarded the OBE, for many years guaranteeing him an unassailable position within the company and the confidence to refer to Petter's team as "that carnival lot at Warton". Moreover, post-war, Sheffield was under considerable pressure to boost production in a number of English Electric factories, including reinstating manufacture of diesel locomotive and electrical generation sets (notably in the Strand Road 'West Works'), together with all manner of English Electric domestic electrical goods such as washing machines and cookers. Matters came to a head at the end of 1949 with Petter feeling that he was getting inadequate support. Unable to get the backing of Sir George Nelson and the Board – who were presumably unwilling to alienate Sheffield – to operate a fully self-contained Warton design and development, experimental test, engineering and manufacturing shop, and despite pleas from Page to stay on the basis that it could only be a matter of time before matters improved, Petter made a peremptory departure for the second time in his career. Among several colleagues who subsequently joined him at Folland were Dave Walker of Flight Test; designers Allan Constantine, Tony Fewing and Peter Kubicki; Denis Smith and, later via RAE Bedford, Roy Fowler. With amazing prescience, on leaving, Petter forecast to colleagues that they and English Electric would still be working on the Canberra 30 years later. How right he was – Canberra refurbishment continued at Samlesbury until the late 1980s! In the same way that English Electric's wartime earnings had enabled the company to consolidate its postwar position in the industry and resource the Canberra, so would income from domestic and overseas sales of the Canberra in due course generate the investment necessary to develop the P.1/ Lightning. At Folland, Petter became the architect of the Midge and Gnat lightweight jet fighter trainers and was appointed CBE. Throughout his life he had been austere and deeply religious, believed to spend a number of his vacations in contemplation at a place of religious retreat. Leaving Folland on its takeover by Hawker Siddeley in 1959, Petter took his then sick wife, and their children, to live in a cult commune in Switzerland. He had nothing further to do with aviation. He died in France in 1968.

Freddie Page went on to occupy many senior positions with English Electric and its successor companies, from 1959 as Director and Chief Executive (Aircraft) of English Electric Aviation; from 1965-72 Managing Director, Military Aircraft Division of BAC (Preston) and, from 1967, Chairman and Managing Director; ultimately becoming responsible for all major British military and civil aircraft as Chairman and Chief Executive of the Aircraft Group of British Aerospace PLC from 1977-82, thereafter to be followed as Chief Executive by former Warton colleague Ivan Yates. Elected Fellow of the Royal Society in 1978 and knighted in 1979, Sir Frederick Page, CBE, MA, FRS, FEng, retired from the Board of British Aerospace plc in 1983. He justifiably took great pride in the fact that the company consistently paid annual dividends to HMG in later years during its period of nationalisation.

Freddie Page in charge, c.1951, not long after Petter's departure to Folland

In Flight Operations at Warton, 1950 began with all sorts of tests on rudder effectiveness, rudder tab oscillation, aileron jamming and elevator flutter. With Beamont at the controls, on 16 January *VN828* became the first Canberra to reach 50,000ft, amazingly without the pilot having recourse to a pressure waistcoat, least of all a full suit, neither of which were at that time available at Warton. With an official Air Ministry limitation of 47,000ft without pressure clothing, such high altitude tests were to continue rather discreetly. Not surprisingly, despite remarkable progress having been made in flying an ever increasing number of prototypes, including expanding the flight envelope into the compressibility range beyond Mach 0.85, operating at heights in excess of 50,000ft and speeds up to 500kt, the unexpected was by no means a stranger to the programme. In January 1950, landing at Warton after a test flight to assess aft C of G handling, with very weak elevator control remaining, *VN813* came to rest sitting on its tail bumper after a fuel balancing miscalculation between the three fuselage tanks had shifted its C of G too far aft – in fact behind its main wheels! The hapless Beamont was left stranded in the cockpit some 12ft above the runway until the emergency services and ground crew arrived. *VN813*, still retaining its dorsal fin fillet, from 1950 served with Rolls-Royce on Nene development, and from 1954 with de Havilland on Spectre rocket trials. On 7 February 1950, flying first prototype *VN799* with Dave Walker, Beamont experienced a grating sensation and stiffening of aileron control at around 15,000ft, leading to complete lock-up at 19,000ft. At that point, with the aircraft stuck in a tight circling bank, ejection became a very real prospect. The problem was consistent with jamming of the system by a 'foreign' body, icing or differential contraction caused, possibly on this particular flight, by the high rate of climb into colder altitudes. In fact it turned out to be the latter, as indicated by complete restoration of control as the aircraft descended to lower levels, proven beyond doubt when Beamont repeated the same sequence of climb and descent, with identical onset and easing of the problem, later in the sortie. Back on the ground, inspection showed evidence of 'picking up' or scoring of control surfaces, a potentially dangerous problem that, once identified by experimental test, was easily rectified on the production line before entry into service. In a later, even more alarming incident, flying at 20,000ft, Johnny Squier inadvertently exceeded the imposed Mach 0.86 compressibility limit at altitude, followed by violent pitch-down and a near vertical dive reaching Mach 0.9 which took 15,000ft to recover, to the accompaniment of an over-stressed airframe. It was a classic example of loss of control due to compressibility and may also have been related to what would become a recurring and serious problem with the Canberra that English Electric would soon have to examine very closely.

In 1950 an Australian technical mission led by RAAF Service test pilot **Wg/Cdr Derek R. 'Jell' Cuming**, who was in the UK also attending an RAF Staff College course, visited Warton to evaluate the Canberra. Cuming's wartime experience had included flying Hudsons in the Pacific, test flying captured Japanese aircraft, together with many experimental and exploratory trials such as evaluating a Spitfire Mk.VIII for towing three eight-man gliders on covert operations. Awarded the AFC in 1944 (with Bar in 1950), he won the McKenna Trophy on the ETPS No.3 Course at Boscombe Down in 1945, where one of his fellow students was the British test pilot Peter Twiss. Cuming, in 1946 the first person to have flown a jet aircraft in Australia (a Meteor), described by the Australian Minister for Air as the RAAF's outstanding test pilot, was also commander of the RAAF's Aircraft Research and Development Unit (ARDU) at RAAF Point Cook and Laverton. An amusing anecdote concerned his returning to RAAF Laverton in civilian clothes late one afternoon, identifying himself to the new airman on gate guard as "Wing Commander Cuming". The guard replied, "Thanks mate, I'll keep an eye out for the bastard."

Testing *VN799* at Warton on behalf of the Australian Government, on his first flight on type, Cuming became aware of a surge in the port engine which was allowed to continue longer than desirable. With the engine on fire, barely able to maintain height in the circuit, he complied with the control tower's urgent command to shut the engine down, extinguishing the flames and coming in trailing smoke to make a skilful single-engined emergency landing. The serious engine surge could have proved disastrous in more ways than one. In another 30 seconds, fire could easily have resulted not only in a burned-out jet pipe but also a catastrophic failure of the main spar, damaging not only the Canberra development programme but also potential sales. If anything, Cuming's successful landing of the prototype under such adverse circumstances served to enhance further the aircraft's appeal to the Australians. With engine surges continuing to affect production aircraft over the next couple of years, albeit on a reduced scale, English Electric eventually got fed up and summoned Denning Pearson and various other senior Rolls-Royce people from Derby up to Warton to sort out issues relating to the Avon's compressor once and for all.

On 12 April 1950 Beamont took *VN799* to 50,000ft. 21 April saw his first flight, lasting 45minutes, of the first of two pre-production/prototype B5/47 Canberras (designated B.Mk.II by internal Company memorandum of 2 September 1949), *VX165*, out of Samlesbury, an aircraft he tested to high Mach No.0.86 on the 28th. The B.2, for visual rather than radar bombing, was distinguished by a glazed nose and provision for three crew members including a bomb-aimer. On 11 May he flew fourth prototype *VN850*, for the first time fitted with drop tanks. Among a series of position error (PE) tests held on 17 and 22 May, Beamont flew *VN828* past Blackpool Tower at 500kt IAS, 45kt above the Service limit, the first Canberra to achieve that speed. *VN828* remained at Warton for the next five years as a development aircraft. Very much the 1950 Canberra display aircraft, on 10 June

VN850 at Antwerp, June 1950. L to R: Taylor, Sheffield, Strang Graham, Sarginson, RPB, Hothersal, Page, Davenport, Chapman, Potter

VN850 was flown by Beamont from Warton to the French Air Force Experimental Establishment at Bretigny in only 54 minutes, thereafter to be demonstrated by him, for the first time overseas, at the Paris Air Show, the *Fête Nationale de L'Air*, held at the newly-opened Orly Airport on 11/12 June. The English Electric servicing party travelled by RAF Dakota via Farnborough and Manston. As ever, *Flight* provided some good words: "Suddenly, from the loudspeakers, came an excited cry – "Voici Canberra" – coinciding with a fleeting glimpse of the magnificent 'English Electric' bomber, immaculate in working dress of glossy grey and black, as it sped low over the field. The thunderous surge of sound from its two Avons had scarcely abated before the Canberra about-turned to complete the same repertoire of speed-plus-manoeuvrability which 'English-electrified' the Farnborough audience last September. The pilot, Roland Beamont, made a final dummy approach and landing before departing."

Flying from Warton to Antwerp in 48 minutes in *VN850* on 24 June, Beamont repeated the display at the Belgian Air Show at Deurne Airport on 24/25th, flying off grass. His display on the second day was set against large patches of blue sky as the weather improved, enabling him to demonstrate the aircraft's spectacular rolling abilities. Spectators and military personnel at both Paris and Antwerp were astonished at the Canberra's performance, greatly admiring its graceful lines which, unusually for a bomber, were unsullied by external aerials, add-on bulges, or other excrescences. On 26 June, Beamont gave Freddie Page a lift back from Antwerp to Warton in *VN850*, the first of Page's many subsequent flights in a Canberra. They sped back over the tops of bad weather in an hour, leaving the support Dakota to slog back to Preston through heavy cloud at 4,000ft. On 30 June Beamont took *VN850* on a three-hour 1600-mile 'operational cruise', the first hour up to 42,000ft, the second at 42-45,000ft and the third at 45-47000ft. *VN850* differed from its predecessors in having the final rudder shape, yet as previously noted retained the dorsal fin fillet which had been deleted from the third prototype *VN828*. It also had fuel lines that permitted the carrying of wingtip fuel tanks, jettisonable by explosive bolts. From 11 May these had been the subject of handling trials, culminating on 31 July 1950 in the first dropping of the tanks from a Canberra. The trial, during which Freddie Page accompanied Beamont in *VN850*, took place over Warton Aerodrome. For safety, in case of any delay in separation and consequent overshoot, they flew on a southerly heading towards the great expanse of the Ribble marshes, but Beamont's wartime ground-attack experience proved invaluable in his successfully hitting the grass between the runways in a test that, in later years, would probably have had the health and safety authorities tearing their hair out! Nowadays it would have to be carried out at an official weapons range.

VN850 was demonstrated by Beamont at the RAF Display at Farnborough from 4-10 July, to a visiting delegation from the American military at Boscombe Down on 11 July, and at the SBAC Show at Farnborough in September along with first Canberra

Close-up of Roland Prosper Beamont (RPB) in the first Canberra B.2 prototype VX165, taken from the tail turret of a Lancaster of the Royal Aircraft Establishment (without telephoto lens) by Charles A. Sims, The Aeroplane, on 25 July 1950 (via BAE Systems)

B.2 prototype *VX165*. Having flown six test sorties in the aircraft earlier in the month, on 18 August Beamont flew the second B.2 prototype *VX169*, which had flown for the first time on 2 August at Samlesbury, from Warton to the USAF base at Burtonwood where he demonstrated it to another party of US Air Force Generals. His display was given under low cloud and in rain, *VX169* trailing spectacular vortexes of vapour from its wingtips in a dramatic low-level demonstration under the worst of conditions. The US delegations could not have been more impressed and on 14 September another American mission, headed by the USAF's Chief Test Pilot Col. Al Boyd (to whom, two years earlier, Beamont had had to apologise for bursting a tyre and surging the engine of a P-80 whilst in the US), visited Warton to evaluate the aircraft for possible acquisition by the USAF. There they were given a further demonstration by Beamont in *VN850*. Boyd later flew the Canberra himself, declining Beamont's offer to accompany him: "Just gimme the numbers!" Such indications of interest from across the Atlantic, before the Canberra had even been accepted by the RAF, were at first greeted with reservation in certain quarters of the British Establishment, who saw it as premature. Their caution was shared neither by English Electric nor the USAF after the displays by Beamont in *VN850* and *VX169*. Subsequently, Col. Boyd and a number of USAF colleagues spent ten days on assessment trials at Warton. Beamont was on sick leave for part of the period, but on one particular day Boyd, with total panache and competence, having confidently determined his own weather forecast for the afternoon of what had started as a very bad day, as conditions improved after lunch flew the first ever sortie of a production Canberra B.2 with full fuel and bomb load. Boyd had to 'loiter' at altitude to allow the USAF Shooting Star 'chase', also up from Warton, to catch up. American interest in the Canberra intensified and English Electric was invited to demonstrate the aircraft in the US early in 1951. Considerable preparation was required before production B.2 *WD932*, first flown at Samlesbury by Johnny Squier on 25 January 1951, could be ferried out to the States by an RAF crew for Beamont to display there in February/March.

[Having been delivered to Rolls-Royce at Hucknall by Beamont on 5 October 1950, on 13 June 1951 *VN850* was to gain the unfortunate distinction of becoming the first Canberra to be totally destroyed when, in the hands of Rolls-Royce test pilot R. B. Leach, it suffered an engine fire on the approach to Hucknall, crashing just outside the perimeter with the loss of its pilot.]

Flying solo, on 1 October 1950 Beamont attained 52,000ft in *VX165* over the Western Isles (some reports put this at nearly 55,000ft). To save weight, Flight Test Observer Dave Walker, usually present on the high altitude tests, was on this occasion 'not required on voyage', much to his dismay. *VX165* was the first three-seater, the first to have a glazed nose and the first with wingtip tanks as original equipment. Two days later Beamont took it to high Mach No. 0.86. Another milestone was Beamont's first flight of the first production Canberra B.2 *WD929* from Samlesbury on 8 October. Three days later he carried out a 50-minute clearance flight in the prototype *VN799* before it was delivered to the RAE at Farnborough and then the Armament and Instrument Experimental Unit (AIEU) at Martlesham Heath, Suffolk, for Mk.9 autopilot evaluation.

[While in the hands of the RAE's Blind Landing Experimental Unit, *VN799* crashed at Martlesham Heath on 18 August 1953, so depriving the Lancashire aircraft industry of the opportunity to preserve a highly significant historic aircraft which today would have had truly iconic status.]

October 1950 was also marked by the initial conversion of RAF aircrew, on detachment to Warton and under the direction of Beamont, Squier, Hillwood and Watson, onto the first production Canberra B.2 *WD929*.

Beamont began 1951 with a wide range of handling tests on several Canberras, including *WD929/ 931/932* and *VX169* fitted with a new fin. Having demonstrated the Canberra to the Americans on several occasions in the UK in 1950, English Electric was astonished to realise that US interest might, subject to further evaluation, even extend to manufacturing the Canberra under licence. Taking up the invitation from the Americans, on 21 February 1951 the fourth production Canberra B.2, *WD932*, an MoS aircraft fitted with wingtip and bomb bay auxiliary tanks, first flown by Squier on 25 January and in which Beamont had conducted tests in January and February, was flown across the Atlantic. Routed from Aldergrove, Northern Ireland, to Gander, Newfoundland, it covered 2,072 statute miles (sm) in 4hr 37min at an average speed of 449.5mph, an unofficial record time, before proceeding to Andrews Air Force Base near Washington. It was crewed by RAF officers from the A&AEE at Boscombe Down, comprising Sqn/Ldr Arthur E. Callard, DFC, Flt/Lt E. A. J. Haskett (navigator) and Flt/Lt A. J. R. Robson, DFC, (radio operator). Callard, a Manchester man, joined the Service in 1940, trained in Canada and later became a Mosquito intruder pilot. In 1947 he joined ETPS No.6 Course at Farnborough and, as a Flight Lieutenant, was one of the seven RAF pilots to evaluate the Canberra at Boscombe Down in October/November 1949. In the US, *WD932's* mission (to be flown by Beamont) would be to compete in evaluation trials against four American types, principally the Martin XB-51, but also the North American XB-45 Tornado, the North American AJ-1 Savage and the Douglas A-26 Invader.

Callard's flight, the first direct Atlantic crossing by a jet-propelled aircraft without refuelling, was far from routine. Arriving at Aldergrove from Warton on 19 February 1951, a hole some eight inches across was observed in the starboard wing leading edge. As *Flight* of 2 March 1951 commented:

'someone's assurance that this was a cabin-air intake could not be accepted: certainly its edges did not bespoke English Electric finish. The station C.T.O. approached, inserted his hand, and distastefully withdrew major and minor components of a seagull. The presence of the remains were soon explained to us by S/L. Callard himself. About three minutes after leaving Warton, in showery weather, he saw a flock of gulls ahead. The Canberra was then clocking about 350kt. Had the birds, as he put it, pressed on, and not behaved stupidly, all would have been well; but, as it happened, one was struck. Callard felt the impact and feared for one of the Avons; Haskett looked out but saw no damage. It was, however (as the Aldergrove C.T.O. soon discovered) serious enough to keep the Canberra grounded throughout the night while repairs were effected. The delay was especially unfortunate as the met.forecast was at that time comparatively favourable. Thereafter conditions were likely to deteriorate…

Having been photographed, filmed, interrogated and stalked for photographs, the crew found sanctuary in the mess: there was nothing for it but to await repair of the gull-sabotaged wing.

Soon after daylight on February 21st we were again out at Aldergrove. The night had not passed without incident. Just before 20.00 hr, Mr. Peter Hillwood, an English Electric test pilot, who had ferried a party over in the firm's Consul, was very wisely making himself comfortable in the mess when word came that the damage was not wholly superficial. A generator cable in the leading edge had suffered. With his navigator, Mr. D. A. Watson, Hillwood lost no time in getting airborne to collect a spare. It was snowing. Cloud-base over Belfast was at 400ft, tops at 10,000-11,000ft., but the Consul forced through to Warton. On the descent through cloud, severe icing was encountered and one sliver from an airscrew penetrated the fuselage. Having landed, the aircraft was still as iced as a Christmas cake but, with the spare aboard, returned in the frozen darkness without further mutilation. By 08.45 repairs were completed in the bitterly cold hangar by RAF and English Electric personnel. These splendid performances were to pass almost unnoticed in the flurry of publicity rightly occasioned by the Canberra's flight.

The "E.E." team at Aldergrove were Mr. D. L. Ellis (deputy chief engineer); H. C. Harrison (chief production designer), R. N. Hollock (aircraft service manager); J. Crowther (foreman); F. Holman (inspector); J. Cookson (electrician); and J. R. Taylor and G. N. Fraser (fitters). Representing Marconi radio interests was W/C. R. R. Stanford Tuck, D.S.O., D.F.C.' [NB: The latter was Bob Stanford Tuck, WW2 Battle of Britain Hurricane and Spitfire fighter ace.]

Flight's report concluded that following all the necessary technical checks and engine runs to test the new generator cable the Canberra was at length refuelled by the station bowsers, during which process 'Quips about "Callard and Bowser" were severely discouraged.' Callard was awarded the Air Force Cross in the Birthday Honours List of June 1951.

Peter Hillwood (wearing cap) in conversation with Dai Ellis, with Bob Stanford Tuck centre right, prior to Canberra B.2 WD932's departure for the USA on a very wintry day in February 1951

A confident Sqn/Ldr Callard enters WD932 to begin the ferry flight to the USA

Callard and crew meet the press on arrival at Andrews Air Force Base, near Washington DC

Sqn/Ldr Callard, Flt/Lt Haskett and Flt/Lt Robson meet G. C. Pearson (President and General Manager of Martin Aircraft) and Glenn L. Martin at Martin Airport, near Baltimore

A series of Martin photographs taken at Martin Field, Baltimore, showing dramatically the lines of the Canberra

L to R: Poplawski (Martin Co), RPB, Brink (Martin) and Sgt Hunt emphasise the wide chord of the Canberra wing

RPB and Flt/Sgt Slade explain the cartridge starter mechanism for the Rolls-Royce Avon engines…

…and an electrical connection hatch for outside power to be supplied when on the ground

Birds of a feather – RPB familiarises Martin's veteran Chief Test Pilot 'Pat' Tibbs with the Canberra's cockpit. Visible is the patched repair made at Aldergrove to the starboard wing leading edge

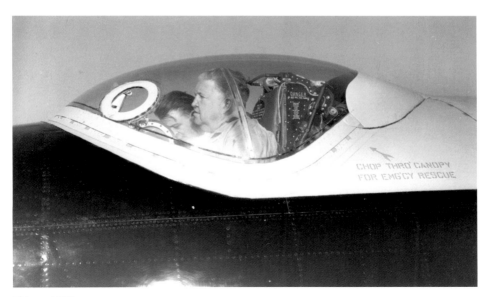

Tibbs and RPB

The burden of responsibility – an impassive RPB prepares to demonstrate WD932

RPB's breathtaking display of WD932 *at Martin Airport easily outclassed the American opposition*

A final commanding pass in front of the Martin Field control tower

Three days after Callard's ferry flight, on 24 February, Beamont, who had gone ahead on 19 February by scheduled BOAC Stratocruiser civil airliner *G-AKGM Castor*, carried out an air test of the Canberra prior to demonstrating the aircraft in what was essentially a fly-off competition held before the US Chiefs of Staff at Andrews Field Air Force Base, Washington on the 26th. All four American aircraft failed to conform to the test criteria within their allocated ten-minute flying slots. But having performed all the specified series of routines, Beamont found himself with three and a half minutes' flying time to spare which he used to dramatically emphasise the Canberra's superiority. The fact that the Canberra's mainwheel tyres both burst as a result of some heavy braking to demonstrate a very short landing on the runway, which it was not realised had been dusted with sand as an anti-icing measure, had no bearing on the outcome. Within days the US Government announced the Canberra to be the best light bomber available. Beamont maintained the momentum with two further 30-minute demonstrations on Tuesday 6 March at the Martin Airfield, Middle River, and again on Sunday 11 March, designated 'Canberra Sunday', before 20,000 Martin employees, families and friends. *WD932* was left in the USA where it was allotted USAF Serial *51-17387*, to be further examined and tested by the Glenn L.Martin Company of Baltimore, Maryland, selected as the US manufacturer under licence.

No less than seven tons of 'loft' plates – thin aluminium alloy master pattern sheets – were subsequently despatched by Douglas DC-4 Skymaster from English Electric to Martins. The USAF also gave *WD932* a thorough workout at the Wright-Patterson Air Force Base at Dayton, Ohio.

After returning from the States, on 28 and 30 March Beamont made his personal first flights in the prototype photo-reconnaissance variant, Canberra PR.3 *VX181*, an aircraft first-flighted by Peter Hillwood from Samlesbury to Warton on 19 March when he encountered increased levels of vibration compared with previous marks. On 13 April, Beamont delivered the fifth production B.2 *WD933* straight off the English Electric line to Armstrong Siddeley Motors Ltd at Bitteswell for use as a test bed, there to have its 6,500 lb static thrust (st) Avons replaced by 7,220 lb Sapphires. *VX181* and *WD933* were both demonstrated at Farnborough in 1951. Beamont later test flew *WD933* on several occasions in May 1952, fitted with uprated 8,300 lb Sapphires, in which form Armstrong Siddeley demonstrated it at Farnborough in 1952. [Fitted with 10,300 lb Sapphires in 1954, it was written off after a crash landing at Bitteswell on 11 November that year.]

Prototype PR.3 VX181 *being refuelled in this busy scene at Warton in 1951*

The choice of the aircraft's name had been an inspired and timely marketing move by English Electric. The jet bomber was officially named *Canberra* by Mr (later Sir) Robert Menzies, Prime Minister of Australia, at a ceremony at Biggin Hill on 19 January 1951. A bottle of Australian 'champagne' was broken against the nose of *WD929*. Bottle-smashing trials had at first proved erratic – some bottles complied, others did not. For the official ceremony the bottle was first weakened by the application of a diamond-tipped glass cutter! After the ceremony, also attended by Lt-Gen Kenneth B. Wolfe, Deputy Chief of Staff of the USAF, the Canberra was brilliantly displayed once again by Beamont, described by Menzies as "the presiding genius who looks just like an Australian tough!" On 16/17 July, Johnny Squier, accompanied by Wg/Cdr Cuming of the RAAF, flew Canberra B.2 ex-*WD939* and in March 1952 Squier flew ex-*WD983*. Both these aircraft were diverted from the first British (RAF) contract, to be sold to Australia and flown there by RAAF crews as *A84-307* and *A84-125* respectively, as pattern aircraft for the production of 48 B.20 aircraft by the Government Aircraft Factory, Fisherman's Bend, Melbourne. Squier also tested *WD935* and *WD942*, two of three additional aircraft made available on loan to the RAAF as *A84-1/2/3*. On 5 August 1951, Wg/Cdr Cuming and his navigator Flt/Lt Harvey departed RAF Lyneham for Australia in *A84-307*, setting an unofficial record covering the 10,235 miles to Darwin in a flying time of 21hr 41min, at an average of 477.62mph with stops at Tobruk, Habbaniya, Karachi, Ceylon and Singapore. [Air Commodore Derek Randal 'Jell' Cuming, AFC*, OBE, born in 1917, died in 2002. *A84-307* ex-*WD939*, the 11th production Canberra B.2 to come off the line at Samlesbury, was the first jet aircraft to fly to Australia and the first Canberra to see service with the RAAF. In Australia it carried out many high altitude, high speed tests with the Aircraft Research and Development Unit (ARDU) and No.1 Long Range Flight, both of which were commanded by Cuming. Damaged in a mid-air incident in 1956, it received replacement wings and was converted to a Mk.21 trainer in which form, among other duties, it served as an instrument rating test and bomber OCU trainer with the RAAF in Vietnam. It is the world's oldest surviving substantially original Canberra, currently (2011) undergoing intensive restoration for static display at the National Vietnam Veterans Museum, Phillip Island, Victoria.]

English Electric hand over B.2 A84-307 to Wg/Cdr Cuming and Flt/Lt Harvey, RAAF, August 1951.
L to R: Shorrock, Strang Graham, RPB

Wg/Cdr Cuming (R) and Flt/Lt Harvey, RAAF, share a joke in front of A84-307 which they flew to Australia
on 5 August 1951

Cuming fires up A84-307 for the flight to Australia

Handover of the second RAAF Canberra B.2, A84-125 at Warton, 16 April 1952. Peter Hillwood (white flying overalls), with Sqn/Ldr Fisher (pilot) and Flt/Lt Sharp, (navigator), RAAF, on his left. The aircraft departed for Australia on 29 April

On 12 April, 3 June and 10/12 December 1951, in order to explore controllability in the event of the loss of the Canberra's one-piece *Perspex* canopy, Beamont, his face taped-up against frostbite, flew four trials flights in B.2s *WD934, 935* and *956*, all without their cabin top/cockpit canopies. The tests showed that the unsatisfactory small secondary glass screen, fitted inside early Canberras to protect the pilot's head from air blast under such circumstances, but at the cost of some reduction in forward visibility, could be dispensed with and replaced by a shallow metal internal deflector plate. In that state the aircraft could just about tolerably be flown at up to 445kt IAS, close enough to the Service requirement of 450kt which itself had been set for aircraft with conventional fixed windscreens. On 25 May 1951, shortly after the type's 'Release to Service', Beamont had the satisfaction of delivering the RAF's first Canberra B.2 *WD936* to No.101 Sqn, RAF Binbrook, where on arrival he gave yet another exhilarating display before presenting the aircraft to the Station Commander, Gp/Capt Wally Sheen and Wg/Cdr (Flying) Pat Connelly. Sheen, who had been given a 1hr 14min familiarisation flight by Squier in *WD931* on 10 January, could not wait to fly the new aircraft himself: "Just show me the taps!" With no dual-control facility, Beamont accompanied him in the jump seat. Sheen coped admirably. But Bomber Command, concerned that enthusiastic displays of the athletic Canberra might encourage too many squadron pilots to emulate them, subsequently wrote to English Electric requesting that, in future, company test pilots refrain from performing inappropriate aerobatics at RAF airfields. They could have saved their typewriter ribbon! On 13 June, Beamont flew *WD934* to West Raynham where he gave a demonstration at the Fighter Convention, an occasion when there might have been some confusion among those present as to whether it was a fighter or a bomber that they were watching display. On 28 June, Squier and Watson made the second delivery to No.101 Sqn, that of B.2 *WD938*.

The culmination of RPB's 'canopy off' trials with B.2 WD956, 10 December 1951, with revised deflector plate fitted, his face taped up against frostbite

RPB and Squier in discussion by B.2 WD934, 'Canberra Day', Warton, 23 May 1951

A larger EE group with WD934 on 'Canberra Day', 1951

Squier and Ground Chief Jimmy Pickthall, 'Canberra Day', 1951

RPB gives an impromptu display on arriving at RAF Binbrook in B.2 WD936, 25 May 1951

RPB hands over WD936 to No.101 Sqn, RAF Binbrook, 25 May 1951.
L to R: RPB, Gp/Capt Sheen, Wg/Cdr Connelly

It was decided that a second Canberra B.2 should be flown across the Atlantic to further facilitate the setting up of the Martin production line, that selected being *WD940*, an aircraft first flown at Samlesbury by Johnny Squier on 31 July. After the usual test flights, including jettisoning of drop tanks, on 29 August Beamont flew a 3hr 25min navigation exercise from Warton, south to the Scillies, then via Manston up as far north as the Orkneys, returning to Warton. On 31 August, **Beamont** with navigator **Sqn/Ldr Dennis A. 'Watty' Watson**, who had joined the company in 1950, and radio operator **R. H. T. (Bob) Rylands** of the Marconi Company, flew *WD940* from Warton to Aldergrove and then across the Atlantic to Gander. For the main leg, Beamont employed the 'cruise-climb' technique, whereby as a fuel-economical aid and, in the absence of an auto-pilot, more restful alternative to manually flying the aircraft all the time, the engines were set at maximum cruise rpm for the optimum cruise speed, on this occasion Mach 0.74, the aircraft automatically cruise-climbing to 50,000ft as its weight reduced with fuel burn. On 4 September the leg from Gander to Martin Airport, Baltimore, included transit over New York at high altitude. On the approach, with the contrails of inquisitive USAF interceptor jets visible ahead, but thrashing impotently thousands of feet below, US Air Traffic Control asked Beamont to confirm his altitude, as "a check on vertical separation". This Beamont refused to do, for security of classified information. Leaving an increasingly frantic Bangor, Maine Sector ATC fading behind, he instead powered the Canberra to probably the greatest height that New York had ever then been overflown. At 51,000ft, he was confident that he was well clear of any other traffic. He was right, but after giving a short demonstration on arrival at Martin Airport, he was called to the Pentagon to explain himself to a roomful of Generals. Beamont reminded them that the Canberra was a British military aircraft, the performance of which was classified secret, not for open discussion on civilian VHF and in any event was operating above the ceiling of any other aircraft then extant in the world. "Just what height was that?" asked one of the officers. "51,000ft, and still not at the Canberra's ceiling" replied Beamont. A collective gasp and "Gee Whizz!" rippled around the Generals.

WD940 was handed over to the Martin Company to become the second pattern aircraft for manufacture under licence as the Martin B-57. Before returning to the UK by Stratocruiser on 11 September, on the 7th Beamont and Watson carried out a test flight in the first pattern aircraft, *WD932*, which had by then been fitted with Martin cowlings. Their delivery flight of *WD940* had established an official record from Aldergrove to Gander, 2,072sm in 4hr 18min 24.4sec at an average speed of 481.12mph. Rylands had made some useful radio contacts with various Northern Ireland stations and an Atlantic weather ship during the first part of the flight but electrical storms over the Western Atlantic denied them similar facilities later on. Their landfall over Newfoundland, just ten miles off track, easily correctable by visual contact with the ground, was a triumph of dead reckoning by Watson.

L to R: Esme Watson, Pat Beamont, Tommy Evans and Peter Hillwood see off 'Bee', 'Watty' and Bob Rylands on their departure from Warton to the USA in B.2 WD940, 31 August 1951

WD940, the second Canberra for America, renumbered as 117352 in USAF markings, over Baltimore, late 1951

It was the first of 22 official internationally accredited long distance point-to-point and altitude record breaking flights, made by company and RAF pilots, which achieved so much in promoting the Canberra around the world during the 1950s. As stated in *Against the Sun*, by Edward Lanchbery: "By less than an hour they had failed to beat the sun; but they had nevertheless set the stage for the days of trans-Atlantic flight in a state of perpetual sunrise or sunset at the travellers' choice." Back in the UK, at the Preston Works on 15 October, Sir George Nelson presented Beamont, Watson and Rylands with gold wrist watches as an appreciation of their achievement.

On 28 November, Beamont flew English Electric's Consul communications aircraft from Warton to Boscombe Down, there to experience once again a North American F-86 Sabre jet in a 1hr 25min handling test.

Sadly, on 21 December 1951 in the hands of a USAF pilot, the first pattern Canberra, *WD932*, crashed during a test flight from Baltimore. Both crew ejected but the navigator's parachute failed to open properly and he was killed. Freddie Page flew to the States a day or two later to show support and on 26 December, Beamont, together with Chief Aerodynamicist Ray Creasey, also flew over to the States in Stratocruiser *G-AKGK Canopus* for discussions with the Martin Company's Chief Test Pilot, O. E. 'Pat' Tibbs and its engineers. On 7 February 1952 at Warton, it fell to Beamont to recreate as far as possible the circumstances of the loss of *WD932*, using B.2 *WD958* straight off the production line. Suspicion that the loss of *WD932* had been due to incorrect handling procedures related to fuel transfer, allowing a dangerous shift of its C of G aft, over-stressing the airframe, required *WD958* to be loaded to give a C of G slightly further aft than normal. When, in that condition, Beamont subsequently pulled 5.2g at 450kt IAS he encountered no problem. In the course of several further visits to the States and attendance at the official enquiry, putting himself on the front line over Chesapeake Bay, Freddie Page acted as flight test observer on the first post-accident flight of the second USAF pattern Canberra, *51-17352* ex-*WD940*, this time flown by a more experienced American crew. It all confirmed that there were no inherent problems providing fuel handling procedures were adhered to.

During 1950, while continuing to production-test large numbers of Vampires, **Johnny Squier** flew all four Canberra B.1 prototypes, B.2 prototype *VX165* and, on 29 December, early production B.2 *WD931*. Accompanied by Watson and Ellis, on 29 June 1951 he took *WD934*, an aircraft in which he had carried out ground runs at Samlesbury on 5 March and flown to Warton on 19 March, to Paris, demonstrating it with Watson at the Paris Air Show on 1 July. Significant also was Squier's maiden flight on 6 July of the Specification B22/48 B.5 prototype target marker *VX185* which had been converted from the aircraft originally designated on the production line as the second PR.3 prototype photo-reconnaissance version.

A typical Canberra B.2 cockpit and panel. WK116, made by Avro at Woodford in 1954, served with No.231 OCU, No.85 and No.100 Sqns, returning to Samlesbury in June 1976 as the first of the RAF's 'Long Term Fleet' for overhaul by BAC. It was lost on 25 February 1982 when both engines failed on take-off, crashing into the sea five miles off Akrotiri. The crew ejected safely

1. Flaps selector switch
2. Ventilation louvre
3. Undercarriage position indicator
4. Wing-tip tank jettison pushbutton
5. Port sloping front panel
6. Undercarriage master switch
7. Undercarriage selector switch unit
8. Undercarriage emergency lowering control
9. Direct vision (DV) panel
10. Call navigator pushbutton
11. Dimmer switch (port UV lamps)
12. Flight instrument panel
13. Emergency amber lamps switch
14. Accelerometer
15. Standby compass
16. Dimmer switch (starboard red lamps)
17. Engine instrument panel
18. Dimmer switch (starboard UV lamps)
19. Miscellaneous instrument panel
20. Tailplane trim cut-in switch
21. Tailplane trim control switch
22. Press-to-transmit pushbutton
23. Wheelbrakes control lever
24. Wheelbrakes lever parking catch
25. Engine starter panel
26. Airbrakes control switch

Explanatory view of a B.2 cockpit and panel. Bottom right is the access to the bomb aimer's position, 'couch' and nose window. The navigator's station, with small fold-down table, is behind the pilot's seat, the two separated by an instrument panel/bulkhead. The bomb aimer/third crew member also had use of a 'jump seat' at the rear of the pressurised cabin

VX185 was also the first Canberra to be built with integral wing leading-edge fuel tanks providing 900 gallons additional fuel, a Dunlop *Maxaret* anti-skid wheel braking system and a 'solid' nose with symmetrical bomb-aimer's window beneath. On 29 January 1952 a further Canberra milestone was reached when Beamont test flew the 40th production aircraft, B.2 *WD980*, the first to be fully flight-tested at Samlesbury prior to delivery, as were all subsequent Canberra production aircraft. Hitherto, Samlesbury-produced Canberras had been first flighted to Warton, there to complete pre-delivery air tests. In another milestone event, having amassed 1,300 hours from 2,500 sorties on Vampires, on 12 February 1952 Johnny Squier first-flighted FB.9 *WG931*, the last of 1,369 Vampires built at Samlesbury by English Electric under contracts with de Havilland going back to 1944. On 12 June 1952 Beamont took Canberra T.4 prototype *WN467* on its maiden flight from Samlesbury and on 12 August also made the first flight of the first production PR.3, *WE135*.

Accelerating production of the Canberra – with the opposite applying to the Vampire, which was terminated in 1952 – meant that from 1950 both Johnny Squier and Peter Hillwood became heavily involved in development flight testing of the new jet bomber. The growing workload required even more pilots and in 1950, **Thomas Benjamin Oswyn 'Tommy' Evans**, DFC, born in 1923, a former Flight Lieutenant in the RAF, joined the company as a production pilot, first flying the Canberra in February 1951. Evans had seen service as a wartime fighter pilot in the Far East and from 1944 until joining English Electric in 1950 was engaged on development-flying jet aircraft for the RAF. He was also No.2 Pilot of the Fighter Demonstration Unit in Fighter Command. Post-war he remained a pilot with the RAF Reserve attached to No.42 Reserve Centre, RAF Fazakerley, Liverpool. Like Squier, Beamont and Hillwood, on joining English Electric, Evans did his share of Vampire production testing at Samlesbury. After flying FB.5 *WA276* on 17 November 1950, he carried out over 350 Vampire test flights before making the final clearance flight of the contract, a 62-minute sortie in FB.9 *WG931*, on 13 February 1952. Having first been flown by Johnny Squier the day before, *WG931* was collected from Samlesbury on 19 February.

On 6 May 1951 Evans accompanied Squier on a 48-minute familiarisation flight in third prototype Canberra *VN828*. In the absence of Roland Beamont in the United States, Evans displayed Canberra B.5 *VX185* at the 1951 Farnborough Air Show where he was commended by *Flight Magazine* for his skill in handling the aircraft after a tyre burst as a result of brake seizure after touchdown. Sadly, on 25 March 1952, flying solo in fine weather, Evans was killed when the new Canberra B.2 he was testing, *WD991*, crashed in open farmland at Cottam to the north west of Preston, on its maiden flight from Samlesbury to Warton. Shortly after taking off at 11.45am the aircraft was seen flying at high speed with wheels and flaps retracted, estimated at 400-450kt, straight and level at 800ft, before entering a steep

Canberra T.4 prototype WN467, first flown by RPB on 12 June 1952

T.4 prototype WN467

80-degree dive into the ground. Debris was scattered for 600 yards beyond the point of impact, causing some damage to property but no other injuries on the ground. Company Flight Test Observer Thomas Burnell, originally rostered for the flight, was prevented from going at the last minute due to a problem with issue of equipment from the stores at Samlesbury. The accident was only English Electric's second to involve total loss since the company had recommenced aircraft manufacturing in 1938 and Evans, with 2,479 hours flying experience, 57 on type, was the first company pilot to lose his life. It was however the fifth Canberra to be lost overall within a twelve month period, including several in RAF service, guaranteeing a thoroughgoing inquiry by the authorities once the much fragmented remains of the aircraft had been retrieved and laid out on the floor of one of the Samlesbury hangars. Various theories were put forward for its cause, including the possibility of a runaway tailplane actuator as happened in a number of other cases, but after failure of the flight controls, engines and even accidental inflation of the pilot's dinghy had all been ruled out, no specific reason was ever determined. Intriguingly, a distorted 2BA box spanner found in the wreckage, damaged possibly by crushing loads in a control circuit, was also considered a possible cause of control column/elevator jamming, but likewise could not be proven.

Peter Godfrey 'Pete' Lawrence, MBE, born in 1920, started his career in aviation in 1937 as a Handley Page apprentice, before joining the Fleet Air Arm in 1939 on a seven-year short-service commission. Qualifying as a pilot, from 1940-42 he served with operational Swordfish squadrons from aircraft carriers HMS *Eagle, Illustrious* and *Argus* and from bases in the Western Desert, thereafter being posted to the Naval Service Trials Unit as a test pilot until the end of the war. During the latter period he made some 450 day and night landings on 25 different aircraft carriers. In 1944 he was appointed to the Firebrand Tactical Trials Unit to work on the single-seat torpedo bomber which was then just entering service. Having practised landings in a Vought Corsair aboard HMS *Glory* in May/June 1945 with No.708 Sqn, Lt P. G. Lawrence carried out a number of deck landings on HMS *Pretoria Castle* in the Bristol Centaurus-engined Blackburn B-37 TF.Mk.4 Firebrand naval torpedo strike fighter *EK602*. That year he joined Blackburn and General Aircraft Ltd at Brough as an experimental test pilot and, after attending ETPS No.4 Course at Cranfield in 1946, was appointed Blackburns' Chief Test Pilot. On 7 March 1946, in a test involving steep dives to investigate aileron oscillation in Firebrand *EK739,* at 25,000ft serious flutter resulted in the wings flapping through three feet at the tips. Lawrence's aircraft started to fracture along the fuselage and wing skins, but as he reduced speed to 100kt and made preparations to bale out, flutter ceased and the aircraft recovered sufficient equilibrium to allow him to make a safe landing, albeit with Category 4 damage. After the appointment of Harold 'Timber' Wood as Chief Test Pilot in 1949, Lawrence's status with Blackburn was, in *Flight Magazine's* terms, 'obscure'. Continuing with the company however, he was awarded the MBE in recognition of his deck-landing trials with the Firebrand TF.Mk.4, 102 of which began to enter service just after the war ended. He displayed aircraft at the early postwar SBAC shows at Radlett and Farnborough. After thoughtfully watching some spectacular aerobatics by jet pilots at the first post-war show at Radlett in 1946, Lawrence took off and notoriously rolled the torpedo-carrying Firebrand TF.5 *EK742* at low level. At the 1948 Farnborough Air Show he demonstrated the Centaurus-powered Blackburn S.28/43 B-48 Firecrest naval strike fighter *VF172*, an aircraft fitted with a cranked laminar-flow wing designed to fold double for compactness onboard carriers, but which did not proceed beyond two flying prototypes. Outside his official duties, Lawrence was a keen competitor in air races, flying in the Folkestone Races Tiger Moth Scratch Race in 1947. In 1949, flying a Firebrand TF.Mk.5A, he won the Air League Challenge Cup Air Race, an event restricted to piston-engined aircraft with a sea level top speed in excess of 250mph. Also in 1949 he came third in the Grosvenor Challenge Trophy Race flying his "faithful old Blackburn B.2." He flew Robert Blackburn's Miles Messenger *G-ALAC* in the September 1951 South Coast Air Race and, on other occasions, aircraft including the B.2 and Proctor. In the 1952 National Air Races he was winner of the Kemsley Trophy at Newcastle and came third in the King's Cup.

With some 2,800 hours on over 80 aircraft types, in June 1952 he left Blackburn Aircraft to briefly fly Canberras for English Electric, moving to Glosters at the start of 1953 to carry out experimental flying of the delta-wing Javelin. Flying from Moreton Valence on 11 June 1953, he was killed near Bristol in a flying accident in *WD808*, one of three Javelin prototypes. During an elevator response trial at altitude, with aft C of G, on lowering flaps at 125kt he entered an irrecoverable deep stall, the first recorded instance of a number of such events that were to plague early jet aircraft with high-mounted 'T' tails when airflow over the tailplane was 'blanked' by the foreplanes. The Gloster Aircraft Co stated that he had died "in heroic circumstances" in that, having been airborne for half an hour and flying at over 20,000ft, when he radioed of trouble he would have had ample opportunity to eject safely. Instead he elected to remain with the Javelin and crash-land it, hopefully with minimum damage to the aircraft and to homes and people on the ground. Descending at 100ft/sec at 50 degrees, in stabilised attitude but with little forward speed, he passed painfully slowly over built-up areas and busy playing fields, staying with the aircraft down to 400ft before ejecting. But he had remained at the controls too long for his own safety and, after the Javelin landed flat in a field, with no damage to anyone on the ground and itself sustaining less damage to the wings and tail than might have been imagined, Lawrence was found 300 yards away, still in his ejection seat. During his career he had flown over 3,000 hours in over 80 aircraft types.

Meanwhile, as previously indicated, Johnny Squier had given B.5 prototype *VX185* its first flight from Samlesbury on 6 July 1951. The B.5 had been designed to meet a specification for a target-marking bomber but, as a result of changing official requirements, no orders were to be received for the variant. Instead, for the next twelve months, *VX185* was used as a development aircraft. During that period, Peter Hillwood experienced a serious bird-strike on the B.5 which he managed to contain and land safely back at base, but which could have had dire consequences. On 15 July 1952, Beamont carried out four Canberra test flights, three handling sorties in T.4 *WN467* and one in B.5 *VX185*, for the first time with its original RA.3 Avon engines replaced by more powerful RA.7s. Each generating 7,500 lb st, 15 per cent more than the originals, they gave significantly enhanced performance. During the next few weeks Beamont conducted a series of engine handling and long-range cruise proving tests, for which *VX185*'s RA.7s and revised 'wet wing' fuel system of integral leading-edge wing tanks extending back to the main spar, with long-range fuel tank in the bomb bay, made it eminently suitable. On Friday 15 August, returning south of Ireland from such a flight, Beamont and Watson were fascinated by a towering black and yellow anvil storm cloud over the south west of England, constantly illuminated by flashes of lightning, rising to well above their height of 45,000ft. Unknown to them at the time, beneath it, the little coastal town of Lynmouth in North Devon was about to be devastated by torrential rain and flooding. Such was the tropical intensity of the rainfall – nine inches fell on Exmoor in 24 hours – many years later in 2001, a BBC radio programme bizarrely blamed the official conducting of 'cloud-seeding' rain-making experiments earlier in the month, referred to as *Operation Cumulus*, allegedly for possible use as a tactical measure in any future European war, a claim refuted by the Ministry of Defence. Meteorologically the storm was attributed to a huge depression several hundred miles across having stagnated in the South West approaches, its moist air then rising to release prolonged heavy rain.

After a number of such round-Britain flights, the decision was taken to add greater purpose (and relieve the monotony) by undertaking not only another North Atlantic flight, but making it a return crossing. Support came from the Royal Aero Club, ever eager to promote an opportunity to break a record. Preliminary range-proving and cruise-climb tests were extended to the East Atlantic British weather ship, Ocean Station '*Juliett*', 500 nautical miles (nm) west of Shannon, at altitudes up to 50,000ft. Two small English Electric service and support teams were put in place, one flown out by Peter Hillwood in the company Dove to the intended start/finish base at Aldergrove, Northern Ireland and the other by civil airliner to the outward destination, Gander, Newfoundland. There, the teams awaited the rather tight flight 'window' imposed by the requirement for both aircraft and crew to be back at Farnborough for the SBAC Show by the beginning of September. On 21 August, in a three-hour sortie from Warton in *VX185*, **Beamont, Hillwood and Watson** flew

RPB, Hillwood (L) and Watson (R) plan the forthcoming Atlantic return crossing at Warton, August 1952

west to '*Juliett*', followed by a triangular proving flight to Manston, onward to the Orkneys and back to Warton, a total of 1,200nm in three hours and five minutes. On 25 August, Hillwood and Watson also carried out a trial flight to Reykjavik, Iceland and back.

The 'window' for the transatlantic return flight opened on 26 August 1952 when B.5 *VX185*, fitted with special electronic, navigation and other aids including Loran, a Marconi radio compass and a Smiths' Mk.9 autopilot, captained by Beamont, with Hillwood as second pilot and Watson as navigator, took off from Aldergrove as the sun came up at 6.34am. That was after a u/s instrument emergency power supply had been thumped back into life with a well-aimed fist applied to the bulkhead, the limited 'window' presumably calling for unconventional methods! Fuel comprised half of the aircraft's overall take-off weight of 21 tons. That in the new leading edge wing tanks, subject to acute chilling at altitude, had to be consumed first before 'waxing' rendered it unusable.

Entering cloud base at 800ft and climbing at 400kt under full power, they broke out into clear skies at 34,000ft, cruise-climbing to altitudes in excess of 47,000ft. Both Loran and the autopilot failed on the outbound leg, leaving only VHF, conventional compass and the trial radio compass as aids. Watson had to work very hard for the first 1,500nm, the navigator's pencil having to be sharpened many times. Moreover, with only sporadic one-way communication received from the Atlantic weather ships, the British *Juliett* and American *Charlie*, Watson was unable to obtain a fix and had to compute the effect of the jetstream headwind as best he could. One of the ships reported having heard a westbound jet aircraft pass overhead but could not see them and, despite arrangements having been made for constant watch, the ships' intermittent radio malfunction meant that two-way contact with *VX185* was not achieved. However, Beamont did make contact with Air Canada Flight 531, an Argonaut grinding its way through the cloud on an opposite heading thousands of feet below. In asking whether he could be of any assistance, its Captain expressed astonishment at the Canberra's mission to complete the return flight in one day – "What a helluva way to spend a day!" Watson was nevertheless able to produce some impressive navigation, some 16 miles north of intended track but easily corrected by a small final adjustment to port on the approach to the Newfoundland coast. Beamont having conducted some straightforward manual flying, the outward flight from Aldergrove to Gander, 2,072sm, took 4hr 33min, at an average speed of 454.9mph. A strong headwind of up to 140kt meant that *VX185*, with more powerful yet more economical engines similar to those of the de Havilland Comet 2 jetliner, took some 15 minutes longer from Aldergrove to Gander than had Beamont when he had set the record in *WD940* the previous year.

A final look at the chart before RPB, Hillwood (L) and Watson (C) depart Aldergrove, 26 August 1952

Piloted by Hillwood, the return trip, riding the 140kt jetstream, was made in a record-breaking 3hr 25min 18.13sec at an average speed of 605.52mph. Communications with the weather ships were far more effective on the return, enabling Watson to plot a more accurate track and confirm the benefit from the jetstream tail-wind. The round trip Belfast – Gander – Belfast, 4,144sm, including a turn-round at Gander of just over two hours, totalled 10hr 3min 29.28sec, averaging 411.99mph. At that point Beamont and the Canberra had secured all three records for crossing the Atlantic: westerly (Beamont, Watson and Rylands in *WD940* in August 1951), easterly and round-trip (Beamont, Hillwood and Watson in *VX185* in August 1952) including the first ever outward and return crossing of the North Atlantic within one day. Having set off from Aldergrove at 6.34am, they had landed back there at 4.35pm in ten-tenths cloud and steady rain, having cruise-climbed in both directions to altitudes over 47,000ft. They had seen nothing of the cloud-blanketed Atlantic, with cloud tops rising to 40,000ft, on either flight. Unlike *WD940*, *VX185* made the flight without wingtip tanks but with the new integral wing tanks and the bomb-bay tank fitted as standard for special flights. Moreover it appeared still to have considerable fuel on board on arrival back at Warton, where its wing tanks were noticeably covered with a frosty condensation.

Air and ground crews at Aldergrove on the return of VX185 from its Atlantic return crossing, 26 August 1952 …

…with hearty congratulations from the Station Commander, Gp/Capt Dennis I. Coote

Freddie Page and Jimmy Pickthall (second, fourth L), among those congratulating the crew back at Warton

VX185 at Warton, carrying the legend 'The Record Breaking Canberra' on its nose, being prepared for Farnborough 1952…

...and in close-up

The 1952 round trip, cruising at speeds of up to 0.85 IMN, was a spectacular aerial voyage of achievement at the dawn of the new Elizabethan Age and resulted in all three crew members receiving the Royal Aero Club's award of the Britannia Trophy – the first time the Award was made jointly to three people – for the aviators accomplishing the most meritorious performance in aviation that year, together with a telegram of congratulations from HM Queen Elizabeth. With the world's first jet airliner, the de Havilland Comet, shortly to enter service, the following day the *New York Times* observed: 'The British jet plane industry appears to be assuming the lead in the Western World in both military and commercial aircraft – and it is a comfort that it is on our side.' Sir Miles Thomas telegrammed: "As contemporaries in jet operations, B.O.A.C. send you warmest congratulations on magnificent achievement. Will soon be after you with Comet."

Beamont superbly demonstrated T.4 *WN467* at the Farnborough Air Show from 1-3 September, with Squier and Watson taking the aircraft over for the latter half of the Show on 6-7th. *WN467* was one of no less than five Canberras participating at Farnborough '52, including B.2s *WD933* (A.S. Sapphire engines), *WD943* (R-R Avons with reheat) and *WD952* (Bristol Olympus). On static display was also B.5 *VX185*, carrying the inscription 'The Record-Breaking Canberra' in gold-lettering on its nose. *Flight* commented: 'Particular mention should be made of J. W. Squier whose exposition of the Canberra T.4 rivalled those of W/C Beamont.' In November,

T.4 prototype WN467, flown by Hillwood with flight observer Len Howatt, poses for photographer Charles E. Brown, November 1952 (via BAE Systems)

flying T.4 *WN467* from the pupil's seat on the port side, Peter Hillwood gave the *Flight* cameraman a splendid air-to-air photo opportunity for the new dual-control trainer. Not conceived as a bombing trainer, carrying no bomb aimer the type was built with a 'solid' nose of similar profile to the glazed units of most other Marks. Production of the T.4 gained momentum in 1953, the prototype being used for type development work and subsequently seeing service with No.231 OCU and No.16 Sqn, emphasising its role of pilot familiarisation rather than combined crew training.

Flying himself from Warton to Woodford in the company Dove *G-ALMR* on 1 December 1952, in a series of one-hour sorties Beamont flight tested the first 'Avro' Canberra B.2 *WJ971*, with another trial on 20 February 1953. He flew the equivalent *WH855* at Shorts' Sydenham, Belfast factory on 27 February. **Johnny Squier** carried out a similar test of *WJ971* at Woodford on 10 December 1952, followed by the first Handley Page B.2 *WJ564* at Radlett on 28 February 1953, testing more Avro and Handley Page-produced machines later that year. Also in 1953, Squier flew Canberra tests accompanied by Mike Randrup and Jock Still. Squier's log entry for 16 June records a 67-minute local flight with Don Knight in Dove *G-AJLN*. The Farnborough and Paris Air Shows were a major part of Canberra promotion. On 2 July he flew B.2 *WH733* from Samlesbury to Warton, then on to Paris where it was demonstrated by Beamont, Squier returning in *WH732* four days later. At Farnborough that year Squier demonstrated B.2 *WJ716*, followed by PR.7 *WJ820* at Farnborough 1954 and B(I)8 *WT328* at Farnborough 1955. On 1 September 1956 he flew the PR.9 prototype *WH793* from Warton to Farnborough, there to be demonstrated by himself and Peter Hillwood.

In a programme of tests during late 1952/early 1953 in the fourth production PR.3 *WE138*, in December 1952 Squier had a narrow escape when he experienced the vibration noted by Hillwood the previous year in comparative handling trials at Warton with the prototype *VX181*. At 2,000ft and 480kt IAS, a severe 24cps vibration induced by aerodynamic buffeting of the longer fuselage caused partial failure of the elevator indicated by a loud bang at the rear and a pitching up of the aircraft. Squier allowed the PR.3 to climb gently to 10,000ft, at which point he felt he had regained sufficient control to attempt what turned out to be a rather heavy landing back at Samlesbury. It was discovered that the vibration had shaken off an elevator mass balance weight, in effect leaving only half the elevator functioning. It was a characteristic of the PR.3 variant that its 14-inch longer fuselage forward of the wing, to accommodate cameras, with redistributed mass, resulted in increased airframe roughness. The problem was overcome to an acceptable degree, though not completely, by stiffening the rear fuselage with the somewhat crude but nevertheless effective technique of 'over-plating'. It was a further manifestation of the original incipient flutter and vibration problems Beamont had encountered with *VN799*, now exacerbated by the PR.3's longer fuselage, requiring Ray Creasey and Ron Dickson to once again address modifications involving larger elevator mass balance weights and a strengthening of the rear fuselage. In another unrelated Canberra incident, flying the third B.6 *WJ756* on 16 February 1954, Squier had to contend with the starboard engine seizing.

After the two pattern aircraft left for the USA in 1951, followed by another two for Australia in 1951/52, the 'Canberra for export' programme really got into its stride two years later when, in February/March 1953, **Beamont** and Squier both flew production tests of B.2s *1-A-39* ex-*WH708* and *2-A-39* ex-*WH709*, the first of six new B.2 aircraft diverted from the second British (RAF) production contract for use by the Venezuelan Air Force, the *Fuerza Aerea Venezolana (FAV)*. The Venezuelan contract stemmed from a highly successful seven-day 24,000-mile tour (Operation *Round Trip*) of 14 South American countries by four Canberras of No.12 Sqn led by Air Vice-Marshal Dermot Boyle, AOC No.1 (Bomber) Group, later Marshal of the Royal Air Force Sir Dermot Boyle, commencing in October the previous year. It was the first of many such overseas orders that the aircraft would secure. *1-A-39* and *2-A-39* were delivered by RAF crews in March 1953, via Gibraltar. The other four, *3-A-39* ex-*WH721, 1-B-39* ex-*WH722, 2-B-39* ex-*WH736* and *3-B-39* ex-*WH737*, left Warton between May and July, ferried by crews including Johnny Hackett and Peter Moneypenny on hire from Silver City Airways. Having been flown to Boca de Rio, Maracay by the RAF, *1-A-39* was demonstrated there on 1 April by Beamont, who travelled to Venezuela from the UK by civil airliner. His display had such impact that he was invited to repeat it in front of President Peres Jimenez at the small airfield of La Carlota, near the capital Caracas, on 6 April. The display was memorable not only for Beamont's style of flying but also, taking off from the rough grass airfield, he had to share airspace, in cloudy conditions, with a continuous stream of C-47 transports coming in to land. Conspiracy theorists among the British representatives present remained unshaken in their belief that the parade of C-47s, together with the blocking of the Canberra in its hangar by a B-25 on jacks, were the unsporting (and unsuccessful) actions of a certain North American power that had been opposed to the Canberra deal! Moreover, with no engine-starter cartridges remaining, after the display Beamont had to depart immediately to Maracay without landing back at La Carlota, a tricky return over

Squier with first Venezuelan Canberra B.2, 1-A-39, *1953*

Venezuelan 1-A-39 with R to L: Dennis Watson, Peter Hillwood, Jock Still and Johnny Squier

mountains shrouded in mist and cloud with no available aids. It all added to the Canberra's reputation, proving a worthwhile precursor to what would become further vital export sales of the aircraft to Venezuela and several other countries in South America.

In July, Beamont spectacularly demonstrated B.2 *WH733* at the Paris Show at Le Bourget. His 408-mile return to Warton, in 42.5 minutes, including climb to and descent from 40,000ft, was achieved at a speed of 576mph without any assistance from a following wind. A few days previously, Johnny Squier had flown the same aircraft from Warton to Le Bourget, taking only one minute longer. Also in July, Beamont tested two Canberra PR3s, *WE140/WE142*, with which No.540 Sqn RAF Air Race Flight competed in the London to New Zealand Air Race in October, a race won by RAF PR.3 *WE139* flown by Flt/Lts R. Burton and D. H. Gannon who covered the 11,796sm London Airport – Shaibah, Basra (Iraq) – Colombo, Ceylon – Cocos Islands – Perth – Christchurch NZ in a record-breaking 23hr 50min 42sec, averaging 494.48mph. On 3 June, the day after the Coronation, in Operation *Pony Express*, three Canberras of No.540 Sqn, including *WE142*, had flown film of the Coronation across the Atlantic for showing on Canadian and American television. On 16 August, in a 50-minute sortie from Samlesbury, Beamont flew the maiden flight of the first PR.7, *WH773*, an extended operational range version of the PR.3, drawing on the B.5 with extra fuel in integral wing leading edge tanks, the resulting extra weight requiring the more powerful RA.7 engines and stronger undercarriage with *Maxaret* brakes. *WH773* was in effect the first production aircraft, as it had

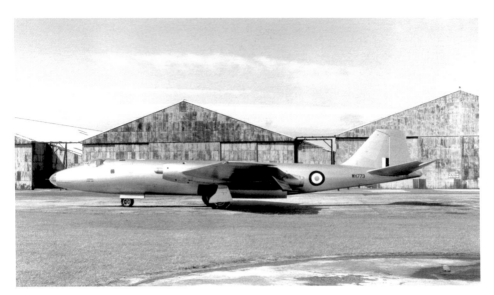

The first Canberra PR.7, WH773, Warton, 1953

been deemed unnecessary to build a PR.7 'prototype'. Similarly there would be no B.6 'prototype'; *WJ754*, the first production B.6, basically a B.2 with integral wing tanks and RA.7 engines, made its maiden flight from Samlesbury in the hands of Johnny Squier on 26 January 1954. Neither was there a B(I)6 Interdictor 'prototype', the first production aircraft *WT307* being given its first outing by Squier from Samlesbury on 31 March 1955.

After PR.7 *WH773*, Beamont's next maiden flight was that of the first production T.4 *WE188* in a 1hr 25min sortie on 20 September 1953. The aircraft has survived intact and is today preserved at the Solway Aviation Museum at Carlisle Airport, where visitors are able to sit in the cockpit. The fuselage of close relative *WE191*, refurbished for the Indian Air Force as *Q497* but embargoed and never delivered is today on display, still wearing IAF roundels, at the nearby Dumfries & Galloway Aviation Museum after being stored for many years at Samlesbury before being moved to Warton in 1988 for fire training. *Q497* was one of three refurbished ex-RAF T.4s (*Q495* ex-*WH847*, *496* ex-*WH845*, *497* ex-*WE191*) ordered by India in 1965 but delivery embargoed due to hostilities between India and Pakistan, both of which countries operated Canberras: India British-built aircraft and Pakistan the American-built B-57. All three were stored initially at RAF Kemble, *495* air-tested on 18 July 1968 by Test Pilot Eric Bucklow and two IAF officers prior to being flown to India at the end of the embargo as *G27-116*. *496* and *497* were bought back by BAC, *496* to be sold to Peru and delivered as T.74 *246 G27-224* by test pilot Tim Ferguson and navigator Jim Evans in February 1973.

Beautiful in black – VX185 reconfigured with offset fighter-style canopy as the B(I)8, on its maiden flight, 23 July 1954, now with only two crew, pilot and navigator/bomb aimer...

...in close up, with RPB at the controls...

...but also menacing as befits its role as an interdictor bomber...

...here portrayed by production B(I)8 WT329 with bomb-bay gun pack and underwing bomb/rocket pod pylons, flown by Hillwood over RAF Millom, 1955

Having once again hopped on board Stratocruiser *Canopus*, at Baltimore on 23/24 September 1953 Beamont carried out three one-hour test flights in the second B-57A to be produced by the Martin Company. At home, in November, December and the first few months of 1954 he conducted a wide range of Canberra production and experimental test flights including work on the power-controlled rudder, the first air test of which he made on 26 November 1953, fitted to B.2 *WD937*. The introduction of the T.4 into service with No.231 OCU at Bassingbourn, Cambridgeshire in spring 1954 could not have come at a better time for the training of RAF pilots, a number of whom had met with accidents during conversion, seemingly as a result of overconfidence in the Canberra's generally complaisant handling coupled with misinterpretation of flight instruments particularly during take-off and landing in poor weather and at night. The resulting training programme set up with the T.4 would serve for decades to come. At Samlesbury, on 23 July 1954 Beamont was again at the controls of *VX185* in which, as the sole B.5 variant development aircraft, he had made the record-breaking Atlantic return flight in August 1952. For the first time this aircraft was now reconfigured as the prototype B(I)8 low level interdictor bomber, painted gloss black overall, with a new fighter-style cockpit canopy offset to port. Keen to check visibility through the new windscreen, Beamont conducted the B(I)8's maiden flight in heavy rain with a cloud base of 300-400ft. As a result he found that raindrops were dispersed satisfactorily and pronounced the aircraft to be "excellent". On 28 August 1954 Peter Hillwood conducted its first flight fitted with the ventral 4 x 20mm gun pack. After the five weeks of almost total preoccupation with the experimental P.1 that followed, Beamont demonstrated the B(I)8 prototype at Farnborough in September 1954, the Press commenting: "The superb Canberra B8 gave what was probably one of the finest-ever displays of a military aircraft". At the same event Johnny Squier and Jock Still shared flying PR.7 *WJ820*. Beamont made the initial flight of the first production B(I)8 *WT326* on 8 June 1955 from Samlesbury. At the Paris Show in June 1955, Hillwood flew a T.4 into Le Bourget amidst teeming rain and drizzle, demonstrating its impressive performance later in the Show in a notably compact display beneath the overcast. Squier flew a PR.7 at the same event.

As early as 1952, having achieved the grand old age of 32 and heading a team of equally 'aged' – in some cases Battle of Britain – veterans including Squier and Hillwood, Chief Test Pilot Roland Beamont was giving thought to what could be termed a succession strategy for English Electric test pilots. Accordingly, in the early to mid-1950s, as word spread in RAF circles about Lancashire's growing aircraft industry, he made a number of new appointments, several it would seem at the expense of No.603 (City of Edinburgh) Sqn, RAuxAF. **Jock Still** arrived in late 1952, **Don Knight** in June 1953 and **Tim Ferguson** in January 1955, all three having been contemporaries in No.603. Both Knight and Ferguson went on to have long test flying careers with the company.

James W. 'Jimmy' 'Jock' **Still**, educated at Boroughmuir School, Edinburgh, started his flying career with the RAF in 1940, seeing action as a fighter pilot in Hurricanes and Spitfires in Britain, Europe, the Middle East and Burma. Flying Spitfires, he was engaged on train-busting raids over occupied Europe and, serving with No.1 Sqn, on intercepting flying bombs. After the war he transferred to the RAuxAF, serving with No.603 (City of Edinburgh) Sqn. In 1950 he was recruited as a test pilot by Brooklands Aviation, an aero-engineering company whose history went back to the earliest days of the industry at Brooklands, Weybridge, Surrey and Shoreham on the South Coast. During WW2 it became a major subcontractor to Vickers-Armstrongs, carrying out repairs to Wellington bombers, relocating to Squires Gate, Blackpool with operations also at Sywell, Northamptonshire, where the company later overhauled and repaired Varsities. Jock Still joined English Electric in 1952 as assistant to Johnny Squier, carrying out some of the early test flying of Canberras from Samlesbury. He went to Venezuela in 1953 when that country became the first overseas customer for the Canberra, staying on to see the first six B.2s, ferried there by RAF pilots and Silver City Airways crews including Johnny Hackett and Peter Moneypenny, into service with the Venezuelan Air Force. Leaving English Electric, he joined Handley Page around the time of the loss of its HP80 Victor prototype *WB771*, with all its crew when, during air speed pressure error tests at low level at Cranfield on 14 July 1954, onset of tailplane flutter caused its detachment. With progressive degrees of structural strengthening still something of a hit and miss affair, Jock Still and another team of flight test observers had the unenviable job of incrementally building up speed to within 15 kt of the suspected critical flutter limit in the second prototype, *WB775*, a task they performed with great dedication and courage. Jock Still demonstrated Canberras at the 1954 and 1955 Farnborough Air Shows and flew Victor B.1 *XA918* at the SBAC Show in September 1957. In 1958 he suffered a serious back injury which effectively terminated his flying career. He had flown over 3,000 hours in 50 different types of aircraft. He then made a successful career in the steel industry at director level, resuming his aviation links when, in June 1973, he joined BAC as Base Manager, Dhahran. In 1975 he was appointed Assistant Chief Executive and Head of Administration, Saudi Arabia.

Donald McM. 'Don' **Knight**, born in Edinburgh in 1931, was educated at Daniel Stewart's College and started his aviation career during National Service, training as a pilot with the RAF in 1949-51. His initial air experience flight was on 7 November 1949 at No.3 FTS, Feltwell, in a Prentice trainer, an aircraft he flew solo for the first time on his tenth flight on 25 November. The following year he progressed to the Harvard 2B, going solo on 1 June on his sixth flight on type. Rated 'above average' as a pilot, he was awarded the flying badge – the coveted RAF 'wings' – on 1 November 1950. He was then posted to No.205 AFS at Middleton St George for advanced training on the Meteor T.7, which he flew solo on 9 February 1951 on his tenth flight. While there he flew a Spitfire Mk.XXII solo on a first familiarisation flight on 8 April.

Rated 'above the average' also on jets, on leaving AFS later that month Knight was posted to No.226 OCU at Stradishall until June, flying the Meteor F.4 and T.7 on a wide range of sorties including battle formation, attack and gunnery. After OCU came his posting to No.603 (City of Edinburgh) Sqn, RAuxAF, initially based at RAF Turnhouse near Edinburgh and later at RAF Leuchars. Knight returned to college in Edinburgh to study printing technology but, as a Flying Officer, remained on strength as a reservist pilot with No.603 until 1954, flying during weekends, summer camps and periods of refresher training, during that time renewing his acquaintance with the Harvard, Spitfire and Meteor. The majority of his flying with No.603 was with the Vampire FB.5, an aircraft he soloed on his first flight on type on 20 July 1951. Typical activities included formation flying, aerobatics, interception, air-to-air and air-to-ground, high and low-level flying, tactics and participating in major air defence exercises.

Today, nearly 60 years after he followed in the footsteps of fellow 603 Sqn pilot Jock Still, joining English Electric in Lancashire on 1 June 1953, Don Knight pays tribute to Roland Beamont for "giving me my chance". Initially, Knight commenced duties as a part-time Canberra production test pilot under Johnny Squier at Samlesbury. His first flight for the company though was as Squier's co-pilot on a local familiarisation trip in the company communications D.H. Dove, followed by many more flights as first pilot, carrying senior personnel including Sir George Nelson, Freddie Page and test pilots Beamont, Squier, Hillwood and Still. His first Canberra solo was in B.2 *WH741* on 13 July. By the end of 1953 he had also flown Canberra PR.3 *WE148* on 29 September, delivered Canberra T.4 *WE189* from Samlesbury to Martlesham Heath on 9 November and flown Canberra PR.7 *WH774* from Samlesbury to Warton on 20 November. The same pattern continued in 1954, with many flights in Canberras of various marks including delivery of T.4 *WE192* to Kinloss on 5 January, test flying B.6 *WJ755* on 21 February and delivery of B.6 *WJ758* from Samlesbury to Kinloss on 7 April. Communications flights continued unabated, Knight also flying Rapide and Anson transports as well as the Dove. Today, Knight recalls English Electric Flight Operations at Samlesbury in the 1950s as reminiscent of an 'outpost' of the Officers' Mess of No.603 Sqn, an impression enhanced further by the arrival of Tim Ferguson at the beginning of 1955. Moreover, Knight speculates that when he joined English Electric as a 22-year-old in 1953, with just over 664 flying hours to his credit and Beamont's record-breaking transatlantic flight to Gander and back the year before still fresh in everyone's mind, Beamont possibly gained rather more youth than he had bargained for in his vision for a younger team! Shortly after Ferguson arrived, on 1 February 1955 Knight introduced him to the Dove which in due course Ferguson took over as part-time communications pilot, freeing Knight to transfer to full-time experimental and development work on Canberra and later projects at Warton. Don Knight's subsequent career encompassed development flying all marks of the Canberra,

Lightning and the TSR2, frequently accompanied by flight test engineers and navigators Eric Oldham, Derek Hargreaves, Peter Moneypenny and P. H. Durrant. Knight's responsibilities on Canberra included the later B(I)8 developments (his first test flight on type was with *WT327* on 20 August 1955) and autopilot system clearance of B(I)58 aircraft for the Indian Air Force, together with contributions to PR.9 aerodynamic and systems development work. On 7 September he flew no less than six separate Canberra sorties on the same day in T.4, B(I)6 and PR.7 variants. In December 1955 and January 1956 he flew a number of Canberra B.2 test flights accompanied by new arrival John Hall.

It was inevitable that the Canberra's high altitude potential would encourage an attempt on the world altitude record. In 1951, Beamont had already cleared the first B.2 to 55,000ft and in August that year, en route from Gander to the Martin factory at Middle River, Baltimore, had overflown New York in B.2 *WD940* at 51,000ft, much to the consternation of US Civil and Military Air Traffic Control. In 1953, **Wg/Cdr Walter F. 'Wally' Gibb**, DSO, DFC, from January that year Assistant Chief Test Pilot of the Bristol Aeroplane Company (Chief Test Pilot from 1955) was engaged on Olympus Canberra test flying from Filton. A Bristol apprentice from 1937, during the war he had been a flying instructor, had flown Mosquitoes over the Bay of Biscay and in low-level attacks over France and Germany and, as C/O of No.239 Sqn, during February/March 1945 he shot down five enemy aircraft on night intruder missions. Gibb returned to the Bristol Company after demobilisation in 1946. He was co-pilot to Bill Pegg on the first flight of the giant Bristol Brabazon airliner *G-AGPW* from Filton, two days before its first appearance at the 1949 Farnborough Air Show. Such was the Brabazon's size and weight (wingspan 230ft, 130 tons) Pegg's aside to Gibb as they thundered down the runway on its maiden flight would go down in aviation history: "Well, my side's airborne, how about yours?" On its 13th flight, his first as Captain, Gibb had to land the behemoth without flaps following a hydraulic failure. With observer F. M. Piper, on 4 May 1953 he was at the controls of Olympus test-bed Canberra B.2 *WD952* when, over Taunton, Devon, it set a new world altitude record of 63,668ft. On 29 August 1955, in the same aircraft, flying without an observer and with all non-essential equipment removed to save weight, he attained 65,890ft over Bristol. Neither flight could be called uneventful, both engines surging out on the first, to be relit back at 40,000ft, while on the second he overcooked the engines so burning six blades. [*WD952* was written off in 1956 after a crash-landing at Filton following an engine failure on take-off.] At Farnborough he piloted the Proteous-powered Ambassador *G-AKRD* in 1954 and the Proteous/Orion-Britannia *G-ALBO* in 1957. On another occasion, when investigating the stalling characteristics of a Britannia, in selecting 'flaps up' the airliner rolled onto its back; unknown to Gibb one of the flaps had failed to retract. After losing thousands of feet he regained control by putting the flaps down, righting and restoring the balance of the aircraft, calmly stating "I undid the last action I had made." In March 1955 he flew a

Britannia to Johannesburg, via Khartoum, in less than 19 hours, two hours less than the Comet jetliner. Gibb retired from test flying and demonstrating the Britannia in 1960, to be appointed Head of Service and Technical Support with the British Aircraft Corporation, from 1978 becoming Managing Director, and later Chairman, of British Aerospace Australia. He died in 2006 at the age of 87.

The Canberra PR.9, with basic design undertaken by English Electric at Warton and detail design by D. Napier & Son at Luton, adopted a modified wing some four feet wider in span than its predecessors, with broader chord and higher incidence inboard of the engines. Its project designation was HAPR.9, signifying 'High Altitude'. It had new powered flying controls and two RA.24 Mk.206 Avon engines, each rated at 11,000 lb st, similar to those powering the early Lightnings. In an era when ever-higher operational altitudes were believed to offer the best protection against interception, it was conceived as a successor to the earlier PR.3/PR.7, capable of increasing their operating ceiling from 50,000ft to 65,000ft. Fresh off the Samlesbury production line, Canberra PR.7 *WH793* which had its maiden flight on 23 April 1954, was flown to Napiers at Luton on 25 May, there to be modified as the 'prototype' PR.9, albeit retaining the original PR.7 canopy rather than gaining the offset fighter-style version of subsequent production PR.9s. In that form, *WH793* was first flown from Cranfield on 8 July 1955 by Napier Chief Test Pilot **Mike Randrup** with test observer **Walter Shirley**. Remarkably, its take-off and climb performance to 30,000ft was found to be two-and-a-half minutes – not dissimilar to that of the Lightning! Roland Beamont also flew it on a flight assessment from Cranfield on 14 July before the aircraft was flown to Warton for the remainder of its test programme. There, during 1955/56, Beamont conducted a wide variety of handling tests but as he was also busily engaged testing the P.1, **Don Knight** was designated PR.9 Project Pilot. However Beamont still remained involved with the PR.9 and, with Peter Hillwood, shared demonstrating the aircraft at Farnborough in September 1956. During the test programme it was found that the PR.9's much improved climb rate to 50,000ft thereafter tailed off disappointingly. On 18 September, wearing a pressure breathing helmet and partial pressure jacket as a concession to the extreme altitude (unusually for him), Beamont took *WH793* to 59,000ft. Don Knight flew the same aircraft, with Derek Hargreaves, for the first time on 16 November. On 23 November, over the Welsh Borders, Beamont cruise-climbed the PR.9 to an altimeter-indicated 59,800ft, finding that the greater drag induced by the broad-chord high incidence wing centre-section was soaking up most of the engines' extra thrust. The PR.9 was at its absolute limit. He was left with very little fuel in his tanks when he got back to Warton. On his return Beamont was adamant that PE corrections *would* confirm attainment of the 60,000ft operating altitude for which the PR.9 had been designed, albeit with no further operational margin.

PR.7-based 'prototype' PR.9, WH793, retaining the original cockpit and canopy, as first flown from Cranfield on 8 July 1955

Prototype PR.9 WH793 showing its original canopy and also the wider wing chord inboard of the engines

RPB displays wide-chord prototype PR.9 WH793, 1955

Hillwood takes off from Shorts' Sydenham Airfield, Belfast, on the maiden flight of their first production PR.9 with offset 'fighter' canopy, the ill-fated XH129, 27 July 1958

More development was essential before production of the PR.9 could be subcontracted to Short Brothers & Harland Ltd of Belfast, who in 1958 began building 23 of the aircraft under licence. Peter Hillwood piloted the maiden flight of the first of Shorts' production PR.9s, *XH129*, by then fitted with a fighter-style canopy offset to port, from Sydenham airfield, Belfast on 27 July 1958.

In 1957, from 6-8 May, Don Knight and Peter Moneypenny ferried Indian Canberra B(I)58 *IF899* ex-*XH227* to Agra via El Adem and Bahrain. On 21 May Knight flew PR.9 *WH793* with Arthur Lewry and the following day with P. H. Durrant. Later that month, and in June, Knight conducted autopilot/ILS trials with *IF908* ex-*XH238* and, from 6-8 September, demonstrated B(I)8 *XH234* at Farnborough. In June 1958, with Derek Hargreaves, Knight flew yet another mark of Canberra, PR.57 *IP988* ex-*WT541*, the first of several of the type he tested for the Indian Air Force.

On 9 October 1958, just seven minutes after taking off from Warton for a low-level test flight, the first Shorts-built PR.9 *XH129* flown by Don Knight was lost in a crash in the Irish Sea off Southport. The accident, during a 5g structural test turn, was caused by failure of the forward pick-up of the new wing at the wing root. As Knight progressively pulled to port, attaining the required 5g, the aircraft suddenly went into an uncontrollable roll in the opposite direction, spiralling down to the sea in flames. Flexing of the wing under load had caused it to fail, accompanied by peeling back of the skin, leading to complete folding of the wing. At very low altitude, with no control remaining, the pilot had no alternative but to eject, which he was only just able to do before the aircraft hit the sea. His parachute deployed just as he entered the water. At that time though, the navigator's station in the nose section of the first production PR.9 variant was not equipped with an ejector seat and sadly the navigator, P. H. Durrant, could not escape quickly enough and lost his life. It was the 56th test flight made jointly by Knight and Durrant in the PR.9, 50 of which in *WH793* and six in *XH129*. Thereafter the PR.9 was redesigned, later production aircraft incorporating revised wing attachments and an ejector seat for the navigator. In five sorties on 13/14/20 January 1960, Roland Beamont briefly returned to Canberra testing from the Lightning to repeat the 5g structural test demonstration on revised PR.9 *XH136*, equipped with full strain gauge and wing deflection instrumentation. By the final sortie, under far from ideal conditions in drizzle just beneath cloud cover at 4,000ft, progressively clearing it to 5.1g and 450kt, Beamont found the modifications to be perfectly satisfactory. Overall, the result was an extremely fine aircraft which served with the RAF up to 2006. Don Knight's continuing involvement with Canberra and in the P.1/Lightning and TSR2 programmes is described later.

Just over two years after making the first flight of the PR.9 prototype *WH793*, on 28 August 1957 **Mike Randrup** and test observer **Walter Shirley** flew a sortie from Luton Aerodrome in Avro-built Canberra B.2 *WK163*, previously a Sapphire test bed with Armstrong Siddeley at Bitteswell, now powered by two 6,500 lb st Avon RA.3

Mike Randrup (R) and Walter Shirley with the Napier Double Scorpion-powered Canberra B.2 WK163, 1957

turbojets. These were augmented by a 4-6,000 lb st twin-chambered liquid propellant hydrogen peroxide/kerosene High Test Peroxide (HTP) Napier Double Scorpion NSc D.1-2 rocket. Igniting the Scorpion at 44,000ft in the climb, some 20 miles south of Shoreham off the Sussex coast, they established a World Altitude Record of 70,310ft. The event required them to wear partial pressure suits and fixed-visor helmets. They were awarded the Royal Aero Club's Britannia Trophy. [*WK163*, retaining its original centre and rear fuselage, but with replacement wings and other parts, is today preserved as *G-BVWC* for heritage display purposes by the Air Atlantique Classic Flight at Coventry Airport, albeit without the Scorpion unit.]

Mike Randrup was born in 1913 to Danish parents; around 1920 his father was Danish Consul General in Shanghai, China, before moving to England to establish an import-export business. Randrup was educated at King's School, Canterbury and Chelsea College of Aeronautics. He started flying in 1935, joined the RAF at the start of WW2 and was promoted to Flight Lieutenant in September 1942, to be posted to No.234 (Madras Presidency) Sqn. He was a production test pilot at Air Service Training Ltd at Hamble in 1943, became an RAF test pilot that year and after various postings finished the war as a Squadron Leader attached to the RAE Engine Research Flight at Farnborough, where he tested captured aircraft such as the Heinkel He177. From 1946 until 1960 he was Chief Test Pilot for Napier Aero Engines, by then an associate company of English Electric, before being appointed personal assistant to the technical director. He assumed British citizenship in 1947. At Napier he flight-tested the company's first gas turbine engine, the Naiad, the compound diesel Nomad and the Eland turboprop. He flew the Eland-powered Varsity T.1 *VX835* at Farnborough in 1954. After the demise of Napiers (the company was absorbed into Rolls-Royce in 1961), in 1963 both Mike Randrup and Walter Shirley came to work at Warton, the former to fly communications aircraft and the latter becoming an associate of Ollie Heath, later to be engaged on the MRCA programme. Randrup then joined Warton's Lightning project office and following the sale of that aircraft to Saudi Arabia, in 1966 then in the Sales Department, he moved to the Middle East as senior resident BAC manager. He remained there until 1974 when he returned to Warton to work on the Saudi support contract. Mike Randrup retired from Warton in 1978 with over 30 years' service with BAe and its predecessors. He died in 1984.

Walter Shirley was born and grew up in Blackpool. During the war years he worked in aero- engineering and flew as an engine observer with Mike Randrup at RAE Farnborough, afterwards going to Germany to assess German wartime aeronautical research. In 1947 he joined Napiers, to where his former Farnborough colleague Randrup had already moved, and in 1952 was appointed Chief Technician. Four years later he was Chief Development Engineer in charge of the design and development of the Scorpion rocket motor. In 1957 he was appointed Deputy Chief Engineer at Luton.

Sqn/Ldr Leslie Morris 'Dick' Whittington, born in 1923, attended ETPS No.9 Course at Farnborough in 1950, after which serving two years as a test pilot at Boscombe Down. On 27/28 January 1953, the then Flt/Lt Whittington, together with Flt/Lt J. A. Brown as navigator, flew Canberra PR.3 prototype *VX181* to Australia to carry out experimental flying at the Woomera weapons test range. In attempting an overall journey time of under 24 hours they established an official London to Darwin record of 22hr 21.8sec, covering 8,608sm at an average speed of 391.2mph. Staging the flight between Fayid (Cairo), Mauripur (Karachi) and Changi (Singapore), within the overall record they also established another for the two legs between London and Karachi, 3,921sm in 8hr 52min 28.2sec at an average speed of 441.8mph. The flight was made at altitudes over 40,000ft, at times close to the aircraft's [unspecified at that time] ceiling, reaching ground speeds in excess of 600mph with 100mph tail winds. The inevitable problems encountered on such an epic flight included temporary loss of flight instruments, very severe turbulence, the cockpit dripping with condensation and misting up during descents, not least the deployment of 'stink bombs' which the authorities at Karachi and Darwin insisted upon for fumigation of the aircraft interior on arrival! It was a case of breakfast in London one day and in Darwin, Australia, the next. The first ever flight to Australia, by a Vickers Vimy in 1919, had taken 28 days. Whittington was awarded the AFC and Queen's Commendation for Valuable Service in the Air (QCVSA). He joined

English Electric as Assistant Experimental Test Pilot in 1953, leaving in February 1955 to go to Folland as assistant to their Chief Test Pilot, Sqn/Ldr E. A. Tennant, DFC. After displaying Gnat F.1 *XK724* at Farnborough on Thursday 6 September 1956, on landing and streaming its brake parachute in wet conditions in a cross-wind (Farnborough '56 was one of the wettest on record), the parachute picked up water from a runway puddle, the extra tail weight causing Whittington to veer off the runway onto the grass, fortunately with no serious consequences for either pilot or aircraft. In November 1962, Whittington delivered the first Gnat trainer to No.4 FTS. From 1961 to 1970 he was a test pilot for Hawkers at Dunsfold, Surrey. It is believed that on 19 March 1971 he demonstrated Hawker Siddeley's preserved Hart biplane fighter bomber at the 50th Anniversary celebrations of the A&AEE at Boscombe Down.

At a time when the Canberra was entering RAF service in large numbers, *Flight Magazine* of 5 June 1953 gave a detailed description of a visit to English Electric to see the aircraft under construction and sample a demonstration flight. Collected from Hendon by the Company's Dove communications aircraft, flown by Jock Still, the journalists arrived in Lancashire, listing the key personnel involved:

'Sir George Nelson (Chairman and Managing Director of the whole group); Warton, having all experimental work, including flying and constructional, with F.W. Page (Chief Engineer and Designer), D. L. Ellis, F. D. Crowe, A. E. Ellison, J. C. King and R. F. Creasey, R. P. Beamont (Chief Experimental Test Pilot), assisted by P. D. Hillwood with D. A. Watson as Staff Navigator. At Preston, A. Sheffield was General Manager; W. Shorrock, Works Manager; and W. Harpley, Works Superintendent, the latter also in charge of the Samlesbury factory where the Superintendent was A. Ainsworth and J. W. C. Squier was Chief Production Test Pilot assisted by J. W. Still. The Aircraft Division in London was headed by A/Cdr. Strang Graham, assisted by J. W. Adderley and R. M. Milne, with W/Cdr. R. Stanford Tuck stationed at Warton.'

Squier gave the journalists a fine demonstration of the Canberra's flying capabilities and Hillwood took them up in the T.4 prototype to experience the aircraft at first hand. After reviewing the factory facilities, the article described the test flying regime; experimental at the master airfield at Warton, equipped with Marconi AD.200 VHF direction-finding radio; with production flying from Samlesbury. Both were constantly ongoing, experimental including ironing out snags, testing new equipment, raising limitations, trying out new control surfaces, eliminating cockpit misting after rapid descents and developing successive marks of the aircraft. For production tests, flights of 1hr 30min continuous flying were normally sufficient if the aircraft performed perfectly from start to finish, although several flights were frequently necessary, with a final flight for every aircraft to check its handling fitted with wing-tip tanks.

Also in 1953, *The Aeroplane* magazine made reference to the 'Amber Airway One' which by then passed over Warton Aerodrome, covering a lane five miles wide, extending between 3,000ft and 11,000ft, even in those days 'out of bounds' to Canberras on test. Yet careful planning, exit and let-down procedures from Warton's location in the flat expanse of the Ribble estuary still allowed good, shallow aircraft movements. But production testing of large numbers of such advanced aircraft presented new issues. Gone were the days when relatively simple heavy bombers could be cleared after one or two flights round the airfield below the cloud base. Now, jet bombers had to be tested to at least 45,000ft, dived and flown level at very high speeds, in the process covering much longer distances. Marconi radio homing aids now allowed continuous production tests in weather that would hitherto have grounded them. Moreover, the Canberra's speed-over-distance performance enabled it to fly in search of weather suitable for test purposes. No longer was it necessary to remain within 25 miles of the aerodrome; if the Lancashire weather was unsuitable for specific tests, within half an hour the Canberra could reach anywhere along the North West Coast from the Isle of Man to Glasgow, the East coast from Newcastle to the Wash, and the South Coast including the Isle of Wight and Portland. Flying at 40,000ft and covering 1,000 miles in two hours, Marconi equipment enabled safe returns to Warton from 200 miles away in quite adverse weather, the total operation, *The Aeroplane* noted, having avoided any major interruption in Canberra deliveries during the unusually inclement weather of the winter of 1952-3.

Timothy Maynard Scott (Tim) Ferguson was born on 4 January 1932, from the age of two spending his early years with his parents in Egypt, returning with them as a twelve-year-old to enter Haileybury College at Hertford. On leaving college he studied electronics with the Marconi Company for a short period before going to Belgium to pursue languages. He joined the RAF on National Service as an Officer Cadet in 1950, opting successfully for pilot training initially on the Prentice and Harvard at No.3 FTS and subsequently the Meteor at No.226 OCU. On completing his tour he then started a career in electronics in Scotland but, as a reservist pilot, joined No.603 (City of Edinburgh) Sqn, RAuxAF, at RAF Turnhouse, flying the Meteor and Vampire. After three years, following in the footsteps of Jock Still and Don Knight, on 1 January 1955 he joined English Electric Aviation at Samlesbury as a production test pilot on Canberra, commencing his duties by flying the company communications Dove, carrying passengers such as Freddie Page and Roland Beamont to meetings at various venues around the country, typically Farnborough and Boscombe Down. During his first two years at Samlesbury and Warton he retained his links with the RAF as a reservist, with periods flying Meteors and Vampires with No.613 (City of Manchester) Sqn, serving until the RAuxAF was disbanded as part of the post-war reorganisation of the RAF. At Samlesbury, Ferguson was soon receiving familiarisation flights on Canberra T.4 and B.6

variants from pilots including Squier and Knight. Soon afterwards, as first pilot himself flying B.2, T.4, B.6, PR.7 and B(I)8, it was Ferguson's task to familiarise other new recruits including John Hall, Johnny Hackett and Keith Isherwood. On 17 April 1956, he was entrusted with flying Freddie Page on a test flight in T.4 *XK647*, an aircraft later delivered to the Indian Air Force as *IQ994*. The following year, from 8-13 June, on the first of his many overseas ferry flights, accompanied by two RAF officers, Ferguson flew Canberra PR.57 *IP987* ex-*WT542* to Agra in India, via El Adem, Bahrain and Delhi. At home he commenced a vast programme of test flights of all variants of the Canberra. At the Farnborough Air Show on 1/2 September 1958, sharing with John Hall and Keith Isherwood, he displayed for the first time T.11 *WJ610*. The aircraft was built originally by Handley Page at Radlett as a B.2, later designed and converted by Boulton Paul Aircraft for training navigators of all-weather fighters in the use of airborne interception radar, for the purpose of which an AI.17 radar set was accommodated in the aircraft's lengthened nose.

John C. Hall, born in 1928 at East Bridgford, Nottinghamshire, joined English Electric from the RAF in December 1955. He recalls being fascinated by aircraft from an early age, ever since having watched an airship from the security of his pram! His first flight, at nearby RAF Newton, was with a New Zealand pilot in an Airspeed Oxford – strictly speaking illegal, for civilians were not allowed to fly in RAF aircraft.

He joined the Air Training Corps immediately on its formation in 1943 and, after Sunday morning parades at RAF Newton, would scrounge whatever flying he could. Summer camp offered opportunities to fly in Lancasters, Whitleys, DC.3s and even Horsa troop-carrying gliders. In 1945, at the age of 17, he was accepted by the Fleet Air Arm for pilot training but the ending of hostilities and resulting cut-backs pre-empted it from even starting. As a result, Hall joined Rolls-Royce as an engineering trainee. In 1948, increasing tension between East and West led to resumption of recruitment by the RAF and Hall was accepted for pilot training, commencing at RAF Wittering and RAF Cottesmore on Tiger Moths and Harvards, followed by officer training.

In February 1950, Hall converted onto the Spitfire Mk.XVI at RAF Finningley and the following month undertook fighter reconnaissance training on the Spitfire Mk.XIV. Between June 1950 and December 1952 he served with the Middle East Air Force in Egypt, based in the Canal Zone with detachments to Khartoum, Habbaniya, Libya, Cyprus, Malta and El Adem, initially flying Spitfire Mk.XVIIIs but after six months converting to Meteor FR.9s. During this time he was a member of a seven-aircraft formation aerobatic team. Between March and June 1953, back in the UK, he instructed on the Prentice and Meteor T.7 at the Central Flying School, also winning the Brabyn Trophy for individual aerobatics. From then until December 1955 he was Flying Instructor on Meteor T.7s and Vampire T.11s at RAF Finningley and RAF Middleton St George.

Leaving the RAF, he joined English Electric in December 1955 as a company test pilot at Samlesbury and Warton. In due course he flew Vampire, Hunter, Canberra, P.1A, P.1B and Lightning aircraft from both airfields. He made a total of 124 Lightning test flights for the company, amounting to 70 flying hours on type. Additionally he flew the company's Dove, Heron, Anson, Marathon and President communications aircraft. From September 1961 to February 1962 he was based at the Bristol Aircraft Co, Filton, by then also part of the British Aircraft Corporation, where he had the opportunity to fly aircraft such as the Britannia, Vickers Vanguard and Valiant.

From May 1964 to December 1968, Hall was Commercial Flying Instructor at the College of Air Training, Hamble, in Hampshire, operating Chipmunk, Warrior, Apache and Baron aircraft. He then joined Caledonian Airways (later British Caledonian) flying the BAC 1-11, Boeing 707 320C and DC-10, remaining there for over 19 years for the period December 1968 to January 1988. From then until March 1991 he was Commercial Flying Instructor at the GB Air Academy, Goodwood, West Sussex, flying Warrior, Tomahawk and Seneca aircraft. After that he undertook mainly private flying of his own Commander and Baron aircraft, trained ex-service pilots to Instrument Rating Standard at Exeter and for a period flew seaplanes off Vancouver Island, Canada. Today John Hall enjoys retirement on Guernsey in the Channel Islands.

Johnny Squier, the second pilot to have flown the Canberra, was made Chief Production Test Pilot in 1954 as yet more pilots joined English Electric at Samlesbury to assist in experimental, development, production test and delivery flying. **Wg/Cdr Desmond 'Dizzy' de Villiers** arrived as Chief Experimental Test Pilot under Beamont in 1955, soon to be engaged on Canberra and the P.1 supersonic development programme. That year, Beamont, while continuing to carry out the duties of Chief Test Pilot, was also appointed Manager Flight Operations, responsible for the co-ordination of all flying and liaison with the Air Ministry, the Ministry of Supply and the Aircraft Establishments. De Villiers, born in South Africa around 1923, joined the RAF in 1940 straight from Bedford Modern School. After pilot training he served with Fighter and Coastal Commands, flying Beaufighters with No.68 (Night Fighter) Sqn. Based in the Middle East with No.252 Sqn, he carried out long-range strike duties in the Mediterranean. On returning to the UK as a Flight Lieutenant, in 1944 he was seconded to the de Havilland Aircraft Company as a production test pilot, later becoming Assistant Chief Test Pilot. De Villiers was released from the RAF in 1946 and the following year was appointed Chief Test Pilot of the Engine Division of de Havilland Propellers Ltd. He had an eventful eleven years at Hatfield, surviving four forced landings. On 12 August 1944, flying Spitfire Mk.XIV *JF316* on a contra-rotating propeller test, the aircraft suffered hydraulic failure necessitating a wheels-up landing. Flying from Hatfield on 24 November 1945, on a propeller Constant Speed Unit (CSU) development trial in Lincoln B.2

RF338, he had a close call when soon after take-off the port inner engine burst into flames. In making a forced landing the port wing hit a tree and the aircraft was burnt out. On 30 June 1947, during propeller braking trials in Hornet F.Mk.3 *PX290*, the aircraft swung on landing and the undercarriage collapsed. The Hornet was written off. On 10 March 1955, a hydraulic failure in Canberra B.2 *WD992*, on charge to de Havilland for Blue Jay programme tests, required him to make a wheels-up landing. During this period he retained his connection with the RAF as a pilot with No.500 (County of Kent) Sqn of the RAuxAF, where he was awarded the AFC. He was later made C/O with the rank of Squadron Leader. As Wing Commander he was appointed a Deputy Controller, RAuxAF, at Fighter Command. He displayed Handley Page (Reading)/(Miles) Marathon 2 *VX231*, an Armstrong Siddeley Mamba-powered test-bed fitted with de Havilland reverse-thrust airscrews, at the Farnborough Air Show in 1951, demonstrating some impressively short landing runs. On joining English Electric, de Villiers was succeeded at de Havilland Propellers by Michael Kilburn, a de Havilland production test pilot at Chester.

Yet another notable 'first' for the Canberra, albeit unplanned, happened in 1956 when Desmond de Villiers was flying one of his early assignments on type over the sea off the Cumberland coast. For some time reports had been coming in from the RAF concerning serious incidents of Canberra aircraft diving steeply out of control, in some instances with fatalities, as on 26 September 1955 (B.2 *WK136*) and 24 February 1956 (T.4 *WJ871*), both from No.231 OCU at Bassingbourn. The RAF demanded that the matter be sorted out – and quickly. All manner of potential causes were investigated, including 'runaway' travel of the tailplane electrical trimmer actuator. The Canberra's entire 'trimming' tailplane pivoted through several degrees on bearings, its graduated variable incidence providing powerful longitudinal nose up or down trim adjustment. Satisfactory at low speeds, at higher ones of over 350-400kt it seemed possible that it might experience uncontrollable runaway, resulting in stick forces beyond pilot control. As an alternative cause, the possibility of the failure of an explosive device fitted in the elevator circuit to sever the mechanical link with the control column was also considered. Designed to be activated in an emergency immediately before ejection, it allowed a spring to pull the column forward, so providing more room for the pilot to depart the cockpit. But the trimmer actuator seemed the most likely culprit and on 6 February 1956, flying production B.2 *WH715* in an intensive programme of trials investigating the matter, in recovering from a dive induced by a simulated runaway, at around 8,000ft de Villiers experienced violent pitch-up, side-slip, yawing and inversion of the aircraft. The sequence of events, alarming enough in itself, was closely followed by a double engine flame-out, the result of erratic compressor function arising from sustained negative 'g', an extreme nose-up attitude also having disrupted airflow into the intakes. Standard relight drills met with no success, both engines and torch-igniters presumably having 'flooded'. Despite its many merits, the Canberra at that time had no record as a glider (although de Villiers was about to find that its low wing loading did in fact make it quite a credible one) and in any event Warton was a long distance away. Having quickly explored all options, he sent out a 'Mayday' to Warton, warning of an imminent forced landing in either shallow water or on a sandbank. However, down to 2,000ft he spotted the then largely disused wartime air observer training aerodrome of RAF Millom not too far away. A gliding landing had never been attempted before in a Canberra and certainly did not feature in the training programme or in "Pilots' Notes". Nevertheless, preferring the more conventional surface, de Villiers approached Millom in a steep glide, co-ordinating perfectly the lowering of maximum flap and, at the last possible moment the undercarriage, to make a bumpy but safe landing amongst the runway debris of the former airfield. It was a remarkable feat of airmanship during which de Villiers badly bruised his head, requiring a precautionary night in hospital. Notwithstanding the extraordinary skill demonstrated by de Villiers, back at Warton Beamont was reputedly less than happy at the prospect of one of his aircraft 'overnighting' on a remote disused airfield, even though it housed a local army training contingent, at first deeply suspicious of de Villiers' intentions. In no uncertain terms Beamont indicated that it would be de Villiers' responsibility to get the aircraft back to base as soon as practicable.

Desmond 'Dizzy' de Villiers with B(I)8

The following day, a team rousted from Warton to check the aircraft out was able to start the engines but discovered that the nosewheel had sustained a slight twist, affecting the steering, which could only be rectified back at Warton. In yet another remarkable feat, de Villiers commenced take-off on a slightly curving trajectory, lifting the nosewheel at the first opportunity before straightening up on the main wheels and easing off the runway. On arriving back at Warton he held the nose up for as long as possible before allowing the Canberra to run gently off the centreline. A very tricky situation had been turned into an example of supreme airmanship. An account many years later in the *Aerospace Heritage* magazine of the BAe North West Heritage Group, concluded: 'All in a day's work…'

Back in 1948 Petter had noted that significant changes of trim were likely to occur for a variety of reasons at high Mach number, influenced by wing, body and nacelle design, together with any bending or twisting of the rear fuselage. Such variations could require quite large elevator angles to trim out, so it was decided to incorporate an adjustable-in-flight tailplane of a type favoured by German designers of high speed aircraft, the tail setting controlled by electrical actuation. Some three months after de Villiers' incident, by July sufficient investigation had been made to enable Beamont to carry out further tailplane trimmer checks on *WH715*. As a result, a wide range of electrical and mechanical modifications was applied retrospectively to the Canberra fleet to eliminate what had by then been shown beyond doubt to be a runaway trimmer problem. These included the reduction of the tailplane trim range to the minimum necessary; clearer separation of the power and signals wiring looms to prevent any possibility of electrically-induced undemanded control movements (suspected as the real cause of the incidents); a revised dipole trim switch to prevent any mechanical 'sticking-on' of the original single-pole switch in the trimming circuit; a redesign of the elevator trim tab controls to provide enhanced capability for the pilot to deal with any runaway, together with the fitting of a stronger mechanical 'stop' to the tailplane. Interestingly, during the maiden flight of *VN799* in 1949, Beamont had noted a 2-3 second time-lag in tailplane actuator response, requiring minor changes to be made. In fact he had routinely made positive use of the 'trimming' tailplane to alleviate the early Canberra's naturally heavy elevator at high speed and in sustained turns, including air displays, without having experienced any runaway issue. Similar modifications were also carried out in the USA, where the Martin B-57 had also experienced the problem. At the time it was speculated that it might have been one of the possible causes of Tommy Evans' crash in 1952. It could also explain an earlier incident involving Johnny Squier.

Yet another record-breaking Canberra flight took place on 16 February 1956 when, taking off from Farnborough, **Peter Hillwood**, with **Dennis Watson** as navigator, en route to Aden for MoS 'tropical' trials, flew B(I)8 *WT329* from London to Cairo, a distance of 2,182.6sm in 3hr 57min 18.9sec at an average speed of 551.8mph.

Hillwood flies Canberra B(I)6 WT307 on test over the Pennines, 1955

Hillwood in Canberra cockpit, possibly B(I)8 WT329, February 1956

The previous record between London and Cairo had been set by the Comet 1 jetliner prototype on 24 April 1950 in 5hr 6min at an average speed of 426.6mph. Having stood outside overnight at Farnborough, where ground temperature was well below freezing, the Canberra had first to be defrosted by washing down with wood alcohol. Powered by Rolls-Royce Avon turbojets built by Napiers at Netherton, Liverpool, carrying a Marconi radio compass, gun pack and full military equipment, *WT329* crossed the English coast near Eastbourne and that of France at Berck-sur-Mer Aerodrome near Le Touquet, passing Rheims and crossing the Swiss frontier at Basle, overflying Verona and the Adriatic, Brindisi, Corfu, Greece and Crete to Alexandria. Conducted mostly at around 45,000ft in forecast air temperatures of between -45 and -50 deg C, with fairly continuous cloud from the French coast to the Adriatic, only the highest peaks of the Alps had been visible. Flying low over the finishing line at Cairo's International Airport, they landed at Abu Sueir military aerodrome 45 miles north east of Cairo. The second leg, some 1,500 miles south to Aden, took three hours.

The success of the initial B3/45 A1 Canberra trials had at once demonstrated both the speed and altitude advantage of the world's first jet bomber. More than that, they were also a stark warning of the urgent need for a fast – supersonic – fighter with an outstanding rate of climb, capable of successful high altitude interception of similar 'new generation' bombers in the future, not all of which could be expected to be 'friendly'. Moreover, Beamont's trials with the Meteor F.4 during 1947/48 had yielded valuable information not only of benefit to the B3/45 A1 test programme but also about high altitude compressibility relevant to future interceptor aircraft. The Meteor trials enabled Petter to report to the MoS that contemporary fighters would have no curve-of-pursuit intercept capability against aircraft like the B3/45 A1 above 30,000ft, would even have difficulty *at* that height, and that successful interceptions in excess of 40,000ft would require an entirely new highly manoeuvrable supersonic fighter. Under such pressure from the industry, with alarm bells ringing in Whitehall, the Government eventually accepted the logic of the argument and at the end of 1947, in a complete 'cave-in' of its position the previous year, launched a new supersonic research programme with the issue of Experimental Requirement ER103, specifying an aircraft capable of exploring the transonic and low supersonic speed ranges. It was not the first Government 'U'-turn in the history of the aircraft industry, nor would it be the last. Having succeeded in putting on the pressure, and with some exciting developments taking place in the United States, in May 1948 – a full year before even the A1 made its first flight – Teddy Petter, Freddie Page, Ray Creasey, Dai Ellis, Ron Dickson, Frank Roe and others at Warton, began studies and design work on the second major aircraft type to be conceived by the company. By instinctively making use of the early principles of what would later become known as the 'Area Rule', the optimisation of cross-sections for supersonic aircraft, they were soon making rapid progress. English Electric was awarded a design study contract in August, for which Page was given overall responsibility. The company's proposals were submitted in November.

On 22 October, Beamont and Squier conducted further tests with a Halifax fitted with a 'Servodyne' powered elevator. Though not adopted initially for the Canberra, the powered elevator would, with modifications, form an important part of the control system of the ER103 supersonic research aircraft, to be known from the end of 1948 as the P.1. Disappointingly perhaps and contrary to statements made by various writers over the years, the 'P' merely conformed with English Electric's new project classification system which Page brought from Hawkers, hence signifying nothing more fanciful than 'Project' – not 'Prototype', 'Pursuit', 'Point Defence Interceptor' – and certainly not, as has been suggested, 'Petter' or even 'Page'! Subsonic wind tunnel tests at Warton in 1948/49 pointed to a degree of instability in English Electric's preliminary design, with low-set wing and high tailplane, the pitch-up tendencies of which were eliminated by drastically lowering the tailplane to the base of the rear fuselage, combined with a later raising of the wing to the shoulder position. Further design contracts followed in the first half of 1949. Air Staff Operational Requirement (OR)268, issued in July 1949, was followed by Specification F23/49 in September for a supersonic-in-level-flight day fighter, carrying cannon and radar as standard and it was for this that the English Electric team submitted a design brochure to the Ministry in October. Remarkably, the English Electric design team had adopted a favoured configuration from early in 1949 and had 'frozen' the principal aspects of its design, including swept-wing planform and low-set tailplane, by the end of the year. From then on it would remain substantially unchanged, testimony to its initial correctness. P.1 emerged as a twin turbojet research aircraft with drag-reducing wings of very thin section, swept back by 60 degrees, fully powered controls including unswept ailerons and hydraulic/spring units providing inbuilt artificial 'feel', with an all-moving tailplane. It was seen as the basis for a future Mach 1.5 supersonic interceptor fighter for the RAF, capable of later development to Mach 2. Sapphire engines were selected as then the most reliable axial-flow motors available, at that time less prone to surging than Avons; supplementary rockets were briefly considered but rejected largely on cost grounds.

But in the event it was not a project that Petter would see through to completion. He departed from English Electric at the start of 1950, joining Folland Aircraft later in the year. Although Petter had been in overall charge of the P.1 design, it was Page [from 1949 designated Assistant Chief Designer (Technical and Projects), effectively Petter's Deputy] and Creasey who had initiated much of the early detail. Petter, favouring a lightweight fíghter, is thought to have become increasingly disenchanted as the P.1 grew in size and weight. Moreover, Petter had had six years of abrasive relations with the production management at Strand Road. In overall charge at Folland, he would get what he felt had been denied him at English Electric, the freedom not only to design but also make an experimental prototype and manufacture the lightweight Gnat fighter/trainer in quantity. Meanwhile, in April 1950, English Electric had received a contract for construction of the P.1 prototype…

At Farnborough, the RAE, as adviser to the MoS, had serious misgivings about the P.1's design, notably its severe 60-degree swept-back wing and low-set tailplane, preferring instead the high-set 'T' tail as used by a number of other aircraft at that time. With the benefit of an early induced-flow supersonic wind tunnel at Warton, designed by Dai Ellis and powered by a Rolls-Royce Nene turbojet (which first ran at transonic speed on 22 June 1950), English Electric, with Petter's successor Freddie Page at the helm as Chief Engineer with responsibility for design, profoundly disagreed. They cited the 'T' tail as harbouring serious 'deep stall' characteristics if its airflow was blanked off by a wingform at a high angle of attack. English Electric were convinced that the familiar problem of 'pitch-up' being experienced by other swept-wing aircraft at subsonic and transonic speeds at that time, particularly when fitted with a high tailplane, could best be dealt with by setting it as low as possible. However, a nervous RAE and MoS sought confidence by commissioning a low-budget, low speed interim swept-wing research aircraft, the fixed-undercarriage Short SB.5 *WG768*, which first flew from Short Brothers &

Short SB.5, WG768, here in the 'T'-tail configuration strongly opposed by English Electric for the P.1

Harland at Belfast on 2 December 1952. The SB.5's wing and tail layout was capable of being varied, not in flight but on the ground between test flights, with wing settings of 50, 60 or even 69 degrees of sweep and detachable high or low-set tailplane/elevators.

It was deemed desirable that Beamont should gain further familiarisation with swept-wing flying before he got to grips with either the SB.5 or P.1. Accordingly, for the third time in his career, on 26 February 1953 at RAF Abingdon, Beamont flew a one-hour sortie in an F-86 Sabre, this time an RAF Canadair machine en route from Canada to the 2nd TAF in Germany. That was followed on 29 April by a handling flight to Mach 1.01 at Dunsfold in the Sapphire-engined third Hunter prototype F.2 *WB202*, for which Beamont was briefed by Hawkers' Chief Test Pilot, the 30-year-old Neville Duke. On 17 March, as reported in the *West Lancashire Evening Gazette*, flying *WB202* from Dunsfold in an air display at Blackpool where assembly of the Hunter was about to commence in Hawker's vast factory at Squires Gate, Duke had broken the sound barrier before a crowd of 100,000 spectators lining the Promenade. Flying southwards off the Fylde Coast, in a dive from 40,000ft to 20,000ft commencing 15 miles north of Blackpool, Duke exceeded the speed of sound some five miles away from the resort. In so doing he became the first person to 'bang' the skies of Northern Britain. In an event that almost had to be cancelled due to adverse hazy atmospheric conditions, the spectators at that point saw nothing of Duke and the Hunter. But they certainly caught the 'boom'. However, eight minutes later the Hunter appeared in full view in a 600mph low level fly-past from the south, Duke rolling it off northwards into the haze. Minutes later it came in again from the south at 200mph with a final fast fly-past from the north before heading off to land at Warton. At that time the runway at Squires Gate Aerodrome had still to be extended to accommodate production test flights of the Hunter. The display also included twelve Meteors from RAF Linton-on-Ouse in fast but otherwise subdued demeanour due to the weather conditions, together with rescue services comprising a USAF Grumman Albatross amphibian and Sikorsky S-55 H-19 (Whirlwind-type) helicopter, both from Burtonwood. At a luncheon at the Town Hall afterwards, attended by Sir Frank Spriggs, Chairman of Hawker Aircraft Ltd and Hawker Aircraft (Blackpool) Ltd, the Hunter's designer Sydney Camm and civic dignitaries, Neville Duke disclosed that at that time he had exceeded the speed of sound on more than 50 occasions. In its leader, the *Evening Gazette* trumpeted Blackpool's position as the natural air centre of the North, invoking its heritage of Grahame-White, Alcock and Brown, Jim Mollison, Amy Johnson and many others. Only just over 40 years separated Duke's supersonic flight in the Hunter from the exploits of the pioneers of flight who had first lifted themselves off the ground at the Blackpool Air Shows of 1909/10. From 1953-58, the Hawker factory at Squires Gate turned out 299 Hunters and more than 20 refurbished Hawker Furies, production-tested over the Lancashire Coast and the Lake District by Hawker test pilots including Duncan Simpson. The factory had been built at the outbreak of the Second World War when facilities there and at nearby Stanley Park made 3,406 Wellington bombers. Post war, the Lancashire Aircraft Co Ltd also produced a small number of Lancashire Prospector (E.P.9) light utility aircraft at Squires Gate and Samlesbury.

During 1953/54, Beamont flew the SB.5 twenty-four times in stability and control tests in various configurations at Boscombe Down. The first flight was on 29 April, later on the same day after flying the Hunter at Dunsfold; the final one in the series on 19 May 1954. In May/June/July 1954, Beamont had a further ten flights in production Hunter F.1s at Boscombe Down, exploring handling and control in dives at Mach 1+. When the SB.5 was flown for the first time with wings at 60 degrees *and* tailplane set low, by Shorts' Chief Test Pilot Tom Brooke-Smith in January 1954, it was only seven months before the first flight of the P.1, the build of which was already far advanced, its design having been 'frozen' in that configuration since 1949! The SB.5 succeeded only in proving the innate soundness of the P.1 design, something that English Electric had known all along, notably by providing some useful low speed handling data. Although it inevitably increased overall project costs it did not cause any appreciable delay. But the SB.5 exercise would not be entirely without benefits in certain other areas. In identifying issues of lateral control as a result of vortexes migrating along the wing onto the ailerons, it enabled English Electric to hit on an effective solution involving provision of a leading edge slot which neutralised the vortexes without having recourse to the drag-inducing wing fences then favoured by American and Russian designers – not to mention Shorts and the MoS! Beamont found the SB.5 interesting, even enjoyable to fly, but considered it less an aeroplane than a "boiler plate" exercise. He described it as "more like a piece of marine engineering than an aeroplane...with thickets of mushroom-headed rivets all over it!" With the first flight of the P.1 coming up soon, Beamont went to Farnborough to 'fly' the first ever simulator to have been developed (jointly by English Electric and the RAE) for a particular aircraft type. During the summer of 1954 he was also able to 'fly' a test rig at Warton, containing a dummy cockpit with control column and rudder pedals, set up to simulate the P.1's powered flying controls. Some nine years later, on 18 March 1963, Beamont made one final flight in the SB.5, a one-off 25-minute handling assessment.

Initially there were concerns that Warton's runway might not be long enough to accommodate the take-off and landing of an aircraft with the expected performance of the Armstrong Siddeley Sapphire-powered English Electric F23/49 - P.1. Hence, 24 July 1954 saw the first taxying tests, together with streaming of the braking parachute at speeds up to 125kt, of the prototype supersonic research fighter, serialled *WG760*, carried out on the much longer 3,000-yard runway at Boscombe Down. Over the next few days Beamont allowed it to become sufficiently airborne for him to get its 'feel', with the first straight flight of 500 yards just 14ft above the runway, followed by brake trials, achieved on 26 July. The initial tests culminated in Beamont's maiden flight in *WG760* from Boscombe on 4 August 1954, Peter Hillwood providing 'chase' in Canberra B.2 *WD937*. It had been postponed from the previous day when, carrying out cockpit checks for what should have been the first flight, Beamont accidentally activated the engine bay fire extinguishers, requiring a lengthy clean-up operation. He would not have been best pleased with himself! During a successful 33-minute first flight, which attained 440kt and 15,000ft before the sortie had to be cut short due to deteriorating weather and cloudbase, the only significant problem noted by Beamont was slight over-gearing and resulting over-sensitivity of the ailerons. The following day the P.1 was transonic. On 11 August, only its third sortie, flying down the Solent at 30,000ft and Mach 1.02, *WG760* and Beamont became the first British aircraft and pilot to exceed the speed

English Electric P.1 prototype WG760 *at Boscombe Down, the first photograph to be published, July 1954. Built at 'Vineys', Strand Road, Preston, it was taken by road to Boscombe for initial flight testing*

WG760's first engine run at Boscombe Down took place at 11pm on an evening in July 1954, its No.2 Sapphire spitting out flame from a 'wet' start

RPB preparing for the maiden flight of WG760 at Boscombe Down, August 1954

RPB with WG760 at Boscombe wearing, variously, 'bone-dome' and traditional leather flying helmets

of sound in level flight. An audible boom satisfied all those back at Boscombe. Yet Beamont had been unaware of the fact as the Machmeter had appeared to stick at Mach 0.98. The following day, completing their analysis of the flight test results, Don Horsfield and his colleagues in Flight Test were delighted to confirm that Mach 1.02 had indeed been achieved. Beamont replicated the circumstances on the fourth flight on 13 August but with a longer maximum dry thrust run, during which the needle visibly flicked up to Mach 1.02, the aircraft then going fully supersonic to Mach 1.04/1.08 at 40,000ft with more shock waves heard at Boscombe. By the 19th, Mach 1.12 had been reached and on the 26th Beamont carried out a 250nm cruise at 40,000ft in 29 minutes. On the 30th, manoeuvring tests were extended up to 42,000ft. From the very first flight there had been no question of attacking Mach 1 by the then conventional means of a shallow dive. Instead, the aircraft was held level and steady, moving effortlessly and stably through the 'sound barrier'. It was as though English Electric was making a clear statement from the outset that Britain now had the beginnings of a new generation of jet interceptors for which exceeding the speed of sound in level flight would be a matter of routine.

Development testing really got under way in September, Beamont's log for the 11th referring to the experimental prototype for the first time as the 'P.1A'. English Electric was not permitted to demonstrate the aircraft at Farnborough in September 1954 because at that point it did not conform to the Air Show requirement that a prototype should have a minimum ten hours flying time. Instead, flying it from Boscombe on test at 40,000ft over Farnborough during the Show, Beamont had to suffer the frustration of listening to radio chatter between fellow pilots carrying out their displays much nearer the ground. The observant might have noticed his contrail; only the very knowledgeable would have identified it. Not all was lost though as Beamont, together with Hillwood, was still able to participate in the Air Show on certain days by showing off the Canberra B(I)8 *VX185* in public for the first time, with Squier and Still also flying PR.7 *WJ820*. At Boscombe on 15 September, Beamont demonstrated *WG760* before Prince Bernhard of The Netherlands and the UK Minister of Defence, Mr. Duncan Sandys. Having arrived late part way through the display, which it had been decided should not be delayed, the rather irritated Minister seemingly found it necessary to criticise some of the low-flying content of Beamont's display. Test flying of *WG760* continued at Boscombe Down until 23 September when, judged safe to operate from the shorter runway at Warton, nudging Mach 1 all the way, Beamont flew it back to its Lancashire base from where the rest of the programme would be conducted. The following day he demonstrated it to representatives of the USAF. Beamont clocked up the aircraft's 50th flight, totalling some 36 hours, on 28 November. Days later he was off again to the States in Stratocruiser *Canopus*, this time to conduct flying assessments of Martin B57A *52-1418* and B57B *52-1530* at Baltimore on 6 December, finding little difference in their handling and performance compared with British Canberras – in spite of

One of the first series of air-to-air photographs of WG760 flown by RPB, taken from an accompanying Meteor, both flying from Boscombe in September 1954

P.1 WG760, showing clearly its shoulder-mounted wing with leading edge slots and low-set tailplane

Head-on view of P.1A WG760 again showing its shoulder-mounted wing and low-set tailplane, with distinctive ovoid intake, later changed in the P.1B to a circular intake with radar 'bullet'

Prince Bernhard Leopold of The Netherlands, RPB and Freddie Page gloomily awaiting the arrival of Defence Secretary Duncan Sandys at Boscombe Down, 15 September 1954

RPB shows Prince Bernhard the P.1 cockpit. The Prince had been a wartime fighter and bomber pilot with the RAF

L to R: Sir George Nelson, Mr Duncan Sandys, Prince Bernhard, RPB and Freddie Page with WG760 *at Boscombe, 15 September 1954*

some extravagant claims made by the Martin Company! *52-1418* was the first B-57 to fly, having taken to the air at Martin Airport in the hands of Martin's Chief Test Pilot, O. E. 'Pat' Tibbs, on 20 July 1953.

Initial supersonic testing of the P.1 in the North began over the Pennines in November 1954. The authorities at that stage preferred overland rather than maritime test routes, presumably for relative ease of retrieval of wreckage in the event of a serious incident. Objections from those on the ground, notably in the Appleby area, soon forced a *volte face* and test routes were directed out over the Irish Sea, the principal one of which to be designated from December 1958 as 'Test Run Alpha'. Even that was not without its problems and some time later, in the Isle of Man, English Electric had to use all its powers of persuasion in the persons of pilots Beamont and Dell, successfully in the event, subject to conditions, to persuade the House of Keys to withdraw its objection to supersonic testing over the Irish Sea. 'Test Run Alpha' remained in use until 1975 when a sonic boom heard over much of Central and South Lancashire and Merseyside, caused by Tornado P02 flown on a supersonic southerly track by Paul Millett and Ray Woollett inadvertently 'banging' Fleetwood, resulted in the test route being abandoned. Famously photographed at the time by test pilot Allan Love from an accompanying single-seat 'chase' Lightning, their aircraft was shown enveloped in shock waves.

Having returned from Boscombe, RPB and WG760 resume the test programme at Warton, September 1954

The leading edge flap here in operation on WG760 during landing offered no benefits, was subsequently locked 'up' on this aircraft and WG763, and dispensed with entirely on all succeeding aircraft

RPB and WG760 *perform on Press Day, Warton, 1955…*

…it being assumed that the photographers had been warned to leave that male fashion accessory of the time, the trilby hat, at home

A newspaper report referred to 'a queer bang, like an earthquake' which caused a lady in Thornton to have her curtains sucked through an open kitchen window. It would be some 20 years before 'Test Run Alpha' was reinstated.

By the spring of 1955 supersonic test flights had reached one hundred. Returning to Warton following flutter tests and a supersonic sortie over the Irish Sea in *WG760* early in March, Beamont was faced with two green and one red landing gear warning lights as the port leg remained partly hung-up. After failing to drop it by pulling some tight 'g', acutely conscious of the importance of the aircraft to the test programme and the RAF, he opted to make a potentially extremely hazardous emergency landing. On the approach, at 200ft and with only 800yd to go, the obstinate leg decided to do the honourable thing and descended with a reassuring clunk! It was possibly the first recorded instance of what were to become notoriously recurring problems with the P.1/Lightning's undercarriage.

On 9 March 1955 Beamont flew *WG760* back to Boscombe for a wide range of tests to be conducted including low and high speed handling, brake parachute reliability and brake testing, engine relights and dusk handling, together with assessment by pilots of the A&AEE. He returned it to Warton on the 28th. After the aircraft had been laid up at Warton for several weeks for modifications, he commenced general tests again on 25 May at up to transonic speed, including

Second P.1A, WG763, fitted with ventral fuel tank, rolled out at Warton, July 1955

Dutch rolls and 'bonkering', the new system of excitation devised jointly by English Electric and the RAE, involving firing small explosive charges (bonkers) located at various points in the airframe to measure the structure's damping capacity to absorb them. For such a revolutionary aircraft, serviceability proved to be excellent and a high rate of flying, sometimes three or four sorties a day, was soon established, the intervals between flights being governed only by the time needed to read-out the instrumentation and prepare the aircraft and its next flight schedule. After overnighting the aircraft at RAF Odiham, on 7 July Beamont demonstrated WG760 at an event at Farnborough to mark the Golden Jubilee of the RAE. The second P.1 prototype, WG763, with provision for a new ventral fuel tank, guns and foot-pedal (as distinct from hand-lever) wheel brakes, was flown by Beamont at Warton on 18 July 1955. In the first appearance of a P.1 at the annual SBAC Farnborough Air Show, he displayed WG763 spectacularly in public in September. Also at the Show, he shared the flying of Canberra PR.9 WH793 with Hillwood while Squier flew B(I)8 WT328. That month Beamont also carried out canopy pressure investigations on WG760 and, in October, ventral tank handling test flights in WG763.

Reheat was not available for the early flights. An afterburner system, and then only a rudimentary one with fixed reheat nozzle, boosting the 8,100 lb st Sapphires to 10,300 lb, was not incorporated in P.1 WG760 until October/November 1955. Its first flight so equipped, on 31 January 1956, suggested potential to achieve 40,000ft in a remarkable three-and-a-half minutes and Mach 1.4 in level flight. But subsequent handling tests and flight data indicated that speeds much beyond Mach 1.5 would require a substantial increase in the area of the tail fin. A little later in the programme, on 24 February WG760 attained Mach 1.53 (1,000mph), paving the way towards the Mach 2+ performance of the P.1B, later to be named the Lightning. The initial flights had revealed an aircraft of massive potential but, like many others of its era, requiring further design and development particularly of its tail fin in order to improve longitudinal and directional stability and control at higher Mach numbers. Moreover, the first P.1's initial flight endurance of only around 30 minutes pointed to a serious constraint which would require urgent consideration.

With the urgent need to get a supersonic interceptor fighter into production and RAF service, it was particularly important that there should be continuity in the event of the indisposition of the Chief Test Pilot. Such exigencies required an increasing number of English Electric test pilots to familiarise on the P.1 at Warton. However, given that the Canberra and P.1 programmes would run in parallel for a number of years, most would maintain their proficiency on Canberra as well. By early 1955 both Hillwood and de Villiers had joined the P.1 programme, beginning by assisting Beamont with control, handling and stability trials. Hillwood became the second person to fly the P.1 when he flew prototype WG760 on 12 March, following it with a sortie in WG763 on 23 September. Johnny Squier, initially retaining his status as Chief Production Test Pilot on Canberra at Samlesbury, also moved across to the

RPB attends engine runs of WG763, Warton, July 1955. Clearly visible are its gun ports

P.1 at Warton in 1956, where he was introduced by an experience on type sortie in *WG763* on 16 November. A week later on the 23rd he was followed in *WG763* by Don Knight. The total number of test flights, having reached 500 by April 1957, increased to 2,000 by September 1959. By then a Government decision had ensured that, for the first time in the industry, in contrast to the usual handful of prototypes, a large fleet of prototype, research and development aircraft, comprising two P.1A research prototypes (plus one structural test airframe referred to as *WG765* at Warton), three P.1B fighter prototypes and 20 P.1B Lightning pre-production fighter development batch aircraft, was available (though not all at Warton). At that time all other than *WG765* had flown. To keep the development period to the minimum, each aircraft was allocated a specific facet of a complex trials programme. With up to six aircraft airborne at a time, many flying at supersonic speed, all under radar surveillance, air traffic control was indeed complex. Beamont, Hillwood, de Villiers, Squier, Knight, Dell, Ferguson, Hall, Isherwood and Cockburn would all contribute to development and production testing of the Lightning in the late 1950s and early 1960s. Imperative for the RAF was the development of the supersonic fighter's weapons system, an aspect that would receive a major injection of expertise in January 1957 when Sqn/Ldr Jimmy Dell joined the team as RAF Fighter Command Liaison Officer (FCLO), bringing with him invaluable experience of single-seater all-weather radar interception gained on the F-86D during an exchange tour with the USAF. Tim Ferguson joined the P.1 team in 1957, the supersonic programme to be supplemented further by Hall and Isherwood from 1960 and, slightly later, John Cockburn, initially with Ferranti Ltd.

Both Beamont and de Villiers were associated with early flutter testing of the P.1 involving the detonation of 'bonkers' housed in the fin. During 1955/56, in the course of deploying 'bonkers' in transonic and supersonic test sorties, three serious in-flight incidents occurred involving the loss of P.1 cockpit canopies due to the flexing of the airframe. The first, on Friday 26 August 1955, involved Beamont and the next two de Villiers but, in spite of the pilots being severely shaken, in all three instances they were able to land their aircraft safely. Beamont's incident was described in graphic terms in *The Sunday News* of 28 August:

'Jet Plane Canopy Blows Off At 600mph – Dazed and blinded, pilot lands safely – Dazed and gasping for breath, Wing-Commander R. P. Beamont fought to control a 1,000-mph secret jet fighter nearly two miles up over Lancashire – Wing-Cdr Beamont's features were wrenched out of shape. His nose was flattened against his face and he was almost blinded. But he won the struggle to control the plane – An English Electric spokesman told the Daily Mail; "Beamont must have had a pretty tough time. But then he is a very tough pilot used to flying at high altitudes. His physique would probably enable him to stand the effect better than most men" – Last night at his home in Lytham St.Annes, Wing/Cdr. Beamont leaned back in his armchair and said: "Just one of those things."

Beamont's canopy was reported as having 'shattered itself' damaging flagstones in front of an elderly lady's house in Morecambe and his helmet, undamaged apart from scratches, 'thudded' into the garden of a police constable. The first of de Villiers' episodes took place just over six months later on 5 March 1956 when, according to the *West Lancashire Evening Gazette*, on a routine test flight from Warton his aircraft shed its canopy somewhere over the Liverpool area. It was only a month after his successful emergency landing of Canberra B.2 *WH715* at Millom. When, on 15 August 1956 his aircraft lost its lid again over the Irish Sea, *Flight Magazine* of 24 August remarked: 'This is the third time within twelve months that P.1 has suffered similar mishap.' In the latter instance de Villiers achieved the somewhat dubious distinction of becoming the world's first supersonic open-cockpit pilot when the lid blew off at Mach 1.5 at 25,000ft, floating gently to earth to land almost undamaged in a compost heap. Under the stresses of flight, the original manual actuating system and attachment cams had made the canopy susceptible to deformation, the mechanism liable either to stiffen up or jettison involuntarily. It was redesigned with a powered mechanism.

Within the constraints of a demanding test programme, as many demonstration opportunities as possible were taken up and in May 1956 Beamont displayed the P.1 (and de Villiers the Canberra PR.9) at Warton to VIPs including Mr. Nigel Birch, Secretary of State for Air; Air Chief Marshal Sir Dermot Boyle, Chief of the Air Staff and Air Marshal Sir Thomas Pike, Deputy CAS. The event was hosted by Lord Caldecote, a director of English Electric; Air Commodore Strang Graham of the EE London Office and F. W. Page. The visitors inspected the wind tunnels, laboratories and other facilities at Warton. Initial weapons testing took place when *WG763* commenced subsonic gun-firing trials in June 1956, progressing to supersonic firing the following year at the Eskmeals artillery range on the Westmorland coast. As recounted in Beamont's book *Testing Years* (Ian Allan, 1980), local opposition came to a head when a number of 30mm rounds discharged by Desmond de Villiers ended up in the garden of a retired senior Army officer. The trials in that locality ceased. Around that time the two prototype P.1s gave many pilots their first experience of true supersonic flight. In the meantime, Beamont continued to make Canberra test flights and on 21 June, flying with Walter Shirley, test-fired the Napier rocket motor fitted to B.2 *WK163*. As described earlier, in September, following a year of intensive handling tests at high altitude, he demonstrated the PR.9 prototype, modified PR.7 *WH793*, at Farnborough. Shortly afterwards, on 18 September he took the PR.9 to 59,000ft for further high altitude handling, on 23 November cruise-climbing it to 59,800ft. On 15 February 1957, he was once again at the controls of P.1 *WG760*, now fitted with a cambered wing leading edge.

Dizzy de Villiers was in the news again, this time in the *News Chronicle and Daily Dispatch* of 27 February 1957 which reported that, the day before, a supersonic bang had shattered a 12ft x 8ft window in the main operating theatre of the

WG760, fitted experimentally with cambered wing leading edge and extended wingtip chord, February 1957. The successful 'kinked wing' innovations were included in later Lightning F.2A and F.6 versions

Southport General Infirmary. The Chief Surgeon, operating on a patient at the time was able to complete the procedure successfully, reportedly commenting: "We were lucky, too, that the patient's feet pointed towards the window and nobody happened to be at that end of the theatre at the time." The news item stated that house windows in many parts of the town were broken, greenhouses damaged and buildings in the town centre shaken. The Hospital Management Committee sent a letter of protest to the Air Ministry in London. An English Electric spokesman was reported as saying: "There is always the risk in unusual atmospheric conditions of a slight misjudgement by the pilot that the area of the 'bang' may reach the land. The Company regrets any inconvenience or loss caused in spite of all the precautions taken. We shall be letting the people of Southport know the address to which claims should be made. The Ministry of Supply have accepted full responsibility." Said de Villiers afterwards: "I sympathise with those people in Southport. I have suffered the same thing on the ground. I have been startled out of my wits at times, and I am not of a nervous temperament. Have I ever visited Southport? Yes, once. I don't think it would be wise of me to go there again!"

Beamont, Hillwood and de Villiers shared demonstrating both the Sapphire-powered P.1A *WG760* and the Avon-engined P.1B prototype *XA847* at Farnborough in September (*WG760*'s first appearance at the Farnborough Show), all pulling 6g to remain in sight of the crowd and coming within a whisker of Mach 1 along the centreline. In 1960 *WG760* contributed to infra-red measurement trials for Firestreak missiles, before being 'retired' in 1962 to RAF Weeton, near Warton, as an instructional airframe. After various homes including St.Athan, Henlow and Binbrook, *WG760* can today be seen preserved at the RAF Museum at Cosford in Shropshire and *WG763* is on display in the Aviation Hall of the Museum of Science and Industry in Manchester.

The maiden flight of the first P.1B prototype *XA847*, the military fighter development of the two P.1 research prototypes (thereafter officially designated P.1As), was made by Beamont from Warton on 4 April 1957. As the P.1B, the P.1A progressed from a day fighter transonic research aircraft to the basis of an operational day and night supersonic fighter with more powerful engines, advanced radar system, guns, guided weapons and rocket armament, with systems including auto-ILS and auto-throttle. After just a single taxy trial on the previous day, with no further messing about with preliminary 'hops' off the Warton runway – which had in 1956 been extended eastwards by some 2,000ft to nearly 8,000ft overall – during its maiden flight of just 27 minutes the aircraft went straight to Mach 1.2 at 30,000ft in dry thrust. Beamont landed it back at Warton to news of the publication that day of Defence Secretary Duncan Sandys' Defence White Paper, advocating the end of manned combat aircraft after the 'V'- bombers and the P.1B. At that time it was the latest of a number of inept political decisions that over the years had proved damaging to the UK aircraft industry. Fortunately the P.1 programme had been too advanced to cancel and intensive handling trials of the P.1B proceeded. With Rolls-Royce Avon RA.24R engines of nearly twice the power, with reheat, of the original Armstrong Siddeley Sapphire AS.Sa.5s of the P.1A prototype, under full power the P.1B could reach 30,000ft in two-and-a-half minutes from brakes-off on the runway and be supersonic within another 30 seconds. Beamont noted that general handling was an improvement on the P.1A, with smooth and quiet high Mach performance at altitude. On 16 May he made a very satisfactory landing in rain in only 750 yards on a near-flooded runway. De Villiers, on his familiarisation flight in *XA847* also on 16 May, noted the same qualities of greater smoothness, with improved engine control and air brakes, together with superior cockpit layout and vision. At a press conference at Warton on 17 July English Electric announced that over the Irish Sea (on what in December the following year would be established as 'Test Run Alpha') *XA847* had unofficially exceeded the World Air Speed Record of Mach 1.72 (1,132mph) set in 1956 by the FD.2, the Fairey Aviation Company's elegant delta-configured research contemporary of English Electric's P.1. No specific details were forthcoming, but the event probably took place on 15 May on a

P.1B prototype XA847 on engine trials, Warton, April 1957

RPB and P.1B prototype XA847 returning from an early test flight, in a tight circuit round Warton over the Rivers Ribble and Douglas, with Preston in the background, summer 1957. XA847 retains its original flight configuration, with small fin and no ventral tank

sortie by Beamont at Mach 1.75. In so doing, *XA847* had exceeded the requirement of Mach 1.7 that had been called for prior to 'entry into service'. The *Lancashire Evening Post* reported from the press conference that "Among the equipment at Warton was an electronic brain, the most complete piece of equipment of its type in use in the country for aircraft problems. The brain had been of immense value in working out calculations in aerodynamic and other aspects of aircraft development… A new wind tunnel which could work at speeds between 300 and 4,000mph would be shared by the company's guided-weapon division."

On 4 June Peter Hillwood made his first familiarisation flight in *XA847*, one of the aircraft's five sorties from Warton that day. On 17/18 June, Beamont carried out a programme of test flights in *XA847* to establish position error (PE), calibrating the aircraft's pressure instruments against a known standard, investigating the degree of interference from the pressure field around the aircraft on pitot heads and the like. Repeating those carried out previously with Canberra aircraft, they involved low-level runs along the runway at Warton, under observation from the old control tower. A new tower came into use later that year. Other runs along the coast were recorded by a team of English Electric flight test observers ensconced with aneroid instrumentation, cameras and other equipment on the platform of Blackpool Tower. That Great Wonder of the World, rising to 500ft above sea level – ten times the height of the old control tower at Warton – was an ideal vantage point and also provided the pilots with a greater safety margin for high subsonic test runs offshore. The results were then interpreted to give a precise measurement of the aircraft's performance. Typically carried out in the calm atmosphere of a late afternoon or early evening, as the sun started its leisurely descent over the Irish Sea, the sudden and unexpected thunder of a shining silver P.1, fast as a bullet and low, only a short distance out to sea, probably startled a fair number of holidaymakers. A few years later, similar tests but at lower speed, were carried out by Lightning F.3 and T.4 aircraft, approaching from St. Annes and disappearing in the direction of Fleetwood, occasionally generating complaints for investigation by the Blackpool Police. For many a family such events were a high spot of the holiday, possibly complementing a visit earlier in the day to the public viewing enclosure at Squires Gate where they would also have seen Austers, Tiger Moths and Jackaroos, Geminis and Ansons, Silver City Airways DC-3s, or treated themselves to a ten-bob joy- ride round the Tower in an Air Navigation and Trading (ANT) Dragon or Westair Rapide. [Yes, I was there! – Author.] [In a later instance of low-flying along the foreshore, on Friday 5 September 1969, the Blackpool Illuminations were switched on from an RAF Canberra, flying at 340mph and 1,300ft, dropping one million-candlepower explosive flashes at two-second intervals. During the fly-past, the two-way conversation between its pilot and Gp/Capt Douglas Bader and Sqn/Ldr 'Ginger' Lacey, both present in Blackpool as guests, was relayed to the crowd.]

On 27 August Beamont experienced no problems in supersonic assessment and clearance of the aircraft, fitted with ventral tank, to Mach 1.3. *XA847*, together with kinked-wing P.1A *WG760*, was demonstrated by Beamont, without 'g-suit', to the public at the SBAC Show at Farnborough during 5-8 September 1957. His flight in *XA847* set the tone for all future displays of the type, demonstrating its minimum radius 6g turn and exceptional manoeuvrability to the accompaniment of thunder and flame from reheat; an aircraft that could streak past the crowd on the brink of Mach 1 (officially assessed at Mach 0.98) or be held down to 100kt before the famed 'opening-up' and near-vertical climb. At the same Show, Squier, Hillwood and Knight shared the flying of Canberra B(I)8 *XH234* fitted with tip tanks and 2 x 1,000lb bombs on underwing pylons. On 25 October Beamont took *XA847* aloft for supersonic handling at altitude, for the first time fitted with two dummy Blue Jay missiles, followed five days later by handling with Blue Jays and a ventral tank. Jimmy Dell, Fighter Command Liaison Officer (FCLO) at Warton from January, familiarised with *XA847* on 23 November, noting the aircraft's impressive performance and ease of flying. There followed a variety of tests and trials by Service pilots at the A&AEE at Boscombe Down and the Central Fighter Establishment. Returning from Boscombe Down to Warton in *XA847* on 13 January 1958, Beamont attained supersonic speed one minute after take-off and maintained it continuously for 21 minutes before arriving over Warton, a remarkable achievement in those days. Some directional control deficiencies revealed earlier in the programme were improved with the fitting of the larger Stage 2 fin and rudder, in which form Beamont first flew the aircraft on 16 May 1958, finding it very steady and easier to control on the approach in rough air and gusting winds. He flew the aircraft fitted with flight refuelling probe on 11 June.

Desmond de Villiers, *Tarnish 15*, flew the two P.1A research aircraft and the first two P.1B prototypes. Familiarising on *XA847* on 16 May 1957, on 21 June he carried out high-level PE tests in the aircraft, flying a range of high speeds past a specially calibrated Venom from the A&AEE, the latter acting as an observation station. *XA847* was directed to the Venom by ground radar, trailing smoke for visual contact. De Villiers conducted the maiden flight of the second P.1B prototype *XA853*, an aircraft destined mainly for gun trials, at Warton on 5 September 1957. Beamont flew the third prototype, *XA856*, an Avon engine development aircraft subsequently much used by Rolls-Royce at Hucknall, for the first time from Warton on an initial handling flight on 3 January 1958. He took the same aircraft to 60,000ft on a 20-minute high altitude clearance test on 17 February. On 3 April, he flew the first of 20 development batch aircraft assembled at Samlesbury, *XG307*, to Warton, followed by *XG308* on 16 May. *Flight* of 6 June reported that in the course of a test from Warton, de Villiers made a 'fleeting but impressive visitation by the P.1' to an Aeronautical Garden Party held by the Chester branch of the RAeS at Broughton Airfield in Denbighshire. De Villiers made numerous flights in the first

P.1B prototype *XA847*, exploring engine and general handling in various configurations with ventral tanks and missiles. On the ground, de Villiers was a noted Jaguar sports car enthusiast, possibly explaining the presence of an XK150 drophead coupe in various photographs of contemporary aircraft and test pilots at Warton. During the 1960s he owned an 'E'-Type which, occasionally on quiet weekends, he exercised along the main runway at Warton, sometimes 'paced' by a motorcyclist!

In June 1958 Beamont had another opportunity to visit Muroc Lake in the USA – by then named Edwards Air Force Base – where he was able to evaluate some of the 'Century' series of American supersonic jet fighters notably the F-100A, TF-102, F-104A and F-106A. He also visited the Production Flight Test Center of Convair and Lockheed at Palmdale Airport. In his follow-up report he was critical of a number of aspects of the American aircraft, especially the F-104A's wing and handling characteristics, deficiencies that nevertheless did not prevent him from attaining Mach 2 in F-104A *762* on 27 June. He considered the P.1B superior to them all in every aspect of handling and performance, with the possible exception of cockpit design. Two American pilots who came over to the UK in September on a reciprocal visit to evaluate early development P.1B *XG308*, though unimpressed by the confines and layout of its cockpit, pronounced its performance and landing characteristics as excellent. Altogether it confirmed to English Electric's

Desmond de Villiers – conducted the maiden flight of the second P.1B prototype, XA853, Warton, 5 September 1957

Second P.1B, XA853, with single-finned ventral fuel tank and pylon-mounted de Havilland Firestreak infra-red pursuit-course air-to-air guided missiles, originally known as Blue Jay

*After the two P.1A and three P.1B prototypes, XG307 was the first of 20 development aircraft and the first
Lightning to fly from Samlesbury, from where RPB made its maiden flight to Warton on 3 April 1958*

RPB balances on XG307's ladder for the maiden flight on 3 April 1958

satisfaction that with the P.1B they were on to a winner. Back in the UK in July, Beamont made initial contacts with the side-mounted flight refuelling probe in *XA847*. Beamont and Dell displayed *XA847* and *XG308* at the SBAC Farnborough Show in September, under circumstances described in more detail later. Dell flew *XA847* back to Farnborough on 22 October where, the following day, it was the centrepiece for a ceremony performed by the Chief of the Air Staff, Marshal of the Royal Air Force Sir Dermot Boyle who, accompanied by Sir George Nelson and with the assistance of a well-aimed bottle of champagne, officially named the aircraft 'Lightning'. Afterwards, Beamont spared nothing in displaying *XA847* to the assembled VIPs, before handing it over to Dell who made a spectacular departure from Farnborough for the return flight to Warton.

With Mach 1.7 successfully, albeit informally, 'in the bag', officialdom was reluctant to encourage even higher speeds, concerned that the ram temperature – the friction between the airframe and airflow – might have uncharted consequences. It was estimated that it would be 120 degrees C at the cockpit at Mach 2, with an absolute limit of 135 degrees C believed to be sustainable before the likelihood of canopy distortion and loss. In fact, eight days before *XA847*'s naming ceremony at Farnborough, flown by Beamont in a sortie of only 28 minutes' duration, on 15 October the same aircraft had thundered along 'Test Run Alpha' at Mach 1.9 with no apparent problem. The matter of even higher speeds was left very much to the discretion of English Electric Flight Test who, in November 1958, with particularly low temperatures of minus 70 degrees C forecast at 40,000ft, saw their next opportunity. On 25 November when Beamont took Lightning *XA847* to Mach 2 (1,280mph) at 42,500ft over the Irish Sea off St.Bees Head (a prominent natural feature off the Cumberland Coast, not named after the Chief Test Pilot!) in good weather and with no turbulence or cloud, carrying a ventral tank but no missiles, he became the first pilot to fly a British aircraft at twice the speed of sound in level flight. Beamont kept a very close eye on the ram temperature sensor specially rigged in the cockpit which, at Mach 2, could have been expected to reach the critical 120+ deg. C skin temperature but, in the colder air on the day, topped out at 94 deg. C. The air temperature had been minus 76 deg. C at 44,000ft. The Lightning was the third aircraft type in the world to attain such speed after the Lockheed F-104 in the USA and the Dassault Mirage in France. In three minutes and forty seconds from the start of his run over the Irish Sea, Beamont had achieved Mach 2 and travelled from the North Wales coast to the Solway Firth. Beamont felt that even at Mach 2 the aircraft had considerable performance in reserve. On pulling 2g to starboard at the end of the run and disengaging reheat during the turn, his speed falling from Mach 2 to Mach 1.8, Beamont was hurled forward in his straps. Overall, from the North Wales coast to that of Scotland, round to Windermere and the South Lakes, had taken less than eight minutes.

Pictured in 1957 with ventral tank, XA847 was flown by RPB at Mach 2 on 25 November 1958 when fitted with the larger Stage 2 fin, but carrying no missiles

Another view of XA847

...the event commemorated by an inscribed plate riveted to the port side of its fuselage

But such speeds came at the price of heavy fuel consumption. Having identified the Lightning's limited fuel carrying capacity, and hence range, as its Achilles' heel, Beamont considered that he and his fellow test pilots had been instrumental in securing essential design changes involving provision for in-flight refuelling and enlarged fuel tanks. In fact, the flight refuelling requirement had been included in the Ministry specification from an early stage. Such changes would be incorporated in later versions culminating in the Lightning F.6, the prototype of which, *XP697* – the fifth production Mk.3 modified with a long ventral tank as the prototype Mk.3A/Mk.6 – Beamont flew from Filton on 17 April 1964. [On 25 November 1983, exactly 25 years to the day since that first Mach 2 flight by a British aircraft, a small ceremony took place at Warton attended by pilots 'Bee' Beamont, Johnny Squier and Jimmy Dell. They were photographed together with engineering and production colleagues, including Len Dean who had been in charge of the original *XA847* ground crew, in front of Lightning *XP693*.]

Beamont first-flighted pre-production development batch aircraft *XG313*, *XG329* and *XG328* from Samlesbury to Warton on 2 February, 30 April and 18 June 1959 respectively. On 6 May it was the turn of the Lightning T.4 (initially designated by English Electric as the P.11) two-seater prototype *XL628* from Warton, followed by second prototype *XL629* on 29 September. In between, he displayed *XG313* at Paris in June, flew Air Marshal Sir Thomas Pike in *XL628* in July and demonstrated

L to R: Knight, de Villiers, Hillwood, Dell and RPB with development batch Lightnings including XG309 with Stage 2 fin (background) and XG310 with Stage 1 fin at Warton, January 1959

Cockpit of fifth development Lightning XG311, first flown by de Villiers on 20 October 1958

the latter aircraft at Farnborough in September. The year continued with a wide variety of handling and development work, Red Top missile, canopy 'off' and jettison trials and included the maiden flight, from Samlesbury to Warton, of the first production Lightning F.1 *XM134* by Beamont on 30 October. The Lightning entered service with the RAF in December 1959 when the CFE at Coltishall took delivery of three late pre-production aircraft, *XG334/335/336*, 'A', 'B' and 'C', for operational evaluation by the AFDS. The second production F.1, *XM135*, first flown by Ferguson on 14 November, was released to the CFE to become aircraft 'D' in May 1960. The third, *XM136*, first flown by Hall on 1 December and delivered to CFE by Beamont on 21 June 1960, became aircraft 'E'. The fourth and fifth, *XM137/138*, first flown by Isherwood on 14/23 December became 'F' and 'G'. F.1 *XM165*, first flown at Samlesbury by Beamont on 30 May 1960, ferried to AFDS at RAF Leconfield by Jimmy Dell (by then Deputy Chief Test Pilot at Warton) on 29 June and then on to Coltishall by Flt Lt Bruce Hopkins, became the first Lightning to enter RAF squadron service, as 'A', later 'F' of No.74 Sqn.

Peter Hillwood carried out a variety of general handling, gun firing, engine relight and early reheat trials, demonstrating *WG760* at Farnborough in September 1957 and P.1B *XA847* to NATO correspondents in July 1958. He was much involved in the experimental flying of P.1B/Lightning development aircraft over the next few years, his activities including flying *XG313* to the Paris Air Show in 1959, working on

First prototype Lightning T.4, the ill-fated XL628, on an early flight from Warton by RPB, May 1959

RPB signs for second prototype T.4, XL629, before flying it to Boscombe Down for Service trials, 13 June 1960. With him is Len Dean, long-serving Senior Flight Shed Superintendent on Lightnings

RPB climbs into XL629 for the flight to Boscombe

Build-up of transonic shockwaves on Lightning F.1 XM165 'F' of No.74 Sqn, RAF, motto 'I fear no man', in a pattern indicating a speed of Mach 0.98 in a low level display c.1960

Debriefing at Warton. L to R: RPB, Atkin, de Villiers, Eaves, Horsfield - and members of Flight Test, c.1960

trials as diverse as handling, flight refuelling probe, weapons handling and firing, the first Red Top rocket firing in 1960, the 2-inch rocket programme and, with *XG311*, 'tropical' trials in Aden in 1961. Hillwood carried out early air-to-air refuelling trials, notably handling sorties in October/November 1959 in *XA847* with flight refuelling probe fitted for 'dry' contacts with a Valiant tanker. Hitherto this had been largely unexplored territory in which the prospect of the tanker's drogue waffling around in the vicinity of the Lightning's engine intake had been the cause of some debate. The late Keith Emslie, a former Head of the Wind Tunnel Department, recalled that this was resolved one day when Hillwood came to the Warton wind tunnel which contained a one-eighth scale model of the aircraft. There, with the engineers, he was able to simulate the circumstances by lowering a 'drogue' from an opening in the tunnel roof into the airstream ahead of the model. This predicted a safe outcome, subsequently confirmed satisfactorily in actual flight with the aid of a slightly lengthened probe. Beamont and Dell participated in further refuelling trials with *XA847* in 1960 prior to assessment by Service pilots at the A&AEE. On another occasion, during an early test of the Blue Jay missile, the predecessor of the Firestreak infra-red pursuit-type homing device, the weapon misfired and came back at Hillwood, bouncing along his wing before disappearing aft into the yonder. He was fortunate not to have shot himself down. It was immensely satisfying for Hillwood when, on 14 December 1960, he delivered the first Lightning F.1A variant to enter RAF service, *XM172* '*B*', to his former Battle of Britain unit, No.56 Sqn at RAF Wattisham. The second Lightning squadron to be formed in Fighter Command after No.74, No.56 later adopted its well-known 'Firebird' aerobatic team red and silver livery scheme incorporating the Squadron's phoenix emblem. *XM172*, one of 24 F.1As built, was first flown at Samlesbury by Keith Isherwood on 10 October 1960. After its withdrawal from service in 1972, from 1981 it remained *almost* airborne, supported on a plinth as a 'gate guardian' at RAF Coltishall. Today it is preserved on static display in Cumbria by former RAF helicopter pilot Sqn/Ldr Neil Airey, now of the North West Air Ambulance Service.

After Beamont made the first flight of the second T.4 prototype *XL629* from Warton on 29 September 1959, later that day he carried out a performance and rolling clearance test in the first prototype *XL628*. Three days afterwards, *XL628* was lost over the Irish Sea as a result of a catastrophic structural failure when being flown by Johnny Squier, an event described in more detail later. Only days after the loss of *XL628*, in a demonstration sortie on 6 October, Beamont flew *XL629* on a general handling and cockpit assessment sortie with Managing Director Freddie Page in the right-hand seat. Page's first flight on type sent out a clear message of their confidence in the aircraft. Early in November Beamont made a flight in *XG313* with its canopy removed, as a precursor to two canopy jettison tests. There was a certain irony when, on 19 November, *XL629*, which had been retained by the company, sustained a canopy breakaway on take-off when being flown by Beamont

Peter Hillwood with fifth development Lightning XG311, with Stage 1 fin, at RAF Khormaksar, Aden for tropical trials, October 1961 (see also Pages 210-212)

and de Villiers. It was an unwelcome reminder for the two pilots of their spate of canopy losses from single-seaters three years earlier. Beamont, recently acclimatised to such conditions in *XG313*, brought the aircraft safely round for another open-cockpit landing back at Warton. 1960 saw work on OR946 assessment, rocket and ventral stores packs, gun-firing trials, flight refuelling and more first flights of F.1s and T.4s. On 13 June Beamont delivered *XL629* to Boscombe Down for preview assessment and a successful flight test programme by 'A' Squadron of the A&AEE. The aircraft served back at Warton as the two-seater development aircraft, on Jaguar 'chase' duties and with ETPS until 1975. On 15 July he made the maiden flight, from Samlesbury to Warton, of the first of 20 production T.4s, *XM966*, together with *XM967* later converted at Filton as the two T.5 prototypes in a programme to meet the RAF's requirement for a two-seat trainer version of the Lightning F.3. On 16 August 1960 he flew the first production F.1A, *XM169*, from Samlesbury to Warton, the first to be fitted with a production refuelling probe and used subsequently for in-flight refuelling trials. By then Deputy Chief Test Pilot of the British Aircraft Corporation (BAC) and Chief Test Pilot of its operating subsidiary, English Electric Aviation, Beamont demonstrated F.1 *XG332* (with Hillwood and Isherwood) and T.4 *XL629* at Farnborough in September, when the latter was also flown by Dell and Knight. 1960 was the first time in twelve years that the Canberra, though still in production for the RAF, was not displayed at Farnborough. Freddie Page made his second flight with Beamont in *XL629*, a directional trim investigation, on 28 November 1960.

1961 included a test flight on 4 January in T.4 *XM966* without its canopy, production first flights and tests, high altitude tests with Red Top and the start of handling and production tests of the Lightning F.2. During the year, Beamont visited Australia and New Zealand on a marketing mission to promote TSR2. Returning across the Pacific courtesy of Qantas in a Boeing 707 fitted with new Pratt & Whitney by-pass engines, he spent three hours on the flight deck, 50 minutes of which in the captain's seat. Not only did he enjoy the experience but he wrote a detailed appraisal which he forwarded to Sir George Edwards at Vickers as input to the VC10 programme. During Farnborough Week, on Tuesday 5 September, and on the Friday and Saturday, Beamont displayed T.4 *XM974*, Jimmy Dell flying the same aircraft on the Wednesday and Thursday. On 22 September the Rt Hon Julian Amery, MP, Secretary of State for Air, accompanied Beamont on a supersonic production test flight in T.4 *XM987*. 1962 began with test flights of *XG310* fitted with the Mk.3 fin, including handling, flutter and resonance, longitudinal and directional stability. He carried out a number of 'low level route proving' investigations to and from Boscombe in Canberra B.2 *WD937* and later in Lightning T.4 *XM996*. On 13 March he took development batch *XG336* to 62,000ft on a high altitude 40-minute engine handling sortie. Beamont flew *XG310* together with T.5 *XM967* at Farnborough in September, delivering T.4 *XM991* to the OCU at Middleton St George on the 20th. In an interesting assignment on 20 November he flew a Vulcan test bed aircraft to assess the Olympus 22R engine, an indication, together with his low-level route proving trials, of the build-up of the TSR2 programme. Beamont achieved his 1,000th Lightning test on 3 April 1963, particularly satisfying for him when in the course of an engine/reheat performance test in Lightning F.2/3 *XN734*, an engine development aircraft on charge to Rolls-Royce, he attained Mach 2.105 at 39,000ft, then the highest speed reached in a Lightning. At that point he had flown supersonically more than 800 times. 1963 saw the start of a large series of production flights of the F.3, Beamont first-flighting some 14 during 1963/64/65, others being flown by Dell, Knight, Ferguson, de Villiers and Isherwood. On 10 April 1963 Beamont carried out the first flight of *XA847* fitted with an extended ventral tank pack, Red Tops and a dorsal fin to restore directional stability. Overall, the aesthetically unattractive fin fit did not merit adoption on later F.6 production aircraft which instead gained twin ventral fins at the rear of the tank pack. It was however retained on *XA847* which in that form remained suitable for target duties in AI.23 trials in the hands of pilots including de Villiers, Cockburn, Knight, Carrodus, Ingham, Houston and McEwan. In 1966, on its 468th flight, the whole having totalled more than 205 hours, that historic aircraft, the first British aeroplane to fly at Mach 2, was flown by Keith Isherwood to Farnborough for loose gravel trials. It was donated to the RAF Museum in 1972. During 1963 Beamont carried out a number of Lightning tests with overwing fuel tanks fitted and also gained experience flying the Vickers VC10, BAC 1-11 and HP.115.

Two dramatic studies of RPB flying fourth development aircraft XG310, here with the Stage 3 (Mk.3) fin in June 1962

In an abridged article for *Airframe* of 25 October 1963, Beamont gave an insight into flying the Lightning. Having completed the pre-start checks, both Avons started almost simultaneously within a few seconds of pressing the starter buttons. After rotation off the runway and retraction of the undercarriage, with speed building up quickly, climb attitude would be reduced slightly at 1,000ft, with minor trimming and engagement of autostabilisers (though not essential), resulting in fine trimming being completed in all axes. In resuming the climb at maximum cold thrust or reheat, the Lightning's climb angle could easily exceed 40 degrees at full power, retrimming only being required in the transonic phase. Mach 1.0 was exceeded during the push-over at the tropopause. Supersonic acceleration in maximum reheat was smooth and fast – very fast indeed in cold air. By virtue of its high speed, manoeuvrability and remarkable zoom-climb, in accelerating to attack speed at the tropopause the Lightning had a considerable advantage against fast targets. Responsive controls and efficient cabin conditioning made flight at Mach 2.0, despite ram-air temperature of 100 deg C, enjoyable and undramatic – even when slow or fast rolling. At either supersonic or subsonic speeds, the aircraft could be trimmed accurately to fly 'hands and feet off'. High speeds however demanded constant attention to navigation in relation to the airways, control zones, other traffic and the consequences of sonic booming. Beamont referred to the success of introducing autostabilisers, particularly for controllability in rough air in the landing configuration. He stated that the Lightning settled on finals as if on rails and was easy to land, but if turns were made too steeply the rapid increase in induced drag of the highly swept wing necessitated use of up to 90 per cent cold thrust to maintain correct approach speed. Combined use of tail parachute and *Maxaret* wheel braking could reduce the landing run to 850 yards from the threshold. Overall, he concluded, the Lightning, although a densely equipped radar fighter, was fully aerobatic and a fighter pilot's aeroplane.

At Filton on 17 April 1964 he made the first flight of F.3 *XP697*, its first sortie after full conversion at Filton to an F.6 with long-range ventral tank and cambered leading edge, flying the aircraft back to Warton later the same day. Also in April, with the maiden flight of the TSR2 getting closer all the time, he carried out a number of TSR2 flight simulation profiles in Lightning T.4 *XM968*, these continuing into August.

During the design stages and prototype build of the P.1, between 1950 and 1954 the English Electric test pilots were heavily engaged with development flying and large scale production testing of B.2, PR.3, T.4, B.5, B.6, PR.7 and B(I)8 Canberra variants. With manufacture and assembly of the Canberra in full swing, ever greater demands were placed on production flight testing and delivery arrangements from Samlesbury. At peak, sometimes exacerbated by delays arising from periods of bad weather, it was not unknown for up to 16 aircraft to be bunched up awaiting final clearance and delivery to customers. In an initiative designed to alleviate the problem, English Electric entered into arrangements with the Silver City Airways subsidiary of British Aviation Services (BAS/Britavia) Ltd of London.

These and the following two photographs show third production Lightning F.2 XN725, first flown from Samlesbury by Jimmy Dell on 31 March 1962, which was retained as a development aircraft. Here with Stage 3 fin, de Havilland Red Top collision-course air-to-air missiles and extended ventral tank, it is about to be test flown by RPB

Development aircraft and F.3 prototype XN725 *in overwing tank trials, probably in June 1963. The drag-inducing tank fins were later removed. Designed for speeds up to Mach 0.9, the tanks were tested safe to Mach 1.1*

Capt. John Walter 'Johnny' Hackett, one of Silver City Airways' most experienced pilots, together with navigator **Peter Moneypenny**, were among several Silver City crews to work with English Electric. Hackett was widely experienced in delivering many types of aircraft all over the world. One of Silver City's sidelines, established by Hackett, was the operation of a ferry unit of former RAF aircrew with experience of jet-powered aircraft, primarily for hire to the manufacturing companies to assist in the delivery of aircraft to overseas customers. The Meteor was among many aircraft types flown by Hackett during his previous RAF service and in 1953 he, Moneypenny and another Silver City crew, pilot Barry Damon and navigator Mac McLaughlan, were sent by Silver City for refresher training on the Meteor F.4 and T.7 at RAF Driffield. They then converted to the Canberra B.2 at RAF Bassingbourn OCU. The links between Hackett and Moneypenny with English Electric were forged from May 1953 when they both began a long involvement delivering Canberras to Venezuela and elsewhere.

Johnny Hackett was a true aviator of the 'old school'. An ebullient personality exuding burly geniality and bonhomie, the generously moustached Hackett was rarely out of the air, had gained extensive flying experience and possessed a proven natural ability to fly an extraordinarily wide range of aircraft types, large and small, military and civil. Born in London in August 1923 and educated at Stonyhurst College in Lancashire, he served throughout the war as an RAF pilot on night fighters and also with Coastal and Training Commands. On leaving the RAF in 1946 he spent eight years with BAS during which time he was personal pilot to Winston Churchill. In October and November 1948, flying up to three return trips a day in Silver City Airways Bristol Type 170 Freighters and Wayfarers, he made 24 return trips between Hamburg and Berlin on the Berlin Airlift. In July 1950, with M. V. 'Mike' Cole of Britavia, he ferried Grumman Mallard amphibian *N2966*, destined for the King's Flight of the Royal Egyptian Air Force, from New York via Goose Bay, Bluie West One in Greenland, Iceland, Stavanger, Deauville and Paris. At Tousson, south of Paris, they were able to compare notes with another crew demonstrating the British equivalent, a Short Sealand amphibian *G-AKLO*. Hackett also delivered Heron aircraft to Japan for use by Japanese Airlines. With Silver City Airways, operating between Blackbushe, Lydd, Lympne, Le Touquet, Deauville, Ostend and Gosselies, from 1950 to 1955 he flew DC-3 Dakotas and pioneered cross-Channel car ferry services with Bristol Freighters on Channel Air Bridge routes.

During 1953, Hackett ferried Bristol Freighters *G-AMRU*, *CF-TFX* and *CF-TFZ* in stages from Filton across the Atlantic via Prestwick, Keflavik and Goose Bay to Montreal, Canada. Though immensely functional as a cargo and utility transport aircraft, the ungainly twin-Centaurus, blunt-nosed, clam-doored and fixed-undercarriage Freighter, its wing reminiscent of a huge plank set atop a

Silver City Airways Bristol Type 170 Freighter as flown by Johnny Hackett

Hackett at the controls of a Bristol Freighter in the early 1950s

commodious slab-sided fuselage, was *not* among the more elegant of the designs produced by the post-war British aircraft industry. After making landfall on the first of these occasions, lumbering in on the approach to his destination, Hackett's headphones crackled into life, followed by an incredulous transatlantic voice from the control tower: "What the hell kind of airplane is that?" demanded the voice. "This, Sir, is a Bristol Type 170 Freighter!" boomed the somewhat miffed Hackett, possibly with an aside to his co-pilot concerning the intelligence and lineage of the inquirer. A pause ensued, another crackle, then again from the control tower: "Did ya' build it ya'self?"

During his years with BAS, from 1953 Hackett was frequently on detachment to English Electric. In a long association with the Canberra he broke a number of world records in the middle and late 1950s. At the beginning of 1953, Venezuela, the first export customer (as distinct from overseas production licence-holder) for the Canberra, ordered six new B.2s for the *Fuerza Aerea Venezolana (FAV)*, all diverted from the second British (RAF) production contract. Work on the order, which had been anticipated, had commenced in 1952. The first two aircraft, *1-A-39 ex-WH708* and *2-A-39* ex-*WH709*, were delivered by RAF crews departing from Warton on 20 March 1953 and routing via Gibraltar. The next two, *3-A-39 ex-WH721* and *1-B-39* ex-*WH722*, left Warton on 6 May in the charge of the two Silver City crews Hackett and Moneypenny / Damon and McLaughlan, respectively, who delivered them to

Caracas and then Boca de Rio via Gander, Baltimore and Jamaica. Hackett and Moneypenny also delivered the last two B.2s of the Venezuelan contract, *2-B-39* ex-*WH736* and *3-B-39* ex-*WH737*, departing Warton on 9 June and 11 July respectively. *3-B-39* arrived within one day, routing via Gander and Baltimore to Venezuela in twelve-and-a-quarter flying hours. Leaving Warton at 3.52am GMT, they were circling over Caracas at 7.05pm, having covered 5,862 miles averaging 487.5mph. Their Atlantic time Warton-Gander of 4hr 46min compared with Beamont's official east-west record of 4hr 18min in August 1951. They achieved Gander-Baltimore in 2hr 50min and Baltimore-Maracay in 4hr 47min. Like Beamont, Watson and Rylands two years before, Hackett and Moneypenny

Hackett (C) and Moneypenny (L) about to deliver Canberra B.2 3-A-39 to Venezuela, pictured with RPB at Warton, May 1953

L to R: Hackett, Moneypenny, Damon and McLaughlan with Canberra B.2 1-B-39 at Baltimore, en route to Venezuela, May 1953. In the background is 3-A-39

Some serious final 'chart checking' by the two crews in another posed photograph with 3-A-39

were amused to see trial interceptions by USAF Sabres from Bangor, Maine, fizzling out two miles beneath them. Not as reticent as Beamont had been on the subject of the Canberra's performance, Hackett took delight in informing air traffic control: "We're at Mach 0.78 and 50,000ft, and we've still got some to spare!"

Long range ferries to South America came to feature large in the workload of English Electric and its successor companies. Two routes were used, subject to the time of year and weather. That across the North Atlantic followed staging posts at Santa Maria in the Azores, Gander in Newfoundland, Baltimore, Nassau in the Bahamas, sometimes Jamaica, then on to Venezuela, Ecuador or Peru. The South Atlantic alternative involved Dakar, in Senegal and Recife in Brazil.

English Electric received its second contract from South America in May 1954 when Ecuador ordered six new Canberra B.6s. With Johnny Squier as Captain, Hackett flew the second of these, *E802*, on test from Samlesbury on 3 March 1955. The aircraft were then flown out in pairs to Quito via Gander, Baltimore, Jamaica and Salinas in April, June and July 1955 by Hackett and Moneypenny (*E802* 18 April, *E803* 16 June, *E805* 14 July) and variously by M. V. Cole of Silver City Airways and Majors G. Barreiro and R. Sandoval of the *Fuerza Aerea Ecuatoriana (FAE)*.

Most notable among the point-to-point records set by Hackett, then aged 32, was his transatlantic return flight of 23 August 1955. At a time when other English Electric pilots were too occupied flight testing the P.1 and later marks of

The Venezuelan Air Force Fuerza Aerea Venezolana (FAV), *one of the more colourful overseas operators of the Canberra, as shown here by Hackett and Moneypenny, this probably a B(I)8 of the second (1957) Venezuelan contract (see Page 197)*

Ecuador Air Force Fuerza Aerea Ecuatoriana (FAE) Canberra B.6 with delivery crews. Centre L to R: Moneypenny, Sandoval, Hackett, Barreiro and Cole with, extreme L to R: Hothersal and Hackforth of EE, 1955

Canberra to be spared for such an attempt, he and navigator Peter Moneypenny (28), both on loan again from Silver City, achieved a London – New York (Brooklyn Floyd Bennett Field) – London return flight over a distance of 6,915.92sm in 14hr 21min 45.5sec at an average speed of 481.52mph. Their time included a 35-minute refuelling stop at New York carried out by an Anglo-American team under the direction of Doug Potter of English Electric. Hackett described the American co-operation as "simply terrific". Their record would stand for more than 14 years. Both components of the transatlantic return flight were themselves world records; outward from London-New York 3,457.96sm in 7hr 29min 56.7sec at an average speed of 461.12mph; their return, with a favourable wind, covering the same distance in 6hr 16min 59.5sec at an average of 550.35mph. As noted by Captain Hackett in his aviation papers now lodged with the BAE Systems Heritage Department at Warton, the previous one-way-only east-west UK-USA record, set by the Americans Merrill and Lambe in a Lockheed Electra on 9/10 May 1937, had stood at 20hr 29min at a speed of 169mph. [In 1952, Captain Charles Blair, a US commercial pilot, established an unofficial west-east record of 7hr 35min flying a Mustang fighter from New York to London.] Hackett and Moneypenny's transatlantic return flight, taking off at 07.10hr BST and returning to land at 21.40hr at London Airport, making full use of radio compass but carrying no autopilot, was officially timed 'out' and 'back' across a start and finish line at

PR.7 WT528, Hackett and Moneypenny, bound for New York, dispatched from Warton by RPB, Page and Hillwood, first stop London Airport, August 1955

Croydon Airport. Having been provided with chicken and egg sandwiches (in Moneypenny's case tongue sandwiches, "his favourite flying food" according to his wife) they were supposed to have been seen off from London by both their wives, but in the event Mrs Hackett lost her direction at the Airport and had to wish them "Godspeed!" by radio.

Westwards, the aircraft carried wingtip tanks which, not required on the return leg, were jettisoned at 12½ deg W. The explosive release of the tanks blew out the starboard navigation light – the only malfunction they encountered. Their feat, in Canberra PR.7 *WT528*, was the subject of enthusiastic worldwide news coverage by a press captivated with the thought of being able to have breakfast in London, lunch in New York and dinner back in London all in the same day. According to the New York Herald Tribune of 24 August 1955, on their arrival at Floyd Bennett in rain and poor visibility, Hackett and Moneypenny were overwhelmed by newspaper, television and newsreel men. Lunch was a very rushed affair. After giving various interviews in which they described the outward leg as "routine", "excellent", "very pleasant" and specifically thanking Idlewild control for a wonderful descent from over 48,000ft and a hundred miles out over the Atlantic, Hackett concluded " Let me get the hell out of here!" as both dived back into the aircraft for the return flight.

PR.7 WT528 *takes on Shell Aviation Turbine fuel at London Airport (Photo: Shell Aviation)*

BBC interviewer Ivor Jones talks to Hackett and Moneypenny before take-off

Hackett and Moneypenny with a final photo opportunity for the press before take-off

WT528 *is towed out between lines of BEA Viscounts, Vikings and Elizabethans…*

...taking off at 07.10hr BST, 23 August 1955...

...landing back at London at 21.40hr, 23 August 1955, Hackett and Moneypenny escorted through the crowds by some very 'period' policemen

They were international celebrities and champagne flowed on their return to London Airport, where 10,000 people turned out to welcome them back. The New York *Daily Mirror* described the flight as a "stirring accomplishment…the British have been ahead of us for years in jet development and thus deserve to be able to claim the first round-trip Atlantic record." Hackett's papers contain the Royal Aero Club certificate confirming the record flight together with numerous telegrams of congratulation including one from the Prime Minister, Sir Anthony Eden – "a brilliant flight" – and others from colleagues at English Electric including Peter Hillwood and Desmond de Villiers. Hackett and Moneypenny were awarded the Royal Aero Club Britannia Challenge Trophy and the Geoffrey de Havilland Trophy; to receive both in the same year was an exceptional achievement. The latter was awarded for attaining the fastest speed during the year in an official British record or race, on this occasion for the return journey at a speed of 550.35mph. Hackett and his wife, who lived in Marylebone, London, were guests on the Saturday evening BBC Radio show *In Town Tonight*.

PR.7 *WT528* was handed over to the RAF Flying College (RAFFC) – formerly the Empire Air Navigation School (EANS) – in a ceremony at Manby in Lincolnshire on 14 June 1956. Named *Aries V*, the aircraft joined Canberra B.2 *WH699 Aries IV* of the RAFFC which, in the hands of RAF crews, during 1954/55 had made a number of notable Arctic and North Pole flights and established records between London and Cape Town, Ottawa and London. *Aries IV* had itself succeeded the RAFFC's Lincoln B.2 *RE367 Aries III*; Lincolnian *RE364 Aries II*; and Lancastrian *PD328 Aries I. Aries V* went on to make a number of long-range navigational training flights and on 25 May 1957, again with an RAF crew, set up a new Tokyo-to-London record, flying via Alaska, northern Canada and the North Atlantic. During April and May 1958, *Aries IV* and *V* made, respectively, a return flight to New Zealand and a round-the-world flight of over 28,000 miles, both with the purpose of developing navigational methods in areas of the world without navigational aids. PR.7 *WT528*, ex-Hackett/Moneypenny, ex-RAFFC *Aries V*, sold back to BAC in 1962 for refurbishment and modification as PR.57 *BP746*, was delivered to the Indian Air Force in spring 1964.

In 1956 Hackett accepted a permanent post with English Electric as a test and ferry pilot working Canberras out of Samlesbury and Warton. Moneypenny was appointed administrative assistant to R. P. Beamont, Chief Test Pilot and Manager of Flight Operations. During 1955, Moneypenny had also obtained a pilot's licence in his own right, enabling him to participate on long haul delivery flights as both pilot and navigator. On 4 April Hackett familiarised on Canberra B(I)8 *VX185* at Samlesbury. In May, Hackett and Moneypenny established three unofficial point-to-point records ferrying the first of eight new Canberra B(I)8s ordered by Peru, *474* ex-*WT343*, departing Warton 25 April via Shannon, Gander, Baltimore, Jamaica and Panama, arriving at Lima on 4 May. Shannon to Gander was achieved at 507mph, Montego Bay to Allbrook Field 514mph, and Allbrook Field to Lima 485mph.

They also delivered two more of the eight B(I)8s, *476* ex-*WT367* departing on 19 June, and 478 ex-*XH206* departing on 30 July. When transiting through the tropics, Hackett routinely ensured that the Canberra's engine starter cartridges were stored overnight in the hotel bar's refrigerator to keep them in optimum condition! During the latter part of the year and early in 1957 he was engaged on production test at Warton and Samlesbury, with further demonstration flights and liaison in Venezuela and Ecuador. The first of five contracts received for Canberras for the Indian Air Force in January 1957 required Hackett to deliver three new B(I)58s, *IF895* ex-*XK953, 898* ex-*XK959* and *903* ex-*XH233* to Delhi and Agra on 15 April, 13 May and 25 May respectively, followed by PR.57 *IP986* ex-*WT539* on 25 July, all routing via El Adem and Bahrain.

English Electric received a second order for Canberras from Venezuela in February 1957, the first overseas repeat business, comprising eight new B(I)8s and two new T.4s. The B(I)8s were all delivered by January 1958, Hackett having ferried *4A39* (shortly afterwards renumbered *FAV 3216)* ex-*XH244, 4B39 0923, 1C39 0240* and *4C39 0453* on 5 June, 19 June, 13 November 1957 and 11 January 1958 respectively. The first T.4 *1E39 0619* departed on 14 December 1957 in the hands of Hackett and Moneypenny. Together with a Venezuelan Air Force officer, Lt Leba, on 14 February 1958 they ferried the second T.4 *2E39 0621* via Santa Maria, Gander and Baltimore. On the final leg between Friendship Airport, Washington D.C. and Maiquetia Airport, Caracas, on 22 February *2E39* established a point-to-point speed record of 2,062.39sm in 4hr 10min 59.7sec at an average speed of 492.95mph. It was the nineteenth and last of such point-to-point records set by the Canberra which, together with three World Altitude Records, gained it worldwide fame.

As Chief Delivery Pilot, between May 1953 and July 1964 Hackett made a total of 27 Canberra overseas ferry flights from Warton, 17 of which to Venezuela, three to Ecuador, three to Peru and four to India. Hackett's duties involved him spending significant periods of time in Venezuela, where he trained and instructed FAV pilots on general handling and tactics, easing the Canberra into operational service. Additionally he made 13 return ferries from Venezuela to the UK, bringing back FAV Canberras to Warton and Samlesbury for refurbishment. Such was the scale of the business that over the years in a number of instances the same aircraft was flown backwards and forwards across the Atlantic several times for repeat refurbishment and redelivery. One in particular, the record-breaking T.4 *2E39*, supplied new when first delivered by Hackett from 14/22 February 1958, he subsequently redelivered on two further occasions (18 June 1963 and 4 July 1964) after he and others had brought it back for refurbishments in the UK. Heavily worked as a trainer, *2E39* renumbered as *FAV 0621* was returned again in 1976 when BAC overhauled and converted it to T.84 standard, before redelivering it for the third time, then as *G27-265* in April 1978. It finally ended its days when it was withdrawn from service in 1990. Similarly B.2 *3-A-39*, renumbered as *FAV 6409*, delivered new by Hackett in

May 1953, was flown back by him on 12 September 1958 for overhaul. Returned a second time for overhaul in 1968, it was flown back by Dave Eagles and Jim Evans in May 1969 as *G27-158*. Returned again in 1978 for conversion to a B.82, in August 1979 it was redelivered for the third time as *G27-304*, eventually to be preserved at Generalisimo Francisco de Miranda AB, Caracus, in 1990.

Between 1961 and 1963, during several periods back at Warton between Canberra ferries to and from Venezuela, Hackett flew the BAC communications Heron *G-AREC* and Dove *G-APSK* to many UK destinations including Boscombe Down, Farnborough, Filton, Hatfield, Luton and Wisley. In 1964 he transferred to the British Aircraft Corporation (BAC) Commercial Aircraft Division and the One-Eleven airliner flight test programme, becoming BAC Captain in charge of delivery flights. He also contributed to development flying of VC10 and Concorde. At the conclusion of his flying career, between 1972 and 1975 Hackett flew on nearly 100 Concorde test flights, mainly captained by a number of eminent BAC test pilots including Brian Trubshaw and John Cochrane who had been Captain and co-pilot respectively on the first flight of the British Concorde prototype *002, G-BSST*, from Filton to Fairford on 9 April 1969. Hackett's first test flight in Concorde was from Fairford with Captain McNamara in *G-BSST* on 4 February 1972. His first flight as Captain was on 7 August 1972, also in *G-BSST*. His final Concorde flight and last test flight of all was on 23 October 1975 as Captain of *G-BBDG* on a noise measurement test from Heathrow to Fairford. After a long test flying development programme Concorde acquired its Certificate of Airworthiness in December 1975 and began airline services with British Airways on 21 June 1976. Johnny Hackett subsequently became Flight Operations Manager with British Island Airways, based at Gatwick Airport.

J. Keith Isherwood, born in 1932 at Chatburn, Lancashire, first entered the Merchant Navy before joining the RAF to begin flying in 1952. He became a fighter pilot with No.19 Sqn at RAF Church Fenton where he was also a member of No.609 (West Riding) Sqn, RAuxAF. In April 1956 he joined English Electric as a communications and trainee test pilot, sharing with Ferguson and Hall the display of Canberra T.11 *WJ610* at the 1958 Farnborough Air Show. Moving on to the Lightning in 1960, he demonstrated F.1 *XG332* at Farnborough that year and, as a BAC pilot, was present there again in 1962. Somewhat unusually for a civilian test pilot, during 1962/63 he attended the Empire Test Pilots' School (ETPS) Course No.21 at Farnborough. It was at a time when the authorities wished to increasingly 'professionalise' test pilots by ensuring that they had graduated from an approved training school rather than having just been 'headhunted' as a result of their known expertise within the RAF or RN. As a result, Isherwood progressed from mainly production test to development test flying. On 11 February 1963, Isherwood's 328th test flight in a Lightning, a final production clearance of an F.2 before delivery to the RAF, was of considerable significance as the company's 5,000th Lightning test flight from Warton.

Keith Isherwood with a prototype/development batch P.1B Lightning, its nose art indicating either XA847, XG313, XG325 or XG331

Isherwood's 328th Lightning test flight was the company's 5000th Lightning test flight from Warton, 11 February 1963

On 13 August 1963, Isherwood, call sign *Tarnish 9*, made a wheels-up landing at Warton in the company's long-serving Canberra B.2 development aircraft *WD937*. Having set course for Filton on a flight continuation training sortie, on arrival he discovered that the landing gear wished to remain indoors. After attempting unsuccessfully to persuade it otherwise, with plenty of fuel on board and no immediate emergency, he opted to return to his home base for an emergency landing. There he circled for another hour to burn up fuel while the Warton fire services laid a 500-yard carpet of foam on the runway, with the Preston and Lancashire County Fire Brigades also in attendance in case further supplies of foam were necessary. After burning off as much fuel as possible, with Beamont watching intently from the control tower, Isherwood gently slid the Canberra's belly down the runway, switching everything off as it came to a halt, releasing his harness and jettisoning the door. The first fireman to arrive, having just grasped the handle from the outside, was astonished as the door instantly came away in his hands. Isherwood was able to walk away unharmed. The incident resulted from fouling of the undercarriage operating cable. Afterwards Isherwood maintained that, thanks to training, his first emergency landing had been virtually routine and that his main concern was to minimise damage to the aircraft. That he succeeded was evident from the fact that the aircraft was in the air again within a week. As a training flight, the sortie must have been deemed to have exceeded all expectations! Keith Isherwood's wife had watched her husband's apparently interminable circling around Warton with some bewilderment, he having made no mention of putting on a display that day. *WD937* was an interesting first production batch aircraft, having been retained by the company as a development and trial installation aircraft after excessive vibration was found during its production test flights in 1951. It went on to serve in that capacity until 1968, notably in the hands of Beamont during 1953/54 trialling the power rudder as later fitted to the P.1. It was used extensively as a chase and photographic aircraft in the Lightning, Canberra export, TSR2, Strikemaster and Jaguar programmes. Towards the end of its career it was bought back from the Government by BAC, re-registered as the civil *G-ATZW* and painted overall black to be operated as the company's private chase and support aircraft. Isherwood's skilful emergency landing was the only serious incident to affect it during its long service at Warton. Having made 938 Lightning test flights for the company, totalling 591 flying hours, Keith Isherwood left BAC in 1967, entering civil aviation with Britannia Airways. He died in November 1993.

Emergencies with the Lightning were not unknown and **Johnny Squier** had more than his fair share. His experience on type dated from 1956 when, in order to gain familiarisation with swept-wing jets, on 9 April he flew Hunter *XF388*, the usual English Electric prelude to flying the P.1. But it would be 16 November before he actually got behind the controls of second prototype *WG763* for his initial 32-minute familiarisation flight. Further flights followed early in 1957 and on 11 October he took the first prototype *WG760* on a handling test. All the time, Canberra testing continued unabated including machines for the RAF and others for export notably B(I)58s, PR.57s and T.4s for India. During 1958 and the first half of 1959 he flew the second P.1B prototype *XA853* together with most of the pre-production aircraft from *XG307* onwards. On 29 August 1958 he flew *XG308* to Farnborough where, together with *XA847*, it was displayed by Beamont and Dell. On 29 December 1958 – no blanket Christmas holiday in those days – following a reheat take-off from Samlesbury on the maiden flight to Warton of sixth pre-production development batch aircraft *XG312*, he experienced speed indicator and undercarriage problems which required a Canberra, returning from test over the Lake District, to maintain station with him on his approach and landing at Warton. For the first time, Squier's log entry for 13 February 1959 referred to the aircraft as 'Lightning' rather than 'F23/49'. On 26 February, flying the eighth pre-production batch *XG325* on its maiden flight at Mach 1.7 at 37,000ft, Squier heard a loud bang from the rear of the aircraft as a large part of the inner casing of the No.1 reheat pipe and its burner failed, to be summarily expelled from the aircraft which, again, he was able to bring back safely to Warton. A manufacturing fault was deemed to be the culprit. With effect from 1 April 1959 he was appointed Chief Production Test Pilot, also acting as Crew Station Liaison Pilot dealing with requests for pilot advice on crew station layout, cockpit and crew equipment matters.

On 18 June he tested the two-seater T.4 prototype *XL628*, the aircraft having first been flown in a 30-minute sortie from Warton by Beamont on 6 May during which it exceeded Mach 1. On another occasion in *XL628*, Squier had to contend with a double engine flame-out at 25,000ft but was able to relight No.1 and get the aircraft back to Warton in one piece. Over the two days 9/10 July, Squier flew *XL628* five times, variously accompanied by Hillwood, Knight, Horsfield, Burns and Moneypenny. On 4 September he flew *XL628* to Farnborough for the 1959 Air Show. There, on 7 September, carrying Ferranti Airpass and twin-Firestreak pack but without the upper Aden guns of the F.1, *XL628* was at the centre of things when it was flown by Beamont in a synchronised duo display with Squier, who was at the controls of development batch single-seater F.1 *XG331*. The latter, with a twin-Firestreak pack, two Aden guns beside the cockpit, a straight leading-edge, enlarged fin, finned ventral tank and Ferranti Airpass fire-control, was by then representative of the production F.1. *Flight Magazine* reported: 'These aerodynamic meat cleavers (so mighty is their drive and so solid-looking their structure) the Lightning F.1 and T.4…performed *a deux*, beginning with a ferocious reheat getaway.' At one stage, due to a change in wind direction and landing pattern, Beamont crossed in front of Squier who was approaching in the opposite direction from Laffan's Plain at Mach 0.9. The resulting synchronisation was a little too close for comfort. To add to the unease at Farnborough, landing at a high angle of attack, Beamont ran onto the overshoot area after the aircraft lost its braking parachute when it brushed the ground. *XL628* sustained slight tyre damage. During the week, Beamont shared flying the T.4 with Hillwood, and Squier the F.1 with Knight. Much of the drama went apparently unnoticed by the press.

It was with T.4 prototype *XL628* that Squier would experience the greatest and most dangerous drama. All previous incidents involving *XL628* paled to insignificance compared with the events of 1 October 1959, when only weeks after it had been demonstrated at Farnborough and six months after its maiden flight, it was lost over the Irish Sea. Flying the aircraft solo at 40,000ft 15 miles off St. Bees Head, Cumberland, carrying missiles, Squier was repeating a previous test carried out on 29 September by Beamont in the same aircraft at Mach 1.6. Eleven minutes after take-off from Warton he was concluding a 360-degree maximum aileron starboard roll at Mach 1.7 when he heard a very loud bang at the rear, followed immediately by violent flicks and yawing. There had been a catastrophic structural failure of the tail fin. As the aircraft broke up and disappeared from Warton's radar, Squier was acutely aware that no other pilot in the world had successfully escaped from an aircraft at such a speed. Holding the blind tightly over his face, in ejecting at over 1,000mph at 40,000ft, experiencing intense pain, Squier became the first British pilot to escape at more than the speed of sound. A yachtsman sailing to the north of the Isle of Man saw the Lightning hit the water. Squier's Martin-Baker seat separated at 10,000ft but his parachute failed to open automatically. Plunging into cloud he fell out from beneath the cloudbase at only 1,000ft, urgently deploying the parachute manually. His RFD single-seat liferaft inflated but the rest of his emergency aids, including SARAH homing beacon, either failed or worked only spasmodically. After two hours of his entering the water, a USAF Grumman SA-16 Albatross amphibian, searching out of Prestwick, passed within 100 yards but failed to spot him. On several occasions he saw various other search aircraft, including a Meteor and a Shackleton maritime reconnaissance aircraft from Kinloss, but they also failed to see him before darkness descended. Within an hour of the incident, Squier's wife had been told there was little hope and the following day English Electric announced that he was missing presumed dead: "The loss of Johnny is a very great shock for us all." On 2 October, flown by Don Knight, the English Electric Company's Dove communications aircraft *G-APSK* was also airborne between Warton, RAF Jurby (IOM) and RAF Bishopscourt (NI), carrying a team of four look-outs including Freddie Page. At one point during the protracted search the Dove itself appeared destined for the 'drink'. A fuel flow issue may have been the cause of the brief loss of both its engines before they spluttered back into life, one after the other, allowing its search to continue.

Meanwhile, with spinal and other injuries, erecting the roof to keep out the rain that had started to fall, Squier floated in his dinghy for over 28 hours in a sea state with 20-foot swell and poor visibility, still unable to be located by the rescue services. After surviving a very wet night, using a piece of orange-box driftwood, at around

T.4 XL628 flown by RPB, with F.1 XG331 by Squier, at the Farnborough Air Show, September 1959. Both carry Firestreak missiles, the F.1 also showing gun ports

A sight to alarm any adversary! Firestreak-carrying T.4 XL628 flown by RPB, at Farnborough, September 1959. But less than a month later XL628 lay at the bottom of the Irish Sea after it was lost following a structural failure during a test flight by Johnny Squier

3.00pm on 2 October he paddled ashore near Garlieston in Wigtownshire, Dumfries and Galloway, 30 miles from his point of ejection. Seeing someone collecting driftwood, Squier blew his emergency whistle to attract attention but, imagining him to be the police, the beachcomber ran off. Having crawled up the foreshore, soaked through, Squier staggered into a garden where the lady of the house, the local school-teacher, was cutting roses, announcing that he had "come from the sea!" She appeared relatively unsurprised, having just been reading about the incident in the morning paper. His helmet and various items of wreckage followed him ashore several days later. At Warton there had been intense frustration and much champing at the bit when the official emergency services insisted that, apart from the Dove, only they should conduct the search. Suffering from exposure, compression fracture of the spine, slight deafness and bloodshot eyes, but otherwise remarkably intact, Squier was hospitalised in Stranraer for two weeks before being flown back to Warton in an Anson air ambulance on 15 October to complete his recovery in the Preston Royal Infirmary. There he remained for another two weeks to overcome air pressure damage to his ears and generally to recover from the buffeting that he had sustained. Squier's log book, with true test pilot laconicism, reads: "Test 1.7 IMN at 40,000ft. Bailed out after structural failure. Landed in Irish Sea. Walked ashore at Garleston, Wigtonshire [sic], 28 hours later. Fractured spine, damaged ears and eyes. Bruised legs & arms." Thereafter, he derived considerable amusement from the fact that he had departed Warton in a Lightning on 1 October for a 1,000mph flight at 40,000ft over the Irish Sea, returning along a similar route two weeks later in an Anson flying at 125mph at 2,000ft!

During Squier's convalescence, with effect from 7 December 1959 Desmond de Villiers was appointed in his place as Chief Production Test Pilot, Squier being redesignated as Chief Crew Station Liaison Pilot responsible for Lightning and Canberra Crew Station liaison, safety equipment standards and crew training. Having made a remarkable recovery he resumed desk duties at the beginning of 1960 and after a gap of seven months returned to flying in April with a local flight in the company Dove. Search operations for the main sections of *XL628* continued for some six months until they were abandoned in March. The circumstances of Squier's amazing escape inevitably made him an attractive subject for investigation by RAF aviation medicine specialists. Moreover, after a visit by Squier and his wife to the Martin-Baker factory towards the end of 1959, when the Company Chairman gave them a works' tour and showed them in detail a Mk.4BS ejection seat as used in the Lightning, a close working association developed between Squier and James Martin which lasted many years. Sadly the accident brought to an end his solo flying days in Lightnings although in May/June 1961 he made three more flights in the right-hand seat of T.4s *XM970/973*, piloted by Tim Ferguson. He continued to fly Canberras, including New Zealand B(I)12s *NZ 6110/6111*; a sortie on 1 May 1961 in *WH734* converted as an aerial tanker; target sorties in Hunters; with an

Johnny Squier ascends a Lightning ladder on 30 September 1959, the day before his accident in XL628

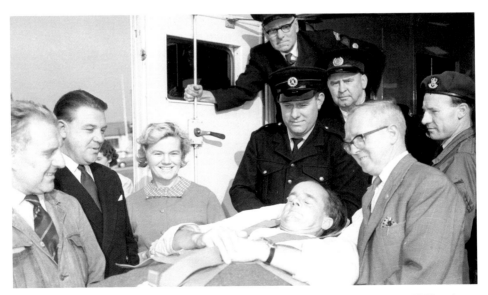

Johnny Squier being transferred to Preston Royal Infirmary after the loss of XL628. Mrs Squier and RPB are in attendance, 15 October 1959

Shortly after the loss of XL628, RPB and Freddie Page show their confidence in the Lightning T.4, preparing to take off in the second prototype, XL629, 6 October 1959

increasing workload flying the company Dove and Heron. On 10 February 1966, a test sortie with Flight Test Observer Derek Leeming in Canberra *WH983* became Squier's 3,000th Canberra flight. In September/October 1966 he undertook trials at the Flight Refuelling Ltd base at Tarrant Rushton with Canberra TT.18 *WJ632*, a target tug fitted with underwing Rushton target-towing cable and winch capable of towing a target ten miles behind the aircraft. Developed by Flight Refuelling and BAC, the system provided aerial targets capable of generating an adequate radar response for surveillance and weapon system training radars; an infra-red source; facility to record accuracy of air-to-air and ground-to-air weapons and a means of enhancing visual acquisition of the target. The two companies converted 18 Canberra B.2s as TT.18s. Also in 1966 Squier was awarded the Queen's Commendation for Valuable Service in the Air. He was unable to attend the September investiture until the following year because of previous commitments, on 12 and 22 September respectively, to deliver two Canberra B.2s, *YA+153* ex-*WK138* and *YA+152* ex-*WK137*, out of three ex-RAF aircraft ordered for experimental work by the West German Air Force at Manching, near Munich. The ferry flights took place at a time, it has been alleged, that colleagues noted coincided with the annual Munich Bierfest…

Squier remained a test pilot until the end of 1966. From 18-29 November, he ferried refurbished Venezuelan Canberra B(I)2 *1280 G27-305* ex-RAF *WH881* from

Warton to El Libertador, via Rabat, Dakar, Recife and Zanderey. His final flight for BAC, a 28-minute production clearance sortie accompanied by Reg Stock in Canberra T.4 *Q496* ex-RAF *WH845*, intended for the Indian Air Force, was on 30 December 1966. *Q496* was subsequently embargoed from delivery to India but later sold to Peru as T.74 *246 G27-224*, ferried by Tim Ferguson and Jim Evans in 1973. Flying with English Electric and BAC since 1946, Squier had carried out 2,500 test flights in Vampires, 3,200 in Canberras and 130 (58 hours) in Lightnings. He had amassed 6,000 flying hours in the course of a 27-year flying career during which he piloted 75 different types of aircraft. He then joined BAC's engineering development team as Cockpit Design Liaison and Safety Equipment Officer with specific interest, not surprisingly, in cockpit escape systems and safety equipment, a role that involved working closely with Martin-Baker. His work included design of the escape systems for the TSR2. After contributing also to the Anglo-French Jaguar fighter-bomber system he retired in December 1983. Having been appointed a Justice of the Peace in 1965 he continued to serve as a local magistrate, eventually retiring as Chairman of the Preston Bench in 1990. A keen poultry farmer, gardener and motor car mechanic, he lived at Little Broad Oak Farm, Penwortham. Johnny Squier died on 30 January 2006 aged 85.

Don Knight, on Canberra development and experimental work at Warton from 1955, had his first direct flying involvement with the P.1 supersonic research fighter project when he flew a pacing flight on 22 July that year in Canberra B.2 *WH715*, alongside Beamont who was flying P.1A second prototype *WG763* on a general handling sortie. With the Canberra continuing to present a major workload, the pressures associated with the P.1 programme also made it necessary to familiarise as many of the test pilots as possible with swept-wing, supersonic flight. Accordingly, from 1-3 May 1956, Knight was attached to the Rolls-Royce Flight Test Establishment at Hucknall, Nottinghamshire, where he flew Hawker Hunter F.6 *XF388*, fitted with the RA.28 Avon engine, on familiarisation and test. His personal first familiarisation flight in the P.1A was a 24-minute sortie in *WG763* on 23 November 1956. He flew the aircraft again in January and March 1957 and in September/October/November also flew the first prototype *WG760*. Although the Lightning, as it would become, was fitted with an autostabilisation system, the original design was inherently stable and easy to fly, proved by the fact that most pilots, having made only three or so flights in other swept-wing aircraft such as the Hunter, were able to convert to the new P.1A with relatively little difficulty. Tim Ferguson flew both *WG760* and *WG763* in 1957 and subsequent development aircraft in 1958. On 30 April 1958 Knight familiarised on type with two half-hour sorties in P.1B second prototype *XA853*, later flying first prototype *XA847* and early pre-production batch P.1Bs *XG307, 308, 309* and *310*. John Hall and Keith Isherwood, both of whom had spent several years on the Canberra, would also soon contribute to test flying the growing number of development and production aircraft.

Don Knight

Tim Ferguson

April 1959 saw Knight making frequent test flights in *XG310*, followed by other development batch aircraft – now named Lightnings – including *XG311, 313, 325* and *330*. On 9 July he accompanied Johnny Squier in two-seater T.4 *XL628*. As the development programme proceeded, Knight flew various support sorties in Hunter F.6 and Meteor NF.14 'target' aircraft, and in October/November carried out spinning practice in Jet Provost, Hunter T.7 and Vampire T.11 aircraft, the latter on loan from de Havilland at Hatfield, as a prelude to spinning trials in the Lightning itself. With Canberra work remaining ongoing, notably on PR.9, in August *XH131* was flown by Knight, accompanied by an RAF officer, Flt/Lt Westell, from Warton to Bahrain via Nicosia, for tropical trials. The pattern continued into 1960 with much PR.9 and Lightning development batch work. The Lightning T.4 featured increasingly, together with continuing communications flights in the company Dove. On 25 May 1960 Knight delivered the first of four F.1s, second production *XM135 'D'*, to Leconfield for onward transit to the AFDS at Coltishall. At the end of the month, with Jimmy Dell he carried out spin recovery practice in the Vampire T.11 prior to commencing a programme of stalling and spinning trials, with Dell as lead pilot, the two working closely together, mainly using development batch aircraft *XG308* fitted with a spin-recovery parachute for use in an emergency. Some relevant preliminary information had been produced by the vertical wind tunnel facility at Lille in France; actual trials showed the Lightning to have a slow spin of five seconds per 360-degree revolution, but very oscillatory with recovery often beyond the vertical and sometimes supersonic. It was at the time the telemetry process was being introduced, with the airborne pilot in close radio contact with another seated with the flight test engineer in the telemetry caravan on the ground. Between them, Dell and Knight conducted over 200 spinning sorties, recovering safely from all. In contrast to the later Jaguar and Tornado trials they never once had to resort to the anti-spin 'chute. The recovery procedure was subsequently written up for inclusion in "Pilots' Notes" and an instructional film produced for the squadrons, something for which future RAF Lightning pilots would have cause to be grateful. Jimmy Dell recounted a later occasion, probably on 18 February 1963 in T.4 *XL629*, when he was checking Keith Isherwood out in a stalling and spinning sortie, Isherwood occupying the right-hand seat. Spin had been induced after a particularly violent flick of the aircraft. While it was usual for recovery to be completed in a steep attitude, on this occasion Dell thought "we were going downhill rather fast." All was explained when control called urgently to say "*Tarnish 6* … you're still in reheat!!"

Knight and Dell shared the demonstration of T.4 *XL629* at the Farnborough Air Show 1960. Knight also participated in Lightning aerodynamic, systems and weapons clearance programmes with particular responsibilities associated with the new generation OR946 integrated flight control and instrumentation system assessment, autopilot clearance (essential to make flying the aircraft as straightforward as possible, allowing the pilot to concentrate on intercepting his target), engine handling, flight clearance, telemetry/rolling/stalling, AI.23B, Red Top missile jettison and overwing tank trials. Having flown the Lightning F.1, F.1A *XM169* and a number of prototype and production T.4s, on 2 September 1961 Knight flew Lightning F.2 *XN723*. On 6 October 1962 he flew F.3 *XP693*. In 1963 his work continued with directional stability, rolling clearance, missile handling and in-flight refuelling trials with the T.4 two-seaters and on 18 July he piloted F.3 *XP697* on its maiden flight from Samlesbury, the latter aircraft later flown to Bristol for full conversion to F.6 standard.

On 31 July 1963, Don Knight, call sign *Tarnish 5*, had to eject from an aircraft for the second time in his career at Warton, on this occasion from pre-production batch Lightning *XG311* over the Ribble Marshes. His sortie had been intended to provide a supersonic 'target' for another development batch Lightning, *XG327*, flown by *Tarnish 10*, the then FCLO (either Sqn/Ldr John Tritton or Sqn/Ldr 'Mac' McEwen) over the Aberporth range in Wales. Just after 09.35 BST, on take-off as the gear came up, Knight immediately felt uncomfortable with the pitch control of the aircraft, manifested by unevenness of tailplane control and limitation of forward stick travel, so much so as to scrub the trip. In turning to Warton and selecting 'gear down' he was presented with two greens and a red as the starboard leg obstinately refused to descend beyond 30 degrees despite his strenuous efforts to free it by use of the emergency release mechanism and repeatedly pulling 'g' in tight turns around Warton. Desmond de Villiers, *Tarnish 15*, was also airborne in the area in Canberra *WD937* at the time, returning to Warton from a pilot continuation training sortie accompanied by company photographer Gerry Peet who was trying out some new camera equipment. De Villiers was instructed to join formation with Knight, maintain close visual contact and report on the state of the gear and Knight's efforts to free it. Eventually Knight had no alternative but to act in accordance with the plethora of advice received from a control tower packed with air traffic controllers, pilots and technical staff, including Jimmy Dell, then Chief Test Pilot, all under the overall direction of Roland Beamont, by pointing the aircraft out to sea, shutting down the engines and exiting 'courtesy of Martin-Baker' in an ejection from 5,000ft at 230 kt. The aircraft descended into shallow water seven miles west of the aerodrome, well out into the estuary on sandbanks just south of the main Ribble channel.

Don Knight ejects from Lightning XG311 over the Ribble estuary, 31 July 1963. XG311 was one of the few pre-production development batch aircraft to retain the Stage 1 fin throughout its life

It was an occasion when the BAC Search and Rescue Whirlwind helicopter *XG597*, piloted by **Fred Ritchie** with navigator **R. Lockert**, having been warned of the situation, was already in the air and overhead before Knight had even unbuckled his parachute harness. With the Lytham Lifeboat standing by, helicopter winchman **Arthur Lewry** was lowered to pick up the Lightning pilot in a 'double lift' within a minute of his feet touching the ground. It was a copybook ejection and rescue, a classic abandonment of an aircraft under controlled conditions within a time scale that had allowed every avenue to be explored, enabling ground control and rescue services to operate to perfection, and an example of fine airmanship on the part of the pilot. He had been airborne for 55 minutes, baling out at 10.21 BST and stepping out of the helicopter back at Warton at 10.30. Knight recalls that, covered in malodorous estuary mud, he was encouraged to leave 'Ritchie's helicopter' as quickly as possible on arrival back at Warton. After a medical examination which showed that he was uninjured, in spite of having had a "hefty kick in the seat of the pants", Knight was home by mid-day, in a Blackpool theatre celebrating his wife's birthday that evening and back at work at the usual time next day, albeit on administrative duties. An RAF Belvedere twin-rotor heavy-lift helicopter recovered the Lightning from the marshes at low tide and returned it to Warton where the incident was found to have been caused by failure of the main undercarriage side-stay bracket. The investigation was helped by film taken from the aircraft flown by Desmond de Villiers. It was a portent of recurring problems of sequencing failures with Lightning undercarriage systems, interaction between the u/c loads and the hydraulics system resulting in reduced fatigue life which subsequently required close investigation. Knight was later told that his experience with *XG311*, by alerting the authorities to the problem, had saved them a lot of money. At the time, with well over half a million pounds-worth of Lightning wreckage embedded in the estuary, it seemed to him to be a rather odd way of putting it!

Knight was back in the air only two days later, carrying out a structure temperature test in T.4 *XM967*. The rest of 1963 and much of 1964 was filled with every imaginable test, including extensive work on AI.23B, OR946, various trials relating to subsonic reheat, Red Top missile handling, lateral and directional stability, rolling, general handling, undercarriage strain measurements using Auto/ILS approaches, Autopilot and Auto Attack. Knight, appointed Senior Experimental Test Pilot after Peter Hillwood left the Company in March 1963, was further promoted to Deputy Chief Test Pilot in January 1964. In August 1964 he participated in tropical trials with F.3 *XP699* at the USAF Wheelus AFB in Libya. Knight's subsequent involvement in the TSR2 and Saudi Arabia Lightning programmes is described later.

Frederick George Ritchie joined the RAF in 1937 at the age of 17, was commissioned in 1942 and flew Wellingtons and Lancasters in Bomber Command during the war. After five years he transferred to Coastal Command, later training as a helicopter pilot at Yeovil, becoming a member of the RAF's first search and rescue squadron. He acquired seven years' helicopter experience with No.22 (Search and Rescue) Sqn before being seconded in 1959 to BAC at Warton as Flight Lieutenant in charge of the RAF crew which at that time operated an MoD Whirlwind rescue helicopter based there in support of the P.1/Lightning test programmes. That year he received the Queen's Commendation for Valuable Service in the Air for his helicopter rescue work. He left the RAF in 1962 but remained at Warton to head up the special BAC (later BAe) helicopter unit which was being set up to be operated by the company under contract to MoD to cover possible emergencies involving test flights from Warton over the Irish Sea. It also provided back-up for tests over certain remote inland areas and frequently assisted in civil emergencies. Navigators including Brian McCann, Ray Woollett, Roy Kenward, George McAuley, Paul Kelly and Les Hurst, while retaining their fast jet aircrew roles, also served at various times as navigator/winch operators. The team also included Jim Eaves, Brian Hennerley, Adrian Jeffs, Derek Leeming, Arthur Lewry, Roy Lockert, Victor Malings and Robin Tayler. In 1962 Ritchie and his crew carried out their biggest rescue when they saved two of the three survivors of a crew of six from the coaster *Druid* which sank in the Ribble during a gale. Ritchie was also the holder of an airline transport pilot's licence for helicopters and a commercial pilot's licence for passenger-carrying fixed wing aircraft. In 1971, while his priority duties remained helicopter rescue, following the retirement of Gordon Moorhouse he was also appointed Senior Communications Pilot responsible for the operational aspects of all the Military Aircraft Division's communications flying. At that time Ritchie had logged 4,000 hours on search and rescue 'choppers' and 1,200 hours flying the company's HS.125 executive jet to and from the Continent, taking his overall pilot time to 15,000 hours on 20 different aircraft types. He was joined in 1978 by ex-Royal Navy helicopter pilot Chris Bowyer who took on similar duties which that year included, together with Kenward and Malings, flying an injured potholer rescued from a deep cave in the Yorkshire Dales to the Airedale General Hospital. On 9 July 1980, Warton's helicopter, crewed by Fred Ritchie, navigator Vic Malings and winchman Brian Hennerley, completed its 1,000th mission – a standby sortie while Tornado P02 undertook spinning trials.

Between 1959 and 1981 there were only four major test flying emergencies at Warton, but many mercy flights were made in support of the civil authorities. Three Whirlwind helicopters had been used, initially the 750hp Leonides piston-engined Mk.7 *XG597* until replaced in the mid-1970s by the turbine-powered Mk.10s *XJ409* (its original Pratt & Whitney Wasp piston engine substituted by a Rolls-Royce Gnome derated to 730shp) and *XP356*. The Mk.10s were 10kt faster, had longer range and were able to carry ten people including three crew. One of them was collected from Wroughton by Fred Ritchie with navigator Robbie Tayler on 17 November 1975, flying into headwinds of up to 45kt which more than halved its maximum speed of 95kt to an average of 44kt (Mach 0.066) at a time when

Fred Ritchie (fourth from right) with long-serving Warton rescue Whirlwind XG597 *and crew*

Warton's Tornados were nudging Mach 2.0! At one point, with groundspeed reduced to 35kt, the helicopter was outpaced by a friendly moped rider! All three helicopters were maintained from start to finish by fitter Roger Read.

The helicopter service was terminated in 1981 when, after 22 years, its funding became a casualty of defence cuts. The MoD stated that the ageing single-engined Whirlwind was being phased out in favour of the larger, more powerful and faster twin-engined Wessex, which in future would provide air-sea rescue services from Valley and Leconfield. The final routine flight took place on 3 August although an emergency flight was made on the 20th, prior to the last of the Whirlwinds being collected by the RAF and flown to Farnborough on 3 September. Fred Ritchie retired as Senior Communications Pilot at the end of August 1981 at the age of 61, to be presented with a cartoon, picture and model Whirlwind by Paul Millett, before taking up a ground post as a supply engineer working on the Tornado in the Stores Department at Warton. In 1982 he was presented with a second Queen's Commendation in recognition of his record of mercy and rescue flights in the area.

The Lightning was one of the few British military aircraft to survive the defence cuts that came in the wake of Duncan Sandys' 1957 Defence White Paper. Although the budgetary climate would limit the number to be ordered, the pressure was still to get the RAF's first supersonic fighter into service as soon as possible. In January 1957 **Sqn/Ldr (later Wg/Cdr) James Leonard 'Jimmy' Dell** was posted to English

Electric at Warton as Fighter Command Liaison Officer (FCLO), RAF Project Pilot and Operational Requirements Liaison Officer (ORLO), to familiarise with the P.1B and, reporting both to the C-in-C Fighter Command and Roland Beamont, to ensure that it was developed to meet the needs of the Service. It was the first time that a Fighter Command operational pilot had been seconded to a flight test team at such an early stage of the programme and would prove to be of great benefit particularly for weapons systems development.

Jimmy Dell, born in Liverpool on 23 August 1924, was inspired for a career in aviation as a ten-year-old boy after seeing one of Alan Cobham's Flying Circus shows. He joined the RAF on his eighteenth birthday in 1942, volunteering for training as a pilot. After initial induction at the appalling Padgate Camp near Warrington (it was generally acknowledged that to survive recruitment there fitted one to survive service anywhere) and the Aircrew Recruitment Centre, London, in April 1943 he sailed from Liverpool to Durban, South Africa, in the SS *Otranto* to undertake initial pilot training in Southern Rhodesia. He remained there for nearly two-and-a-half years, his elementary, basic and more advanced flying training revealing skills in airmanship which resulted in his being retained by the RAF Central Flying School (CFS), Southern Rhodesia, to instruct other cadet pilots. Dell's personal first familiarisation flight was in a Tiger Moth at RAF Induna on 20 September 1943, going solo on his 15th flight on 1 October. He rapidly progressed to the Harvard, Oxford and Fairchild Cornell, training at airfields including Thornhill, Norton and Belvedere. In 1944, as a Sergeant Pilot, he was assessed 'exceptional' as a flying instructor. On 23 January 1945, flying with a trainee cadet, he carried out a successful forced landing after the propeller of their Cornell broke off at the hub. After service at CFS Norton, mostly training pupils on the Cornell, Dell returned to the UK in August 1945 on HMS *Athlone Castle*.

Back home, like many other service personnel potentially redundant after the end of hostilities, he found himself at risk of demobilisation. Keen to keep on flying, but with opportunities few and far between, in November 1945 he was one of only three pilots to volunteer for posting as flying instructors at Elementary Flying Training School (EFTS) centres such as Perth, Sealand and Rochester. From there, by then a Flying Officer, Dell volunteered as a Pilot Gunnery Instructor at the Central Gunnery School (CGS), RAF Leconfield, which involved some short order conversion onto the Spitfire Mk.XVI, one of which he soloed for the first time at RAF Spitalgate near Grantham, Lincolnshire, on 19 June 1946. At that time Britain had just sold surplus Spitfires to the Turkish Government which had an urgent requirement for pilot training. Accordingly, despite having only recently qualified on the Spitfire himself, Dell's instructor rating resulted in the temporary interruption of his posting to the CGS in order to instruct the Turks, initially on Harvards, at Spitalgate during November and December. Back on track as an instructor at the CGS from December 1946 until 1949, he flew extensively in the Spitfire Mk.XVI, completed the Pilot Attack Course, was promoted to Flight Lieutenant and made his first jet flight, a solo familiarisation in a Meteor F.3, on 18 January 1949, describing it as 'Terrific!' Dell flew a Vampire FB.5 on 29 July. He left CGS in December 1949 with an impressive 'above the average' rating as a Pilot/Instructor, Pilot-Navigator, in bombing and air gunnery. He was then posted to No.43 Sqn at RAF Tangmere, flying the Meteor F.4, T.7 and F.8, also attending the two-month No.12 Day Fighter Leaders' Course (DFLC) at the Central Fighter Establishment (CFE), West Raynham, for instruction on squadron leadership. Six months after returning to No.43 Sqn, in October 1950 he was posted back to West Raynham as an instructor, remaining there until June 1952. His assessments at both No.43 Sqn and DFLS/CFE ranged between 'above average' and 'exceptional', particularly in air gunnery. During this period he also participated in some of the great air offensive exercises of the early 1950s, battle formations, high and low-level interception and bombing and offensive-sweep exercises over the Low Countries.

Still aged only 27, at a pace that could only be described as fast-tracking, in June 1952 he was selected for the British-US Military Exchange Programme and in July he and his family found themselves aboard the RMS *Queen Elizabeth* bound for New York. Dell was assigned to the USAF 60th Fighter Interceptor Squadron at Westover AFB, near Springfield, Massachusets. Within days of arriving, on 24 July he flew a familiarisation solo on an F-86E Sabre jet. On only his ninth flight, a camera gunnery sortie in F-86E *611* on 5 August, he was in formation with his leader whose aircraft, unlike Dell's, had underwing fuel tanks. As they sought to avoid a line squall of thunderclouds, Dell reported to the leader his concern about his fuel state, something the leader apparently failed to appreciate. As they entered the bad weather over Hartford, Connecticut and lost contact with each other, Dell's engine flamed-out. With the weather too bad to attempt a landing, he was ordered to eject. Having struggled to release the canopy he left the aircraft at only 500ft over hilly terrain. Alighting safely and disengaging his parachute, with a plume of smoke from his aircraft's crash site visible in woodland in the distance, pursued by a large number of local schoolchildren eager to help, Dell set off on foot along a highway to seek assistance. In later years, he recalled coming upon a drugstore where his enthusiastic acceptance of the proprietor's kind offer of a drink turned to disappointment when only a milk shake was produced. Even so, he reckoned that it was the best milk shake he had ever tasted! From mid-November he attended the USAF All Weather Instrument School at Moody AFB, Georgia for instrument flying training on the T-33A. After returning to Westover in February 1953, in June he made his first 'transition' flight of many sorties in the F-86D with pilot-operated radar interception system and air-to-air rocket armament. As a fully operational pilot with the 60th, Dell made over 500 sorties in the course of his two-year assignment, covering aspects of navigation, instruments, aerobatics, formation flying, scramble interception, combat simulation, air-to-air gunnery and radar interception by day and night. He visited USAF bases in many parts of the country, seeing much of the USA in the process.

At the end of his tour of duty, returning to the UK in RMS *Caronia* in August 1954, Dell held the unique position of being the only pilot in Britain with experience of single-seat all-weather jet interceptors equipped with airborne radar. Following nine months with HQ No.81 Group, Rudlow Manor, Wiltshire, including a month with No.66 Sqn, flying a number of sorties in RAF Sabre Mk.4s, he was posted to the Fighter Weapons School (FWS) at Leconfield. By then a Squadron Leader, he instructed there from July 1955 until the end of January 1957. During that time he flew the Meteor F.8, Vampire T.11 and Venom FB.1, familiarising on the Hunter F.1 for the first time in September 1955. He also spent some time at the Officers Advanced Training School (OATS) at RAF Bircham Newton in Norfolk. On the conclusion of his posting to FWS, on the staff of HQ Fighter Command he was invited to become project pilot on the P.1, attached to the English Electric Company at Warton as Fighter Command Liaison Officer (FCLO). With Beamont's initial test flying of the P.1 well under way, it was a critical stage in the development of such an advanced aircraft. In an instance of inspired thinking, officialdom decided it would be advantageous to have an operational fighter pilot, particularly one with experience of a pilot-operated radar system (as distinct from a Boscombe Down test pilot as was usually the case), to be attached to the English Electric development team as Operational Requirements Liaison Officer (ORLO) to ensure that the aircraft was developed to meet the specific needs of the RAF. In effect Dell was the RAF's Lightning Project Pilot, charged with reporting to both the C-in-C Fighter Command at RAF HQ and to Roland Beamont at Warton.

On 19 February 1957, for the first time, Dell flew the second prototype P.1A *WG763*, following it with a Mach 1.25 run the following day. His first impression was that the cramped nature of the early version cockpit and canopy was incompatible with a rigid 'bone dome' helmet which, through contact with the canopy, during take-off could transmit vibration to the pilot in the form of eyeball resonance. Somewhat disorientated as a result, but past the point of no return, on the take-off run Jimmy kept his head down as far as possible and let the aircraft do the work! For this reason Chief Test Pilot Beamont frequently preferred to fly wearing an old-fashioned soft leather helmet. Moreover, Beamont had little time for the 'anti-g' pressure suits as first 'modelled' by Jimmy Dell at Warton around 1960. After years of acclimatisation to the rigours of wartime fighters at the extreme limits of their performance, followed by post-war experimental fast jet flight, Beamont had trained himself to withstand forces of up to 7.5 g without g-suit protection, compared with the average pilot's limit of 5.5 - 6 g. Nevertheless he acknowledged that such suits were a must for RAF pilots in extreme manoeuvrability combat situations where it was vital not to miss an opportunity to destroy the enemy. For routine testing however, Bee's personal solution was a heavy, wide brass-buckled belt drawn tightly around his midriff, a device that he had used throughout the war and which he maintained served him well throughout his testing of the Canberra, P.1 and Lightning, even including his later back seat 'retirement' test flights in the Jaguar. Dell's flights in *WG763* were followed by AI.23 handling trials in the Canberra B(I)8 and on 25 April he flew the first prototype P.1A *WG760*, followed the next day by a Mach 1.45 run, climb to 40,000ft and general handling tests. When on 3 June Her Majesty Queen Elizabeth presented Dell's former RAF Squadron with its Standard at RAF Leuchars, to where No.43 Sqn had relocated from Tangmere, Dell had the honour and satisfaction of performing a fly-over in *WG763* at 100ft and Mach 0.96. On the ground, after showing Her Majesty around the aircraft, during which she graciously and with keen interest took up his offer to look inside the cockpit, Sqn/Ldr Dell was informed by a senior officer that "the Station Commander will see you later." Expecting to be congratulated for his attention to duty, he was somewhat surprised to find himself 'carpeted' for having not only offered an unsolicited handshake but also varying the itinerary by assisting Her Majesty up a rather rickety ladder! He flew P.1B prototypes *XA847* on 23 November, *XA856* on 17 January 1958 and, in April, *XA853* on a handling with missiles trial and in a constant Mach 1.3 climb to 50,000ft.

On 8 May 1958 Dell survived the first of a number of serious incidents in the P.1/Lightning. This time it was at the controls of P.1B *XA853*, an aircraft much used for trials of the Aden gun, on its 51st flight. The series had acquired notoriety for fire warnings, most of which proved to be false. On this occasion however, less than 15 minutes into his flight, climbing through thick cloud over the Irish Sea a loud explosion at the rear of the aircraft was followed by onset of control problems manifested by a slight sideways trajectory, together with a major electrical system failure including loss of radio contact. Unaware that smoke had started to issue from his aircraft, with superb airmanship Dell brought *XA853* back safely to Warton, operating the emergency undercarriage mechanism, making a fast landing without flaps or airbrakes seconds before the controls seized solid as the aircraft came to a halt on the runway with smoke and flames pouring from the rear. Thereupon, leaving the aircraft to Warton's emergency fire services, he abandoned the cockpit, legging it away onto the grass as fast as he possibly could. The incident was the subject of an official RAF citation as an 'Instance of Avoidance by Exceptional Flying Skill or Judgement, of Loss of, or Damage to [an] Aircraft or Personnel'. It read: 'A serious accident was narrowly averted on the 4th prototype P.1 (*XA853*) while carrying out gunsight trials on 8th May 1958. The intermediate jet pipe on No.2 engine fractured and a large panel of the pipe was blown out, with the effect of a minor explosion. Considerable damage was done, resulting in hydraulic and electrical failures. Scouring of the rear fuselage by the hot exhaust gases caused further failures, and caused a fire to break out when the aircraft landed. Sqn/Ldr Dell, under difficult circumstances was able to save the aircraft and thus establish the cause beyond doubt.' Ironically, it was later reported that had Dell been aware that he was on fire and been in radio contact and able to report it, he would have received an immediate award of the Air Force Cross! Later in his life, Jimmy Dell would cite this incident, of many others in an eventful career, as the one that had caused him most anxiety of all. With Category 4 damage sustained, the aircraft was able to rejoin the development fleet after extensive repairs including the fitting of a new rear fuselage and modifications including the new increased-area Stage 2 fin.

On 29 August 1958, in formation with *XG308*, Dell flew P.1B *XA847* to Farnborough where several days later he was demonstration pilot on three occasions at the SBAC Air Show. The 1958 event would be memorable for a number of reasons, not least as the year of No.111 Sqn's spectacular 22-Hunter line-abreast loop led by Sqn/Ldr Roger Topp. Describing the events at the Show on Thursday 4 September, *Flight Magazine* reported: 'Dell has shown himself well able to display the Lightning in the best Beamont tradition, with fast rolling runs and the tightest turns at speed seen at the show this year.' However, a few days later, during his display on the final day, Sunday 7 September, Jimmy blotted his copybook when the reheats lit unexpectedly, *XA847* accelerating through Mach 1.0 at 100ft and, quoting from his log book, "unfortunately" shattering windows over a wide area – including those of the Farnborough Control Tower! It was indeed "unfortunate" given the attempts by the SBAC show organisers at that time to ban sonic booms, having read the Riot Act to the extent of threatening to send home any disobedient pilots with their aircraft. The fact that it was the final day, and Dell was flying *XA847* back to Warton after the display anyway, rendered this an empty threat. Several senior RAF officers, most of whom Dell knew, attempted to discipline him, mostly it seems quite without conviction and barely able to conceal their mirth. One pointed out that the windows of the Show Director's office had also shattered – "Unfortunately he wasn't in it!" Another concluded that, as Dell was so deeply involved in the P.1 project, he could not possibly be relieved of his responsibilities. Someone considered whether the cost of re-glazing part of the town should be deducted from Dell's pay, but decided that Dell would be unlikely to live long enough! Such was the number of small claims submitted that years later, whenever recounting the incident, Dell could not be shaken from his belief that the opportunity had been taken to replace every pane of glass that had been cracked in Farnborough and gone unrepaired for years! Some years later, *Flight International*, in a short profile of Dell, stated that 'In this capacity [FCLO] he accidentally dropped a bang at Farnborough 1958, [the] only man to go supersonic at the show.' In fact other reports suggested that Dell was not the only miscreant 'boomer' at Farnborough that year, pointing the finger also at certain Hunter and Scimitar aircraft diving in proximity to the airfield.

Dell was at the controls for *XA847*'s flight from Warton back to Farnborough on 22 October, where, the following day, the only sound of breaking glass was that of a champagne bottle shattering across appropriate nose-art when the aircraft was officially named 'Lightning' by Marshal of the Royal Air Force Sir Dermot Boyle, accompanied by English Electric Chairman Sir George Nelson. As previously described, the ceremony was capped by one of Beamont's customarily dramatic flying demonstrations, followed later by an awesome reheated departure of the aircraft, piloted by Dell, on its return to Warton. By then the type had been flown by over 30 pilots from establishments such as the RAE, A&AEE and CFE. Beamont had flown it over 300 times and Dell over 50. Later in the year, on 10 November at RAF Wyton, Dell demonstrated *XA847* to NATO officials. In November/December he carried out practice sideways jettisons under 'g' and with sideslip together with simulated firings of the Blue Jay missile from *XG309*. On one occasion the aircraft stalled, entering an incipient spin from which Dell recovered without difficulty. He launched another Blue Jay from the same aircraft at Mach 1.3 and 40,000ft on 13 April 1959. A few days earlier he gave a demonstration take-off from RAF Cottesmore when the station was visited by the Prime Minister, Mr Harold Macmillan, to mark the 41st anniversary of the RAF. The occasion also included a demonstration Quick Reaction Alert (QRA) take-off of four Victor bombers in under four minutes. On 24 April 1959 he climbed *XG312* on test to 55,000ft.

The RAF Ensign falls away to reveal the name 'Lightning' as Marshal of the Royal Air Force Sir Dermot Boyle, with Sir George Nelson, operates a 'Heath Robinson' device to crack a bottle of champagne against XA847, *Farnborough, 23 October 1958*

Jimmy Dell in a Lightning

From around April 1959, though remaining on attachment to English Electric as FCLO, Dell's RAF unit was once again the Central Fighter Establishment where he was appointed O/C, Air Fighting Development Squadron (AFDS) and promoted to Wing Commander. In that capacity he followed in the footsteps made by Roland Beamont 14 years earlier.

At that time, it was customary for a team of Boscombe Down test pilots to travel annually to the USA to gain first-hand experience of some of the latest USAF military aircraft. Although Jimmy Dell had not been on a test pilot course (later in life he would modestly maintain that he had learned all his test flying skills 'on the job'!), he was selected to lead the 1959 mission, in his case primarily to assess weapons systems, leaving the Boscombe types to evaluate performance. On 14 June 1959 he flew from London to New York by BOAC Britannia, thence by EAL and TWA Constellation and Boeing 707 via Washington and Los Angeles to Edwards Air Force Base, where he was able to fly the F-100F Super Sabre, F-104A Starfighter, F-105B Thunderchief and F-106B Delta Dart. Flying solo in the F-105B, he attained Mach 1.7 on his familiarisation sortie. After less than a month in the USA, Dell was urgently recalled to undertake a similar assignment at the French Air Force Test Centre at Mont de Marsan, south of Bordeaux. Returning to the UK on 8 July, by the 20th he was in France and the following day flew a Super Mystere solo on a familiarisation sortie, the first of four, followed by flights in a Vautour IIA and Morane-Saulnier MS.760 Paris trainer, liaison and light strike aircraft.

At the end of a hectic six weeks in the USA and France, he returned to the UK on 25 July. After just over two years as FCLO at Warton, in August 1959 Wg/Cdr Dell took over full time as O/C, Air Fighting Development Squadron (AFDS), in fact as the first O/C of the newly combined AFDS and the All Weather Development Squadron (AWDS), at the Central Fighter Establishment (CFE), West Raynham. There he flew the Hunter F.6, Javelin F(AW).5 and Meteor T.7. On departing from Warton, Jimmy Dell was presented with a 'leaving card', showing him heading back to CFE on a mechanised sled device reminiscent of the 'Time Machine' in the 1960 film of H. G. Wells' novel, with a number of vignettes depicting incidents during his time as FCLO, including *XA853* with its tail on fire at Warton, Jimmy hastily evacuating it with the seat of his pants on fire, his shattering of the fenestration at Farnborough, the whole collage entitled 'Oh Hell, It's Dell!' The ejection seat of this magnificent machine carried the parodical instruction: 'Don't pull the chain while the plane is landing at the station.' Of Jimmy Dell there is more later.

During the late 1950s and early 1960s, **Flying Officer L. J. S. (Len) Houston**, call sign *Soaker 3*, a Ferranti Project Pilot from 1956 to 1973, flew the P.1B radar aircraft *XG312* from Warton and carried out interception by AI.23B-equipped Lightnings against various Lightning and Canberra targets. Ferranti had its own Flying Unit at Turnhouse but its relatively short runway meant that Warton had to be used for Lightning trials. Other AI.23 trials pilots were John Field (Ferranti 1953-1963) and John Cockburn (Ferranti 1961-1966). In 1971, Houston, then Ferranti Chief Test Pilot, together with flight test observer Bill Roberts, also conducted trials with a modified RAE Canberra B(I)8, the nose of which housed the Laser Ranger and Marked Target Seeker under development by Ferranti and the RAE for the Jaguar and Harrier. Houston was awarded the Queen's Commendation for Valuable Service in the Air.

John Moreton Nicholls was seconded from the RAF in June 1959 to follow Jimmy Dell as Fighter Command Liaison Officer, joining English Electric's test flying programme at Warton and reporting back to the RAF with a view to clearing the Lightning for entry into service at the beginning of the new decade. Born in Moreton, Cheshire in 1926 and educated at Liverpool Collegiate and St. Edmund Hall, Oxford, Nicholls joined the RAF in 1945, entering the RAF College, Cranwell and training as a pilot prior to serving with No.28 Sqn on fighter-reconnaissance Spitfires in Singapore and Malaya. Back in England, in 1949 he converted to Meteors on No.257 Sqn, became a pilot attack instructor and served at the Central Fighter Establishment.

In April 1952 he attended Nellis AFB in Nevada, flying the F-86 Sabre. In common with a number of experienced RAF fighter pilots assigned to fly operationally with the USAF and RAAF in the Korean conflict, Nicholls was attached to the USAF 335th Fighter Interceptor Squadron operating from Kimpo Airfield near Seoul, where he flew 100 operations in the 6-month period from June 1952. In fighter sweeps in the infamous 'MiG Alley' he was credited with damaging two MiG-15s on one sortie and on his penultimate operation shot down another, the first MiG to be despatched by an RAF pilot.

On returning to the UK, with a DFC (1953) added to his American DFC and Air Medal, Nicholls flew Meteors and Hunters before becoming a tactics instructor at the RAF Day Fighter Leaders' School from 1953 to 1956. From 1956 to 1958 he flew again on exchange with the USAF, this time on F-100s and F-104s of the 435th and 83rd Sqns in the USA.

During his time at Warton between 1959 and 1961, Nicholls flew many Lightning test flights. On 28 October 1960, flying P.1B *XA853* on a 55-minute sortie during the weapon development phase, he had just completed a gun firing trial and was descending from high level when, having selected the cockpit demister, the canopy was accidentally jettisoned, carrying away the top of the aircraft's tail fin, but he was able to land safely.

In 1961 Nicholls left Warton to attend the RAF Staff College at Andover, prior to pursuing a successful further career in the highest echelons of the RAF. As Wing Commander, he was posted O/C of the AFDS at the CFE, RAF West Raynham, on 2 April 1962, where he remained until 1964. Nicholls was ideally placed to supervise weapons development and missile firing trials. When the AFDS moved to RAF Binbrook near Grimsby and began evaluating techniques for intercepting high-flying aircraft, U-2 spyplanes of the USAF were sometimes used as 'targets' – much to the incredulity of the American pilots when the Lightnings appeared alongside. On 1 January 1964 Nicholls collected the RAF's first Lightning F.3 *XP695* from Warton for delivery to the CFE at Binbrook. The F.3 had more powerful Avon Series 300 engines of 13,500lb dry thrust, 16,000lb in reheat – over twice the power of the P.1A – improved performance, greater range, more advanced Ferranti Airpass airborne interception radar then designated AI.23B, navigation and fire-control equipment. Rather than 30mm Aden cannon, it carried two Red Top collision-course weapons (or two Firestreak pursuit-course weapons, or 48 spin-stabilised two-inch explosive rockets rippled from a pair of retractable Microcell launchers). In February 1964, at a time of tension between Indonesia and Britain, while still at the AFDS at Binbrook, Nicholls instigated some interesting mock combat trials between *XP695* and airworthy Spitfire Mk.X1X *PS853*, to develop tactics to deal with P-51 Mustang fighters then operated by the Indonesian Air Force. The trials concluded that in any such engagements the jet fighter should attack from below to deny the slower, but highly manoeuvrable piston-engined aircraft, any advantage in tight turns.

In 1964 Nicholls attended the Joint Services Staff College before being posted to the MoD to work in personnel and on the Air Staff, being promoted to Group Captain in 1965. In 1967 he became O/C, RAF Leuchars, Fife, responsible for two Lightning squadrons and one of Javelin night fighters. In that capacity, having been present at Warton as FCLO to take delivery of the first Lightning in 1959, he was present at Warton on 28 August 1967 when the RAF took delivery of its last Lightning F.6, *XS938*. The aircraft was flown to Leuchars by 23-year-old Flying Officer Paul Reynolds of Blackpool, the issue being decided between Nicholls and Reynolds on the toss of a coin. After attending the Imperial Defence College in 1970, Nicholls was appointed Senior Air Staff Officer (SASO) at HQ No.11(Fighter) Group at the time the Phantom started to enter RAF service. In 1971 he became Principal Staff Officer to the Chief of the Defence Staff, Admiral of the Fleet Sir Peter Hill-Norton. After promotion to Air Vice-

Air Marshal Sir John Nicholls on a visit to the Saudi Arabia Support Department, Warton, 8 August 1980

Taylor, Houston, Carrodus and Tritton

Marshal in 1973 he went to HQ Strike Command as SASO. He was awarded the AFC (1965), appointed CBE (1967) and KCB (1978). In 1976 he was appointed Assistant Chief of the Air Staff (Operational Requirements) at a busy time for investment and modernisation of the UK's air defence early warning radar and for the introduction of both Tornado IDS and ADV versions. Promoted Air Marshal in 1977, Nicholls joined the Air Force Board as Air Member for Supply and Organisation. Air Marshal Sir John Nicholls was appointed Vice-Chief of the Air Staff in 1979 and retired in 1980. Nicholls flew most of the aircraft types in service with the RAF, including Tornado, Hawk and Harrier, together with those of France and the USA such as the Mirage and F-15. After leaving the RAF he worked for British Aerospace until 1982 as Director-in-Charge, Saudi Arabia, on the support package to the Royal Saudi Air Force and the major procurement deal for the Tornado. Air Marshal Sir John Nicholls died on 17 May 2007 aged 80.

[Subsequent RAF Fighter Command Liaison Officers based at Warton included, from April 1963, **Sqn/Ldr (later Air Commodore) Norman 'Mac' McEwen and Sqn/Ldr John Tritton**. McEwen, formerly of No.56 Sqn, spent much time on weapons trials at Aberporth, flying *XG312* with 2-inch rocket armament and *XG328* equipped with Auto-Attack.]

To be continued...

ACKNOWLEDGEMENTS

Many people have assisted in the preparation of this series of publications.

As may be inferred from the dedication, I should first of all like to record my appreciation for the time, knowledge and encouragement so willingly given to me from the outset by the late Brian Tomlinson, Bob Fairclough and Keith Emslie, all among the founding fathers of the Heritage Department, sadly all three of whom are no longer with us to give a critical welcome to the fruits of their advice and guidance.

Among those active in the affairs of the BAE Heritage Department at Warton today, I thank Dave Ward and John Shorrock in particular. As professionals with the misfortune to have shared an office with a layman, they have been in the firing line of my ceaseless questioning, patiently answering and explaining so many matters over the years. In no particular order my sincere thanks also go to Ian Lawrenson, Mark Atkinson, Keith Spong, Ken Hillman, Rick Hardman, Daphne Seddon, Graham Leather, Bob Jones, Roger Jones, Joe McGrath, Dave Banks, Richard Dell, Gerald Wilson, Dave Hutton and Tom Clayton. Peter Hardman scanned many of the photographic images for which I am most grateful. Dennis Leyland and Brian Sargeant have introduced me to much of the company's heritage, and to new contacts via the outside visits programme, respectively. Ray Troll and Mark Wright of the BAE Systems Photographic Department at Warton, have willingly assisted with some highly specialised scanning of images. It has been my great pleasure to work with Gavin Hawthorne and Tim Harwood of Reid Creative.

In carrying out my research, it has been my privilege to have had several discussions with Mr Frank Roe, formerly Managing Director at Warton, whose vivid recall of events that took place in the earliest days of English Electric over 65 years ago, together with tape-recorded interviews with his contemporaries Ron Dickson, Bob Price, Keith Emslie and Dennis Leyland, have been nothing less than inspirational. Relating to a more recent era, I also thank Alan Matthews (Hon Secretary) and other officers, including Craig Eckersley, and members of the Preston Branch of the Royal Aeronautical Society, for continued access to the Branch's transactions and programme of speakers, Alan not least for introducing me last year to Ed Fisher, formerly of Flight Test, who sadly passed away just recently, whose recall of events was second to none. Among officers and members of the Avro Lancashire Club, I thank Trevor Moncrief, Jim Britton, Bob Studley and many others for information received and access to some excellent speakers over the years, notably from BAE Systems Flight Operations.

Thanks to the good offices of Eric Bucklow (and the late Bob Fairclough) I have benefited from access to copies of the flight logs of a large number of Warton and Samlesbury test pilots and aircrew, documents which are kept for reference under secure conditions in the Heritage Department. I am also grateful to the following former test pilots and aircrew who have provided information and/or commented on my earlier drafts concerning their careers at Samlesbury and Warton: Don Knight, John Hall, the late Jimmy Dell (and his son Kevin and family), Eric Bucklow, John Cockburn, Reg Stock, Pete Ginger, Dave Eagles, Andrew Love (concerning his father, the late Allan Love), Jerry Lee, George McAuley, Keith Hartley, Jim Stuttard, John Turner, Bill Ovel, Bernie Scott, Frank James, Keith Dennison and others. Many of these feature later in the series. As ever, the archives of *Aeroplane* and *Flight* magazines have been rich sources of information and aviation context. All photographs, unless otherwise stated, have been sourced from the BAE Systems Heritage Department Photo Archive.

Finally, last but most certainly not least, my appreciation to my wife Kath and our daughters Helen and Sarah for their support and interest over the several years of this project, enduring the frequent explosions of my wrath directed at the computer, from the clutches of which they have rescued me on so many occasions.

James H. Longworth
June 2012

ABOUT THE AUTHOR

Jim Longworth was born in Bolton, Lancashire and educated at Bolton County Grammar School and Queen Mary College, University of London, where he gained a BSc Honours Degree in Geography, specialising in industrial and economic aspects. He is a Fellow of the Royal Geographical Society (FRGS) and a Fellow of the Royal Society for the encouragement of Arts, Manufactures and Commerce (FRSA). He is a member of the BAE Systems Heritage Department at Warton and of the Rolls-Royce Heritage Trust at Derby. He has worked on regional planning, land use, industrial and economic development matters in Lancashire and the North West throughout his career, for many years in the Lancashire County Planning Department as Head of the Industrial Development and Promotion Unit of Lancashire County Council. With a long-standing interest and involvement in aviation matters, his responsibilities included promoting Lancashire's aerospace industry at the Farnborough International and Paris Air Shows. He now writes on industrial and aviation heritage subjects. His previous book *Triplane to Typhoon* detailed the aircraft produced in factories in Lancashire and the North West since 1910. His other books include a review of the region's contribution to the development of aero-engines and, from a different era, the cotton textile industry. He is married with two daughters and lives in Grimsargh, Preston.

The publication of this book coincides with the Preston Guild Merchant 2012. These images show English Electric's participation 60 years ago in the 1952 Guild, with the front and centre fuselage, rear fuselage and tail of Canberra B.2 WH648 in the Trades' Procession, negotiating North Road and Lancaster Road

WARTON'S HERITAGE DEPARTMENT

The Heritage Department at Warton, previously known as the BAE Systems North West Heritage Group, was established in June 1995 by a group of volunteers following an appeal by the Company to help support its heritage policy. The Department covers the heritage of the Company in Lancashire, namely the sites at Warton, Samlesbury and formerly Preston.

The Department now has over 30 active volunteers whose range of activities include the establishment and management of document, photographic and film archives. The material held by the Department is used to promote the proud heritage of the Company at various displays and exhibitions as well as answering a constant stream of enquiries from within and outside the Company.

This book, the first in a series of publications dealing with the history of test flying at the sites of BAE Systems and its predecessor companies in Lancashire, is a further example of using material from the Department's archives by telling the story of that remarkable group of people who over the years have operated at the pinnacle of the Company's activities by test flying aircraft ranging from the Felixstowe flying boat of WW1 to the Eurofighter Typhoon of today. It follows our previous publication of accounts of the design concept that led to the P.1 and Lightning, and the history of wind tunnel developments at Warton. More publications are planned in the future that will tell the stories of other projects, sites and facilities and most importantly the people who were key figures in the success of the Company over the past decades.

The Department would like to hear from past and present employees who may have material that would be of interest. We are especially keen to acquire more items for display in our new Heritage Exhibition Centre at Warton. We would very much like to hear from those who may have been involved with the P.1 and the Wind Tunnel Department, together with any whose memories will be stimulated by reading the new series of publications on test flying, of which this volume is the first.

Finally, do you have a story to tell that you feel would be a good subject for a future heritage publication? If so, please contact us and we will be pleased to discuss your ideas further.